The Life and Art of François Krige

For Sylvia and Suzanne

NA DIE BRON
VAN ALLES, DIE SON,
ÉÉN BEURENDE DRANG
ÉÉN GOUE VERLANG!

UYS KRIGE, *SONNEBLOM*

François Krige on the *stoep* of his
brother Uys's home in Onrus, 1987.

JUSTIN FOX

THE LIFE AND ART OF

FRANÇOIS KRIGE

FERNWOOD
PRESS

FERNWOOD PRESS, P O BOX 15344, VLAEBERG 8018, SOUTH AFRICA
REGISTRATION NO. 90/04463/07
FIRST PUBLISHED 2000
TEXT (CHAPTERS 1 TO 5) © JUSTIN FOX
    (APPRAISAL) © STEFAN HUNDT
DESIGNED BY WILLEM JORDAAN
SETTING AND MAKE-UP BY EPS&M
REPRODUCTION BY CAPE IMAGING BUREAU CC, CAPE TOWN
PRINTED AND BOUND BY TIEN WAH PRESS (PTE) LTD, SINGAPORE
COLLECTORS' AND SPONSORS' EDITIONS BOUND BY PETER CARSTENS, JOHANNESBURG

*ALL RIGHTS RESERVED. NO PART OF THIS PUBLICATION
MAY BE REPRODUCED, STORED IN A RETRIEVAL SYSTEM
OR TRANSMITTED, IN ANY FORM OR BY ANY MEANS, WITHOUT THE
PRIOR WRITTEN PERMISSION OF THE COPYRIGHT OWNER(S).*

STANDARD EDITION   ISBN 1 874950 48 2
COLLECTORS' EDITION   ISBN 1 874950 49 0
SPONSORS' EDITION   ISBN 1 874950 51 2

THE SPONSORS

FNB
A DIVISION OF FIRSTRAND BANK LIMITED

NATIONAL ARTS COUNCIL

Fernwood Press gratefully
acknowledges the financial contributions of
the above sponsors who, by generously supporting this
publication, are expressing their
interest in the cultural heritage
of this country.

The following abbreviations are
used in the captions to save space;
the full credits appear below:

FNB	First National Bank
Humphreys	William Humphreys Art Gallery, Kimberley
JAG	Johannesburg Art Gallery
Montagu	Montagu Museum
MTN	MTN Institute of Art and Material Culture
Rupert	Collection Mrs Huberte Rupert, Stellenbosch
SANG	South African National Gallery
Sanlam	Sanlam Art Collection, Bellville
SANMMH	South African National Museum of Military History
Transnet	Transnet Heritage Collection
Welz	Collection Stephan Welz & Co

FRONT COVER
STILL-LIFE WITH FRUIT, 1979
OIL ON BOARD
46 x 64,5 CM
PRIVATE COLLECTION

CONTENTS PAGE
JAMES JOUBERT, CEDERBERG
CONTÉ

CONTENTS

Acknowledgements . 6

Foreword by Breyten Breytenbach . 9

Introduction . 13

1. Youth 1913–1933 . 17

2. Travels and Early Career 1934–1940 . 27

3. War 1941–1945 . 47

4. Cape Town 1946–1966 . 64

5. Montagu 1967–1994 . 88

Concluding Remarks . 129

The Art of François Krige: An Appraisal by Stefan Hundt . 132

List of Colour Illustrations . 138

Index . 139

List of Subscribers . 142

ACKNOWLEDGEMENTS

I am deeply indebted to the late Daantjie Saayman for his encouragement and faith in this book, even in the last days of his illness. In the initial phase of trying to get this manuscript published, Daantjie and after him Mike Kantey worked tirelessly to get sponsorship. Their work was taken over by Kerneels Breytenbach at Human & Rousseau and finally by Pieter Struik, who saw the project through to book form.

I am also indebted to a number of friends and colleagues who read the manuscript and offered invaluable advice on pruning and reworking: a special thanks to Breyten Breytenbach, Evelyn Cohen, Neville Dubow, Sandra Klopper, Sarah Nuttall and Robert Plummer for their contributions. My family were also roped into reading and commenting on the progress of the script.

Thanks are also due to Erik Laubscher whose painting classes gave me an inkling of the alchemy required to create an image out of oil and canvas, and to the staff of Cape Town University's History of Art Department under Michael Godby who provided me with the tools and the critical methods with which to read images.

Thanks to all those who offered anecdotes and fond recollections of François, particularly his widow, Sylvia Krige, and sister, Suzanne Fox, for the time they invested in the making of the memory.

The staff of the South African National Museum of Military History and the Stellenbosch University Library archive deserve mention for helping locate many important letters and documents. Thanks must also go to the University of Cape Town for granting a year's post-doctoral research fellowship which gave me the time to complete this book.

Lastly and most importantly, a debt of gratitude to François himself for the inspiring way he made a life, and the beautiful images that adorn these pages.

Justin Fox

ACKNOWLEDGEMENTS

SELF-PORTRAIT WITH BUDDHIST PRINT
1980s
OIL ON CANVAS
65 x 49,5 CM
PRIVATE COLLECTION

FRANÇOIS KRIGE

8

OBIDOS, PORTUGAL
PEN

FOREWORD

The artist at work in his studio in the sixties.

It is often said that François Krige was a retiring person, discreet and unostentatious. Indeed, if we look at how seldom he exhibited and how reluctantly he sold any of his works, it is clear that he shunned the public role or posture.

But, looking at what he left behind, it is as evident that his work grew from an intimate interaction with his immediate environment. He'd divested himself of the frills and the blasphemy of mundane salon agitation, he'd pared his existence down to the essential living discipline of painting and drawing, but he was no hermit. He loved his wine, his pipe, his music, his tennis, his garden, his painting expeditions, his extended overseas trips for a good hard look at the work of his predecessors, and he loved the company he kept.

It is an honour for me to have been asked to write this foreword. Some people walk with you all through your life. You are aware of their existence, their presence even, although you may very seldom meet.

I first knew of François Krige when I was still at school, through the book of his brother Uys, *Sol y Sombra*, for which he'd made companion drawings. An illuminating title for both these brothers, I'd suggest – *Sun and Shade:* the play, the texture of light and closeness, a veritable existentialism of the senses quite different from the more tortured Germanic sombreness rooted in myth and repression; but, as well, in the title and the attitudes inferred, a reference to bullfighting, that deathly art of dappled clarity and surging obscurity, where the seats are priced according to whether you sit in the *sombra* or the *sol*; and where you could watch the sword of sunlight piercing and releasing the flood of nightfall.

Already, I think, I was captivated by his gift of showing light and movement, the way these drawings captured *more* than just form and line, *more* than the scenes depicted. They had the capacity of gently but insistently drawing you in, making you participate; and in this procedure, as I only realised much later, he was showing total generosity, as he would all through his life. He was *sharing*.

Later still, I would come to understand his wisdom in giving only enough for the receiver (or the guest) to become autonomous – because the greater generosity is in neither pretending to give more than you have nor giving more than the recipient can take.

Of course, I was also attracted by the impossible romanticism of this draughtsman (I knew nothing of his paintings then) moving a penetrating eye and a deft hand over faraway exotic places. Who wouldn't have been captured by the traveller and the explorer?

Daar sou twee … : I would like to apologise to François on two counts. First, that I should have the chutzpah, the cheek, the hubris, the effrontery to wish to comment on his work. I am almost certain he would not have been pleased. But, well, he has moved on in the meantime, a bit … into the shadows, and from here on we speak directly to the light of his work. His canvases and drawings embody him, of course, but they also are greater than him and differ from him. The second reason is that even after this apology I insist on continuing, and then not in our shared mother-tongue – which entails that my words sound much grander and more pompous than I would prefer them to be. But we must accept that everybody does not understand Afrikaans, and a pity it is. Yet I would like to make the contentious statement that, in spite of a certain timelessness and universalism both in the techniques of his art and his subject matter, which kept on fascinating him, he worked in Afrikaans. Partly it must have been a matter of instinct – a bird sings the only tune it knows – but it surely was also a matter of choice. This is evident especially in the observations of his pen and brush, his subjects of simple people and things and landscapes, of soil, unadorned, humble, earthy. And in the joy of simple lines, the celebration of colour, the pleasure of paint – as Afrikaans as only that mingling of Boer and Khoi and Asian can be.

Since that time he stayed with me; a space, a reference on my intellectual and artistic horizon. Ultimately, as I'd like to underline here, as an ethical position as well.

Over the later years I had the privilege, only too rare, of spending some moments with him. When we last met a few weeks before the paint on his palette finally dried – he was only 'resting' to get over the 'weakness of the body' before returning to the easel, he said – we spoke of Matisse continuing to create even when dying, lying on his back to draw with long colour-tipped sticks on paper stretched on the ceiling of his room. How François's eyes glittered with excitement and a curious wonder when we discussed the masters. I must stress that we'd be talking about the nitty-gritty of technique, as painters always do – not the contents or the meaning or the intention. Not the theory but the practice, the natural philosophy of the hand.

The metaphysics is all there, fully sublimated in the pigments, the brushes, the surfaces, the lines and the relationships, in the movement. One doesn't interpret; one is. There is nothing outside the being of the workings, of transformation and rendering, nothing beyond the paints and the pencils, but this is not a limitation; it is essence. Indeed, it is the being of awareness continually growing and dreaming and incarnating itself.

Let me confess my habit of appropriating what I deem important. I'd adopted François as an ancestor, family even – in the good African and Afrikaans tradition: somebody with whom one instinctively shares more than could ever be expressed in words, or would ever need to be. To try would be embarrassing, maybe indecent.

Daar sou twee dinge wees waarvoor ek François … om verskoning wou vra. Een – dat ek die chutzpah, die cheek, die hubris, die domastrantheid het om te wil [skryf] oor sy werk. Ek is amper seker hy sou nie daarvan gehou het nie. Maar, nou ja, hy het intussen opsy gestaan, effens … in die skaduwee, en hiervandaan vorentoe praat ons direk met die lig van sy werk. Sy doeke en tekeninge is natuurlik hy, maar ook meer en anders as hy. Die tweede rede is dat ek dit tog doen, en dan nie eers in ons gedeelde geboortetaal nie – wat behels dat my sê daarom deftiger en meer opgeblase klink as wat ek dit graag sou wou hê. Maar ons moet aanvaar dat nie almal Afrikaans verstaan nie, hoe jammer dan ook. Ek wil tog die omstrede stelling maak dat François Krige, 'n sekere tydloosheid en universalisme ten spyt, beide wat betref die tegnieke van sy kuns en die onderwerpe wat hy betrek, wat hom altyd weer bly lok het, in Afrikaans *gewerk het. Gedeeltelik was dit seker instinktief – die voël sing immers soos hy gebek is – maar dit was sekerlik ook 'n kwessie van keuse. Dis sprekend veral in die waarnemings van stif en kwas, die onderwerpe van eenvoud, mense en dinge en landskappe van grond, van onopgesmuktheid, nederigheid, aardsheid. En van die vreugde van die skoon lyn, die viering van kleure, die lekkerkry van die verf –* Afrikaans *soos net daardie vermenging van Boer en Khoi en Oosterling dit kan wees.*

If I may digress for a moment (I actually mistakenly wrote 'regress' here): we should resist the temptation of analysing too much, of reading more in his paintings and drawings than he intended or put there. We live in futile times where the old Romantic impulse reigns supreme – in gaudy theoretical garb, and ever more smothered in the garbage of 'post-modernism', 'deconstruction', etc. (particularly the etc.!). To put it in a culturally incorrect way: we are terrorised by the notion of not being subtle enough to tease forth the shadows of meaning or unconscious intentions hovering below the light of the surface – what older moralists knew as the soul behind the mask of appearance.

The fashionable discourse is the mind-numbing nit-picking of the academics, of those cleverer than we are. And all these exquisite (and boring) explanations are invading and contaminating the clear space of saying, singing, painting. François Krige's work points us in the salutary direction where paintings and drawings speak for themselves. What you see is what you get. Also (if I may be topical): what you see is a dance, not a *toyi-toyi*.

Painting is singing. Matisse said, 'I continue painting until the hand sings'. It is this hand-singing that François Krige has left us, which we have the luck and joy of listening to with our eyes.

I must generalise outrageously and say that South African painting, to my admittedly untutored mind, is too loaded with meaning, often too clever by half, reflecting the ingrown toenails of living in the colonies, mortally afraid of being irrelevant or Euro-centrist (as if we don't all learn from the same tradition!), worried about not being sufficiently committed or ironical or funny.

I'm not just simplistically protesting against the intellectual regime, or worse, the moral-political restraints of which we need to purify ourselves if we wish to continue seeing clearly and feeling strongly. I am pleading, though, for a balance so that (if I may say so) the digestion does not eliminate or obviate the eating of the food.

Surely, when we look at François's paintings and drawings, the first reaction must be: How they glow! How they 'hold' the walls! What presence, what beauty, what a feast for the eyes!

Producing an image or a 'presence' of line and colour on a flat surface (and thus of shapes and relationships) is certainly a complex process. And yet, firstly and lastly, it flows from a simple and non-intellectual necessity: to show, to display, to mark, to *make*, to understand, maybe to reflect.

Again, and at the risk of ruffling some rainbow feathers: in this country there's a whiff of the stench of moral and emotional correctness: the ultimate correct posture is, of course, death. Or suicide. Painting (and writing), on the contrary, when true to the deeper body, is *movement*. And because it moves, it sets off motion in the minds of those who partake of it. François moves our eyes, he moves our memories and our emotions. He knew about the sounds of colours. One needs no formal apparatus to sense the deep empathy and sympathy he had with his subjects (and I include landscapes among these). Witness the dignified portraits of Krisjan, an old drifter. (He was born as Christiaan, by the way, a brother of Ai Byp, a well-respected Montagu character.)

How can one not be touched by the obvious humanity apparent even in his nearly abstract drawings? François knew about comparison, but I rather suspect he resolutely avoided the national pastime of feeling sorry for himself.

Illusion was not his game, except to the extent that all pictorial representation is predicated upon a measure of make-believe. His was a passionate dialectic between the materials (or craft, if you wish) and the looked-at 'reality' – and looked at as if for the first time – with himself, that is, the magic bird of hand and eye, as the vector of the non-intellectualised consciousness.

When he painted pears they were not pears but succulent blobs of colour and shapes, weighing upon space, which in passing may also register with us as 'pears' – and make us look with altered expectations the next time we see 'real' pears! Like Cézanne he could have said that painting apples taught him about constructing the sky (and just listen to the reverberation of those skies!). And like Uys, he knew about singing the sun. He too was a mystic of the surface: that most difficult of disciplines where touch and tone and knowing how not to go too far are all-important. But the sun can be dark at times. Just look at his magnificent Karoo funeral as the tolling of a dark bell.

Does this mean that his work was guileless, without 'message'? Down the ages pictures have conveyed other 'texts' beside the apparent aboutness, if only because they reflect history or were shot through with references familiar to people living at the same time. It is fascinating, for instance, to walk with the eyes over the genre of the still-life, all the way from Greek libations, to the proof of the host's expansiveness, to shows of riches, to Dutch bourgeois but puritan values (as in the hues and in choice of subject matter), or to *memento mori*. Or to look at what portraits were intended to transmit: from the faces of the dead stuck on Egyptian coffin lids to the butchered and smeared head of a Francis Bacon caught with its pose down between looking and seeing.

People (not 'the people') obviously looked knowingly and expectantly at art works. So it was only natural that artists should be aware of these conventions and manipulate the expectations to allow for new insights. Part of the generosity of the painter is, after all, to illustrate how all cultural expressions of all times belong to all of us.

We saw how Michelangelo talked through the echoing chambers of the ages with the Greeks and we can observe how François Krige dialogues with Cézanne, Gauguin, Rembrandt … not through imitation or as some secondary wry comment, not to footnote, but to reclaim (first of all for himself and then for us) what painting is all about.

I'm sure François believed that eyes have memories. Notice how many of his portraits wear hats, or have something on the head, and how this device makes a Rembrandt prophet of a humble Little Karoo labourer. See how he uses outline in his canvases, like Gauguin did – sometimes to start off with, to denote an area to be filled in, sometimes as a final harmonic and structural component. When you look closely you will see how he applied undertone or ground colour as a promise and a promise against which the subsequent tints would be pitched and played out, thus allowing for the work to develop its own dynamic (one could nearly say 'logic'), as in the case of a Picasso. See the feathery touch of the brush stroke capturing light, as on the surface of a Manet statement.

No derivative neo-Impressionist. Neither modernist not classicist. A wide range of intentions – from the 'consciously conceived' masterpieces to light and humorous sketches. A variety of expressions – in motifs, styles, themes, disciplines. The apparent choice of not being 'in the swim', not keeping up with

FISHING BOAT
QUILL PEN

the trendsetters or the commissars. Not interested in career-building. Impervious to recognition. No attempt to interact with the fury of what was happening internationally although he was contemporary to the likes of Pollock, De Kooning, the Ecole de Paris, the Cobra group … Neither recluse nor iconoclast. Neither Protestant nor puritan, certainly no moralist. But with deep ethical concerns grounded in his craft. He was his own man, and thus, paradoxically, he would belong to all of us. He was instinctively *right* – but that was an expression of aesthetics, a sureness of touch, a true eye for composition and colour.

Like all painters he became better as he grew older, the matter of awareness matures, the substance of beauty becomes more malleable, the dictionary of ethics and aesthetics is resolved, absorbed, the flame burns brighter – and we are left with light, texture, calmness, voluptuousness, freshness, an explosion of colours.

From these surfaces of pigment, creating relationships between forms, *statements* are elicited, *invitations* rather, since he's never obtrusive in what he offers – so self-evidently as if we too only now see for the first time. They are the products of what must have been, palpably, the intricate debate between his own looking and seeing, between observation and transformation. He searches for and finds (I think) a dynamic harmony. And what he finds seems natural to us. That is, if beauty be natural. François Krige already lives on differently from when he was alive. Indeed, his life will keep growing and changing. Many of us have a perception of him, a construct or a memory, some snippets of hearsay. He continues to be with us, the way we all move in and out of one another.

And then, more importantly, there is the living matter of his existence – his paintings and drawings. They constitute the primary and collective expressions of the consciousness of an intelligent and sensitive artist-man. They too will change as all living matter does, because our vision and the context of our looking and our situating will alter. But as long as they can be preserved we shall be struck (and caressed) by the fresh and direct impact of colour-laden brushes on canvas.

Breyten Breytenbach

DONKERGAT
CHARCOAL

INTRODUCTION

François Krige died on 19 February 1994. I was out of the country at the time and returned to South Africa and to his home in Montagu a year later.

I pass through the garden of the main house, through sunflower beds, past the old pomegranate tree, the droning wasp-filled wisteria, flowering frangipani and roses: the scent of a Montagu summer. I crunch on apricot-pit gravel round the side of my uncle's house to where his recently harvested apricot trees grow. I unlock the back door and step into the studio, which still smells strongly of paint. His easel stands in the corner, an unfinished canvas upon it; a loaded brush lies to one side. Oil paints and brushes are laid out on the kitchen counter. On a shelf is his collection of art books, and on the wall a Buddhist print, the only decoration. Here is his palette, the colours of his last picture mixed and ready for application.

I feel like an intruder in this quiet place which my uncle always kept private. I open his drawers, page through sketchbooks, leaf through photographs. I find a calabash, used as a prop for the Barakwena paintings, and earthenware jugs for his floral still-lifes. In a cupboard I discover old Krige family letters. François was the last of the siblings to receive these chain letters, usually started by his brother Uys, intended as a means of keeping the entire family informed about the others' doings.

I open a door to one of the back rooms and move the canvases – which are all stacked facing the wall, as was his custom – into the light. This is the Bushman collection his widow, Sylvia, had hinted at. None of these paintings have been exhibited and Uncle François kept them locked away until his death. I line the pictures along the wall: this 'tableau' is one of the private worlds that François inhabited in the last decade of his life.

I step out into his garden and hear the soft plop of tennis balls over the fence where he used to play on Saturday afternoons. A hoopoe flits by, heading for the birdbath François always kept filled with seed and water to entice the birds of the veld into his garden. Here are his roses and vegetables, still tended by Sylvia and Klaas, the old gardener. The apricots have been harvested and the Montagu heat is singing. He would have been having his siesta now.

Would Krige have wanted me to write this book? Would he have been comfortable with my delving into his so very private life and uncovering his past, laying it bare for others to read? No. He would have resisted all attempts. Nonetheless his paintings do deserve to be exposed, images that have received almost no

BARAKWENA WOMAN WITH
CALABASH, 1980S
OIL ON CANVAS
89 x 78,5 CM
PRIVATE COLLECTION

attention from art critics. Today he is known largely for his fine draughtsmanship, but the paintings were rarely exhibited and the bulk of his oeuvre remained in his studio and was shown only to a select few, and then only isolated works.

François Krige was something of an ascetic who nevertheless engaged with the world on his own terms and in his own time. Quiet and reserved, he was wonderfully entertaining in a soft-spoken way when you got him talking, but he seldom talked about himself and never about his work. One had the feeling that he was entirely self-contained and even when he was silent, one felt at ease in his presence. I never heard François say anything derogatory about another painter. He always found some redeeming feature in others' work although he was ruthless about his own failures, insisting on the destruction of paintings with which he was unhappy. He was well-read, had a fine intellect, and expressed his ideas in a lucid and original way in both English and Afrikaans. He also spoke Spanish, Italian and Flemish and could get by comfortably in German and Portuguese.

His reticence to engage with others and his need for privacy speak of a man content with his own company on the one hand, yet at ease with the world. Coming from a large, charismatic and successful family, his first instinct was always to withdraw. His painting was a way of life, a deeply personal act of self-fulfilment which apparently did not need the affirmation of others. But perhaps there was also a certain apprehension at engaging with the public world and the realm of the art establishment. Although he was part of the avant-garde (as attested by his involvement with the New Group), he increasingly detached himself from the mainstream, especially after the Second World War. It may even be partly due to war experiences that he ultimately chose the route of a Braque rather than a Picasso, avoiding the limelight and the accolades of an art world hungry for innovative explorations of style and subject matter.

Krige was an artist of poetic reserve, of exceptional draughtsmanship, and a colourist comparable with the Post-Impressionists. His subject matter remained that of the late nineteenth century: still-lifes, portraits, landscapes and figure studies. But he is not simply a South African Post-Impressionist and no label fits entirely comfortably or consistently and none should be imposed. He was influenced by many styles and traces of artists as diverse as Rembrandt, Van Gogh, Cézanne, Chagall, Matisse and Marc are discernible at various times in his career. But more importantly, it is a personal vision that comes through; an honest, hard-earned 'take' on the world, a private relationship with paint, brush and canvas that makes a Krige work unmistakable.

Krige did experiment in a limited way, but always returned to his trademark style developed over a lifetime. François the person and François the artist were too closely linked for any experimentation for the sake of fashion. His way of seeing and rendering the world is a formidable one; democratic in its breadth, sincere in its intent, humble in its execution and true to a personal vision of beauty. The art critic Neville Dubow concurs:

> *In an age of shoddy painting values, where the fashionable is so often synonymous with the easy way out, Krige's enduring qualities – his thoroughgoing concern for the truth of his work, his deep regard for the dignity of the humble people who form his subject matter – stand out very clearly.*[1]

Krige espoused no theories about art and, if he had spoken out, would probably have insisted only on a 'romantic' truth to the subject and the self. His art was a way of life, not a profession, and if he did not sell paintings for extended periods, he did not mind so long as he had materials and enough to live on. Indeed, as soon as he could remove himself from the city and the art community, he did, settling in a Little Karoo town where he would practise and develop his art in relative isolation.

One area of Krige's painting that critics have commented on is his habit of *drawing* with the paintbrush[2] and his use of dark outlines. Where he over-uses these devices and where he does not allow the outline to 'breathe', the effect can be heavy and the balance between line and 'painterliness' upset. But Krige's line often performs an essential function in the paintings, swelling and tapering expressively, and in his best works the line has a character of its own, imparting a rhythm to the composition.

Krige was certainly attracted to the silhouetted 'outline' so prevalent in Japanese art (indeed he assembled a collection of Japanese prints that must have served as a lasting inspiration for his works). Gauguin would have approved: 'Study the silhouette of every object; distinctness of outline is the attribute of the hand that is not enfeebled by any hesitation of will.'[3] Linear effects and dark outlines are a characteristic of much Post-Impressionist art and the harsh isolation of objects or

---

[1] Neville Dubow, 'François Krige's Paintings Reflect his Permanent Values' in *The Cape Argus*, 13 November 1959.
[2] The painting style of Van Gogh – one of the formative artists in Krige's career – is also graphic, as though he were drawing with colour.
[3] Gauguin, quoted in Robert Goldwater, *Paul Gauguin* (1957; London, 1985), p. 126.

areas and the feeling of monumentality it creates often make for a powerful effect in Krige's paintings.

The great technological advances of the twentieth century go unrecorded in this artist's work. Instead he was convinced of the need for a direct and deeply personal experience and concrete study of nature. He would spend time alone in the wild, often packing his rucksack to walk and sketch in the mountains, sleeping under the stars and meditating in the veld. His art, particularly his line drawings, exhibits this close affinity with nature and the way he can suggest a tree or a landscape with the barest skeleton of lines speaks of a love and an intimate knowledge of the land. He is able to achieve the *essence* of a scene with great economy, another quality he admired in Japanese art. His attention to the details of colour, light and form in flowers, fruit, landscapes and the human figure show us his mastery of the simple facts of our existence, unencumbered by a need to say things that are contemporary or in ways that are ground breaking.

Krige painted this country in a manner informed by European traditions, but his eye was that of an African and the feeling and emotion he evokes are indigenous. His approach is humanist and his subjects essentially rural, traditional and familial. His art is never overtly political, but his representations of the indigenous groups of South Africa do have important social implications. He was an Afrikaner liberal who shunned the world of politics and yet his subject matter belies his 'democratic' eye. His mature art features a great many portraits of Coloured and black people and these are seldom sentimental stereotypes or 'characters'. The images do not reinforce the idea of white superiority over 'indigenous' culture (although in the later work there is an element of romanticism, but this is an idealisation of his own past rather than an 'isolation' of the Other). The native Other is seldom portrayed as an exotic; Krige presents individuals – homeless vagrants, fishermen, farm labourers – whom he respects and whose dignity he stresses.

My task in writing this book has been made difficult by the fact that Krige was a man of few spoken words and almost no written words. His paintings are often the only record of his life and it is through them alone that I have had to piece together certain parts of his career. Family archaeology is full of unique biographical privileges and fraught with its own pitfalls: where to tread lightly, in which cupboards to rummage in search of material, which letters to read, how much should I say? In which instances do I have the right to speak for him? Precious few, I have learnt.

The form of this book has been dictated by the available information, and its emphasis shifts from biography to art criticism as it progresses. In the chapters on Krige's youth and early career, a period in which he did very little significant work, we fortunately have plenty of biographical material stemming largely from family documents, particularly his brother Uys's letters and stories, as well as some autobiographical material. His active service as a war artist was a seminal time and I have devoted a full chapter to this period, using military archives, some personal letters and his war art (almost the full body of his war work is preserved in one place and this provides a unique opportunity to study a concentrated period of creativity). The war also deserves a chapter on its own because it was a crucial time for François, a period when he learnt about isolation and about inhumanity; in some ways it must have sealed his reclusiveness and almost Schopenhauer-like retreat from the world. The subsequent Cape Town chapter balances art criticism and biography and takes a close look at his 'ethnographic' sketching expeditions into the Kalahari and beyond. The final chapter deals with the paintings of his most productive period, his last decades in Montagu: many of these have never been seen, let alone reviewed by critics. This was a time when he withdrew even further from the world and his art became his life. The story of the later paintings thus, in a sense, becomes his biography.

SELF-PORTRAIT
CONTÉ

FRANÇOIS KRIGE

16

A Krige family portrait on the stoep at Mostertsdrif, Stellenbosch, in the mid-twenties. From left: Bokkie, Uys, Mizzi, Japie, François and Arnold.

1. YOUTH 1913-1933

François in the early thirties.

FAMILY BACKGROUND

François Krige was born on 20 July 1913 to a well-known Afrikaner family, the fourth of six children. His family on both his mother and his father's sides had lived in South Africa for over ten generations. The first of the South African Kriges, Wilhelm Adolph, came from Germany to the Cape as a Dutch East India Company official in 1721 and married Johanna de Villiers, daughter of one of the French Huguenot immigrants who had settled in the temperate valleys to the east of Cape Town. For the next two-and-a-half centuries the Kriges, and the small group of families into which they married, continued to have an umbilical connection to the area around Stellenbosch, with its gabled homesteads, oak trees and vineyards. The Krige clan became part of the growth and development of this region and played a significant role in the civil and professional life of the area. François Krige's grandfather was a highly respected Dutch Reformed Church minister who had seven sons, who became doctors, magistrates or high-school teachers.

If the Kriges belonged to the landed gentry of the Cape Afrikaners, many of François's maternal relatives, the Uyses, belonged to another category of Afrikaner, the migrating, independence-loving cattlemen of the frontier. The first Uys landed at the Cape from Friesland in 1704 and his son married a Huguenot woman and moved to the undulating Swellendam district in 1765 to farm sheep and cattle. As the Colony expanded, some of the Uyses trekked eastwards. By 1837 Jacobus Uys and his son Piet were leading one of the four Great Treks to the north, away from British rule. The restless temperament of the Uyses seems to have contrasted strongly with the reason and stability of the Kriges. The Uyses were proud, fatalistic, adventurous folk and their names recur frequently in the pages of Afrikaner history. For instance there were the legendary deaths of Piet Uys and his young son Dirkie, shortly after the assassination of the Voortrekker leader Piet Retief in 1838 (Retief was also distant family, in fact a great-great-great uncle of François Krige).

François's father, Jacob Daniel Krige (1879–1961), was a gentle, retiring man who was reputed never to have said a disparaging word about anyone. He was a magistrate who performed his duties in a number of small towns in the Western and Eastern Cape and the Free State. If his father's nomadic profession meant an unsettled youth for François, it also exposed him to many different parts of the country he grew to love. François's remarkable temperament, his desire for a harmonious and reclusive life style, his need of privacy, his own unwillingness to say anything unpleasant about anyone (other than perhaps the odd politician) were traits inherited from his father and from the Kriges. He recalled how his grandfather would escape from his thirteen children to write his sermons by retiring into the branches of an old oak tree and pulling the ladder up behind him (François was to make similar, Krige-like retreats into his studio whenever company threatened).

Jacob Daniel Krige, or Japie as he came to be known to millions of South Africans, won fame not as a magistrate but on the rugby field. His heyday was in the first decade of the century, a time when he could punch a hole in the defence of any rugby team in the world. He was reputedly 'the finest centre three-quarter of his era and certainly the first South African rugby player to capture the national imagination'.[1] Legends abound concerning his ten-year career (1896–1906). He was only seventeen when he gained his provincial colours and never once played in a losing match for Western Province (the famous Currie Cup final of 1906 was won at the last moment by Japie's brilliance). In 1903, within a year of the South African War, South Africa won a series of matches against the British touring team. Three years later these victories were emphatically confirmed when the South Africans again beat their foes on a visit to the British Isles (it was against Wales that Japie, in the last test match of his career, proved that he was the best centre in the world by out-playing the only other contender for the title, Gwyn Nicholls).

François's mother, Susanne (Sannie) Uys (1886–1976), was brought up by an English governess and then studied music at Stellenbosch. Sannie was a gracious, dignified and formidable woman who was fiercely devoted to her family, but also given to the Uys self-doubt and melancholy. She encouraged her sons to follow their creative inclinations from a very early age, taking the children to their first plays, introducing them to the classics of literature and to fine art, and frequently insisting that they speak English to her. It was she who encouraged François with an unwavering faith in his artistic talent. After she had raised her six children she turned to writing and published her first book of short stories at the age of sixty-two.

It is thus not surprising that Japie and Sannie produced such remarkable children. François's eldest brother was born a year after their marriage in Swellendam in 1908, at which the Western Province rugby team, rather than a team of horses, drew their bridal carriage. Jacobus (Bokkie) went on to win a Rhodes Scholarship and read English at Oxford. He subsequently became a high-ranking aviator and chief inspector of aerodromes for South Africa and made two acclaimed translations of Antoine de Saint-Exupéry's *Vol de Nuit* and *Terre des Hommes* into Afrikaans. Uys, the charismatic second son and the most famous of the siblings, became a much-loved South African figure, publishing dozens of works in English and Afrikaans ranging from poems and novels to plays and travel sketches. Next came the urbane and cultured Arnold, the only family member who had any business sense and, as such, kept his artist siblings afloat during financial difficulties. François was the youngest son and was followed by two daughters, Maria Magdalena (Mizzi), who, before her early death, was a highly regarded actress, and Suzanne, the *laatlammetjie* who inherited her mother's temperament and who became a journalist for *Die Burger* newspaper at age 19 before marrying the architect Revel Fox.

CHILDHOOD

François was born in Uniondale, not far from Oudtshoorn in the Western Cape, where his father was stationed as a clerk of the court. His early childhood was spent in the platteland, resulting in a life-long affinity with rural environments and settings as evidenced in his work. In fact, for the last thirty years of his life he settled in a small Karoo town, reluctant to make more than the occasional journey to the city.

In the early years the Kriges were poor and Japie struggled to provide for his rapidly growing family. When François was very young the family moved to a farm, Zandhoogte, near Bredasdorp in the southern Cape, where they remained during 1915 and 1916. It was here, at the tender age of three, that François held a paintbrush in his hand for the first time (how he cleaned his only brush of its various paints was always a mystery to his mother). At Zandhoogte the first reference to François appears in a letter by his brother Uys: '*Ons het vandag die dyfies yt ge haal en moedr het vandag naar het Dorp gigan met F.*'[2] It is also where the first extant photograph of François was taken. The four brothers pose with 'Red Indian' feather headdresses. The three older boys stand to attention in their culottes, long socks and *velskoene*, while white-haired François keeps to one side with a naughty grin on his face – clearly the baby of the group going about his business independently of the others.

'Ons het vandag … ': 'Today we took out the little pigeons and Mother went into town with F.'

velskoene: raw-hide shoes.

---

[1] Chris Greyvenstein, *Springbok Saga: A Pictorial History from 1891* (Cape Town, 1977), p. 28.
[2] Uys Krige, *Briewe I: 1916-33* (unpublished letters, Stellenbosch University), letter to Mr Howe-Browne dated 31 October 1916, p. 1. Throughout their lives the Kriges were scrupulous about circulating letters and we can safely assume that most letters addressed to one sibling or parent would make the rounds until everyone had caught up on family news.

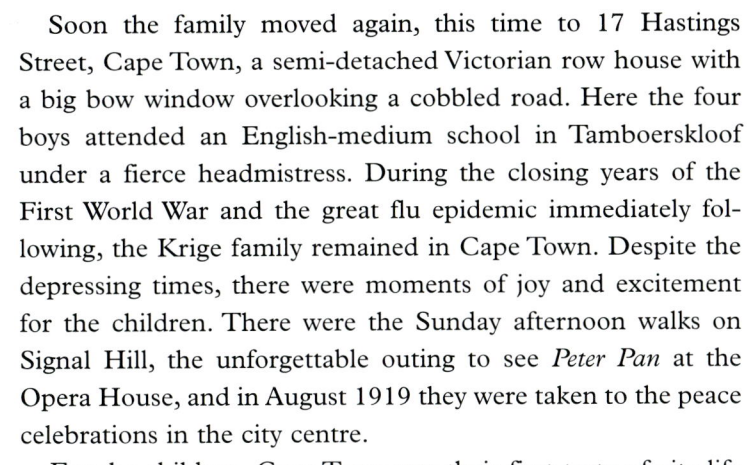

Soon the family moved again, this time to 17 Hastings Street, Cape Town, a semi-detached Victorian row house with a big bow window overlooking a cobbled road. Here the four boys attended an English-medium school in Tamboerskloof under a fierce headmistress. During the closing years of the First World War and the great flu epidemic immediately following, the Krige family remained in Cape Town. Despite the depressing times, there were moments of joy and excitement for the children. There were the Sunday afternoon walks on Signal Hill, the unforgettable outing to see *Peter Pan* at the Opera House, and in August 1919 they were taken to the peace celebrations in the city centre.

For the children, Cape Town was their first taste of city life and it left an indelible impression. In the thirties, Uys wrote a short story, '*Die Stad*', in which he deals with an arrival in Cape Town through the eyes of the youngest of four brothers, clearly modelled on little François. The wide-eyed child is enchanted and then frightened by the bustling streets, the crowds dressed in their 'Sunday clothes' during the week, the towering crags of Lion's Head. The boy compares his experience of the city with visual images he has conjured up from picture books. His eyes drink in the vibrant colours of this new environment: red post-boxes, green lampposts, black shadows cast by tall buildings, pear-yellow trams. It is as though Uys has climbed into his baby brother's skin and painted a visual and emotional portrait of the artist as a young child. We also learn of the poverty of the family living in Cape Town during the First World War and of how the child received his threadbare clothes and playthings fourth hand, passed down through each of his older brothers.

BONTEBOKSKLOOF

Holidays during the war and after were often spent at Bonteboksloof, the Uys family farm near Swellendam at the foot of the Langeberg. Bonteboksloof had a special significance for the whole family and it became a symbol of their farming ancestry, their closeness to the land. It was also a magical setting for a group of young brothers. The children played in the river bed, made clay oxen with the labourers' children and went walking in the kloofs looking for animals. They would watch the shearing and dipping of sheep, the slaughtering, and the hanging of skins to dry in a corner of the wagon-house. They would help with sowing and harvesting and take sickly lambs back to the farmhouse to be raised. In springtime Sannie showed them on which hill the freesias grew, into which kloofs the evening flower poured its scent, where to find *rooi pypies*, cornflowers, *katjietee* – aristocrat of veld flowers – and the fragrant kukumakranka. The child who listened most attentively and acquired his mother's love of nature most readily was François.

Oupa Uys was an eccentric character and a great raconteur who would keep the children spellbound with his stories both of the district and of family folklore. All the Krige children knew about their gentle grandfather's strange habits. For instance the attic of the old home was packed with provisions: golden tobacco leaves hung from the roof, red apples, bags of dried fruit, tea and sugar were piled on the floor and in the middle stood Oupa's coffin, which usually housed cases of tinned food, but occasionally he would unpack these and test his future bed. And it was also Oupa Uys who loaded up the ox-wagon and embarked on a nine-month, thousand-mile trek to the Transvaal to visit relations, with his coffin in the back of the wagon, in case of misadventure.

STELLENBOSCH

After Cape Town the Kriges packed their wagon and moved to Bellville for a short period – the boys walking to a nearby 'country' school – before making a home in Stellenbosch where Japie was appointed assistant resident magistrate. The years in their Mostertsdrif home were a happy time for the family, a settled existence in which the children thrived and an era evocatively captured in Uys's novella, *The Dream*. A 1926 photograph shows Japie sitting proudly with his four healthy boys while little Mizzi reads a book. François, in an ill-fitting suit and tie askew and with big brother Arnold's protective arm around him, can be singled out as having the most serious expression on his face.

The Krige siblings would look back on their childhood in Stellenbosch in the twenties as an idyllic, semi-rural existence. Their home was a semi-detached Victorian house on the outskirts of the town, under the shadow of the Helderberg. It had no fireplace and no electric heater, so the Stellenbosch winter must have been bitterly cold. But there was no lack of familial warmth in this household dominated by the loving Sannie and the soft-spoken Japie. The centre of the home was the living room where the children practised the violin and other

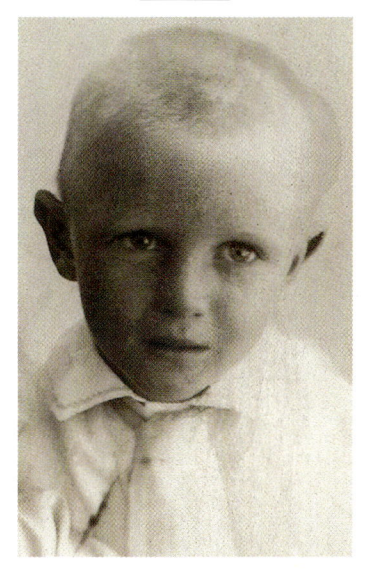

The young François in Cape Town at the end of the First World War.

Die Stad: The City.
rooi pypies: watsonia, red afrikaner.
katjietee: painted lady.

instruments and Sannie held music lessons. Japie's rugby photographs hung on the wall together with a reproduction of C F Watt's painting of *Hope* sitting forlornly upon the globe, a broken lute in her hand. There was the constant clink of cutlery and crockery – the sound of work being done in the kitchen by Marta, the domestic worker – and if the children were lucky, there would be Marta's warm custard for pudding.

Sannie took great pride in cultivating a large garden, as she would do in all the homes they lived in, and this horticultural interest was handed down to her youngest son. In spring the Mostertsdrif garden was at its most beautiful and François would have relished it with eyes that were becoming sensitive to the nuances of colour in nature. A patch of wild poppies stood out red against the green of plants and vegetables behind, while Sannie's three peach trees were wrapped in the cotton wool of early spring, and the De Waal orchard next door was a sea of pink. Uys describes contemporary Dorp Street during a Stellenbosch spring:

> *On either side the water sang in the sluits [irrigation canals]; the tall broad oaks were a mass of pale green leaves; the snow-white and pink orchards looked more like huge flower beds than trees; everywhere in the gardens daffodils and hyacinths nodded in the breeze; dogroses fell like waterfalls over the hedges and in the vineyards patches of sorrel lay like white wisps of mist between the long rows of green vine stalks.*[3]

The boys' year was governed by the school timetable and the seasons. In autumn they would ride into the countryside on their bicycles and watch the harvesters moving through the red vineyards. Rugby practices would start on the muddy Jongensskool fields below snow-capped peaks. At home on the long winter nights there would be swapping and sorting of stamp collections and the flag tops of cigarette boxes, with hours of reading and drawing. Spring brought the Boland to life and the boys would take walks in the mountains above the town, excited by the rebirth of a myriad species of fynbos and watching out for the baboons and leopards that still populated the foothills. Cricket bats would be oiled for the coming season (the boys would don their black cricket caps on which Ouma Uys had sewn the letters 'MCC' – Mostertsdrif Cricket Club) and tennis rackets hauled out of the attic. In the glorious summer weather the boys would take their bicycles and ride out along the avenues of oaks, past the gabled white homesteads and into the countryside. There were outings to the Strand, final exams and then the trek down to Onrus for the Christmas vacation.

Daily life in the Boland town was a patchwork of adventures for the boys. On their way home from school they would play marbles and kick-and-jump with their cousins, the De Wets, and with friends on the large village green in the centre of Stellenbosch known as the Braak. The children would clamber about in the branches of the old pear tree in their garden and sail home-made boats in the village irrigation canals that ran past their house. They were fiercely proud of their BMK and Farley bicycles and would oil and rub them with rags until the frames blinked in the sun. When the children got muddy, Sannie would pile them all into the bath while she stoked the battered old geyser with planks and pine cones. On Saturday afternoons Japie would give each of his sons four pennies for the cinema where they would avidly follow weekly serials for boys such as the cowboy favourite, *The Masked Rider*. Visits from Oom Nols, Sannie's big-game hunting brother who lived in what was then Rhodesia, caused great excitement among the children as he was invariably the bearer of gifts.

The big event for the boys of the town each week was the Stellenbosch University first team (be it cricket or rugby) taking on out-of-town opposition, and usually taking them apart. The brothers would sit on the touchline in the area reserved for schoolboys and shout themselves hoarse. The intervarsity clashes between Stellenbosch and the University of Cape Town would work them into a frenzy of excitement. Although François enjoyed watching (and in later life became something of an expert in the nuances of both cricket and rugby), he did not enjoy playing and was not a fan of group activities. Family lore has it that on his first attempt at his father's game, François left the field after the first tackle and vowed never to play again. Although he enjoyed tennis throughout his life, he left sporting achievements to his athletic older brothers and concentrated on drawing. As the youngest, he usually retired from company and Sannie would often find him under the dining room table, shrouded by the cloth, happily sketching by himself.

He began to acquire a sophisticated sensibility for colour, line and form and even his earliest sketches show considerable talent. In the short story, 'Die Diefstal', Uys considers a child's awakening artistic perception through the character of Fransie, a little boy who displays some of the attributes of young François:

Kleure is vir hom nog mooier as woorde, en baie, baie mooier as klanke. 'n Kleur – en die lyn, die vorm van dinge – voel hy, praat met hom direk sonder dat hy nog, soos in die geval van die geskrewe woord, soms moet nadink en hard probeer verstaan.[4]

But the time in Mostertsdrif was not without its sadness. There were two tragic events in the lives of the Kriges during the Stellenbosch period that were to shatter the happy idyll. The first incident involved the deaths of Sannie's sister, Minnie McKillop, and two of her three daughters, who drowned in a river near Heidelberg in 1922. Minnie's twin girls, Francina and Kathleen, were about the same age as the Krige boys and the cousins often played together. The story of the drowning had to be pieced together from the confused accounts of three-year-old Fredel, who had been found wandering about, crying, on the bank of the river an hour after the tragedy. Francina, who couldn't swim at all, had waded out too far into the stream and Kathleen had jumped in to try and help her. Minnie had just taken off her bathing costume when she heard her daughters' cries and rushed back to the river to rescue them. Her panic-stricken children grabbed her around the neck and dragged her under. Later, two men from the village dived in and found her lying naked at the bottom, her twin daughters clasped in her arms.

The second incident, within two months of the drownings, was even closer to home. Not long after they had moved into Mostertsdrif, Sannie had given birth to a fifth son, but the frail baby contracted meningitis and did not survive more than a few weeks. Kleinboet's death made a powerful impression on the children. The Krige family plot lay in the white-walled cemetery on a hill just outside town, and it was here that Kleinboet was taken in Mynheer van Kerkhof's horse-drawn landau and laid to rest on top of Oupa Krige's coffin. For the sensitive nine-year-old François the early loss of his brother, cousins and aunt must have had a profound impact, and throughout his life he exhibited a fascination with death. There are many depictions of funerals in his oeuvre and one of his most haunting paintings is that of a charred corpse during the war.

ONRUS

Throughout François's early years the family made annual summer pilgrimages to Onrus River where the Kriges had owned a seaside house since the nineteenth century. For the whole family the expedition to Onrus was a highlight and the children loved these long vacations. During their teens the four boys would cycle there from Stellenbosch.

The summer home, Melkbos, was a gabled white house in a grove of *melkhout* and had no electricity. Light was provided by old-fashioned paraffin lamps which hung from the ceilings. The shade of a giant milkwood tree in the garden served as an outdoor living room and the children played like monkeys in its branches. The De Wet brothers used to rail their cows to Bot River from where they would be driven along the road to Onrus so that the extended family could have fresh milk during the holidays.

Relations from all over the country would descend on the seaside hamlet during December. There were only three bedrooms in the house, so the Krige Christmas was an intimate and communal family affair. All the boys slept in the *ramhok* which Oupa had built outside next to the garage, Ouma had a small room on the *stoep* from where she could oversee the running of the ship, and the married couples and their daughters shared the bedrooms. Ouma was a tiny, white-haired, bespectacled old lady who dressed only in black: black skirt, black stockings with black side-button boots. She was not very demanding of her extended clan, but there were certain rules: no smoking in her presence and none of the women was allowed to wear trousers or shorts. Mealtimes were strict (daughters-in-law taking turns to help Ai Rosie, the domestic worker, with the cooking) and while Oupa Krige – the Caledon *dominee* – was still alive, there would be lengthy prayers after dinner (often cut short by Ouma's timely, 'Amen, Papa'). Apart from this the children were free to roam the beach, go swimming or row on the lagoon. It was a perfect environment for them. They had plenty of playmates, a beautiful, unspoilt stretch of coastline, a river and mountains to explore, and long summer days. The younger children would swim in the sea pool near the camp site at high tide or dive off the rocks into the *palmiet*-coloured waters of the lagoon, while the older ones would brave the cold surf of Onrus beach. They would collect shells and peer into the little worlds contained in rock pools where starfish, *klipvissies*, crabs and other creatures lived among the swaying green weed. François was particularly fascinated by this underwater world in the intertidal zone and later in life would paint these submarine scenes as well as images of the rocky Onrus shore.

Kleure is vir … : Colours for him are even more beautiful than words, and much, much more beautiful than sounds. He feels that colour – and the line, the form of things – speak to him directly without having to think it through and trying hard to understand, as with written words.

melkhout: milkwood.

ramhok: rumpus room.

stoep: veranda.

dominee: minister.

palmiet: bulrush.

klipvissies: coral fish.

---

[3] Uys Krige, *The Dream and the Desert* (London, 1953), p. 90.
[4] Uys Krige, 'Die Diefstal' in *Die Palmboom* (Pretoria, 1943), p. 58.

As always, François was reclusive and even as a child would often break away from group activities and go off to walk, paint or sketch alone. When he was still very young he is reputed to have drawn the faces of General Hertzog and General Smuts on the sandy walls of the Onrus house. His earliest significant portrait was also done during a vacation here in the thirties. *Suzanne* is a fine painting of his sister with the beach, rocks and ocean behind. The girl is associated with her environment through a number of devices. Her skin is burnt by the summer sun. Her nose, lips and cheeks are pink and about to peel and these flesh tones reflect the colours of the beach and rocks in the background. Green shadows in her face and hair respond to the foliage behind and the greens in the sea and sky. The loose, free brushstrokes of her white dress are echoed in the sea's white horses and the shapes of the seagulls in the background. The brushstrokes in the sky arch over the girl's head, almost creating a halo effect enhanced by the golden hair and cherubic cheeks. This is a study, even a celebration, of female maturation and puberty. The girl is no longer a child and not yet a woman. There is diffidence here as she does not look at us face on; indeed her serious expression conveys a wisdom beyond her age.

Childhood memories of Onrus were important to François and he returned there for vacations throughout his life, in later years to Uys's home above the lagoon. The sounds, smells and emotions attached to Onrus stayed with the Krige siblings always: the daily walk to the beach through the dense shade of the *melkbos* with the heady scent of their berries, the shrill monotone of cicadas in the midday heat, the blinding white of sand dunes and the rust-coloured waters of the lagoon.

There was one particularly memorable 'expedition' in January 1929, probably the last all four boys ever made as a team. It was a summer adventure that the brothers would reminisce about during the war and in letters from various parts of the globe as a symbol of their idyllic Onrus holidays. The boy-scout plan was to hike for two days along Walker Bay beach beside the windswept strandveld dunes to De Kelders and Gansbaai. Photographs of the hike show the suntanned young men basking in the January sun, swimming naked in the surf and enjoying their sandwiches in the shade of rocks. An early morning black-and-white shows the smiling adventurers reclining on the sand among their rucksacks and blankets. Bokkie holds a bottle of beer and Arnold a pipe, teenagers posing with their symbols of manhood. In the distance is the outline of Maanskynkop towering above Hermanus. A bronzed, fifteen-year-old François is clearly the baby of the group but appears proud to be included in his older brothers' expedition. Years later Uys wrote of that seminal experience: '*Dis of daardie twee dae, die geluk, en sorgeloosheid daarvan 'n apoteose is van geheel ons kinderdae en jongmanskap.*'[5]

UNIVERSITY

In 1927 the family was posted to Cathcart in the Eastern Cape, and Japie, Sannie and the two girls packed up their Stellenbosch home. It was at this time that Sannie encouraged François to begin drawing lessons with Ruth Prowse, then curator of the Michaelis Collection in Cape Town. The boys completed their schooling at the Hoër Jongensskool and the two eldest registered at Stellenbosch University, while François enrolled at the University of Cape Town's Michaelis School of Fine Art at the age of fifteen.

When François was contemplating leaving school to attend Michaelis, Uys wrote to his parents expressing his opinion on his brother's future (something in which he would, perhaps in the self-conscious role of a Theo van Gogh, take a very close interest):

> *François's fate I dimly expected. I think he must go back to school in Junior Matric. Paint in the holidays, have an exhibition in Town at the end of the year. People and newspapers will certainly interest themselves in him and probably subscribe and send him to Europe … Let him do just what he wants to, above all, do not worry a damn … He is going to be a great artist, I am certain he will be acclaimed before he is dust. He is old enough to judge for himself – he is not 16 – but so, really I think Herbert Vladimir Meyerowitch [sic] is a big piece of scab, don't you?*[6]

Whatever Uys thought of Meyerowitz, in the coming years the fine-art lecturer taught François the basics of woodcarving, which proved invaluable in his later rendering of two-dimensional form. Meyerowitz, known for his carved memorial doors in the South African National Gallery, was a Russian Jew who emigrated to South Africa from Germany in 1925 and was soon appointed lecturer in woodcarving at the new University complex in Orange Street. There he guided the Michaelis staff and students in the execution of carved teak panels and fanlights depicting historical scenes of the Cape that adorn several buildings on the University campus.

'Dis of daardie …': 'It's as if those two days, their happiness, their carefreeness, were an apotheosis of all our days as children and as young men.'

[5] Uys Krige, *Briewe I*, letter to Bokkie dated 12 January 1932, p. 68.
[6] Uys Krige, *Briewe I*, undated (1930?) letter to parents, p. 5.

The only extant Krige work of his period at Michaelis is a woodcarving of a young man (1928), possibly a self-portrait. The small figure is clad in shorts and an open shirt and stands barefoot in a casual pose with hand in pocket, a pose deliberately at odds with the monumental 'timeless' figures that were traditionally associated with sculpture. Indeed the sculptor's attention to such details as the young man's belt, his open collar and rolled-up sleeves demonstrates his attempt to make a contemporary statement.

The only other surviving Krige sculpture is a clay piece – one solid mass with no negative volume – of a young calf, curled up and asleep. In this small work Krige shows his understanding of animal form. The spine and muscles are well modelled while the bent neck gives the young creature a look of vulnerability.

The contrast between François's university life and that of his older brothers could not have been greater. Bokkie and Uys were together in digs in Stellenbosch and enjoyed a very social time. They played sport year-round for their university and were very active in campus life. There were dinners, dances, outings into the country and rugby tours. Bokkie played in the Intervarsity tournament and Uys even started a Writers' Club.

By contrast and unlike his brothers, François stayed with relatives in the southern suburbs and withdrew from clubs, societies or anything that smacked of group activity. He commuted by train to the Orange Street campus and there dedicated himself totally to learning the basics of a profession he knew would be his for life.

CATHCART

Cathcart – or Ekatikari, as the Xhosa call it – was a sleepy 'frontier' town in the undulating green hills of the Eastern Cape and the boys used to visit their parents here during university vacations (and later from Johannesburg). It was Japie's first post as full magistrate and from now on the Kriges would have considerable standing in the villages to which he was posted. The residences in which they were housed were often grand, and in Cathcart a German governess could even be hired for little Suzanne. The Cathcart home was a fine old Victorian stone house covered in ivy, with an iron roof, veranda and a pretty garden which François enjoyed painting in a derivative Van Gogh style. Apart from a lot of *plein air* work, François also had a separate white room that Sannie had cleared for him to use and the other children recalled the silence and heady smell of oils that emanated from this space.

Because the boys were spread across South Africa at this time, family gatherings at Cathcart were rare and cherished occasions. It was a time when they could be pampered by Sannie, talk through the night catching up on family news, sleep late, eat home-cooked food and play plenty of tennis. During the initial Cathcart vacations, François would spend hours in the kloofs and rivers with local black children, helping them fashion oxen and rhinoceroses out of clay. When he and his brothers were older, holidays were a very social time. There were Show Balls in the city hall, regular dances in the hotel at which the Krige boys would meet young women of the town, Sunday outings to farms in the district (Suzanne recalls that François was always the driver on these occasions) where there would be teas and tennis parties. The boys used to parade in the main street on Saturday mornings, the only time when the town really came alive and the streets bustled with ox-wagons and activity.

As could be expected, François was reluctant to take part in too many of these activities and Suzanne remembers that whenever there was a knock at the front door, he would disappear through the back gate with a sketchbook under his arm.

François's mother, the writer Sannie Krige (née Uys) at the time of her marriage.

François on holiday in Ladybrand.

François se werk …: François's work has improved amazingly. It seems as if the rascal has genius. So strong, so firm. If he continues like this, nothing on earth will stop him. Already he stands far above most S. African painters – at least to my taste … Franc (sic) will be a great success in the city of gold.

[7] Uys Krige, *Briewe I*, letter to Bokkie dated March 1931, pp. 32-33.

One photograph of this period (1933) shows the blonde, tanned and handsome twenty-year-old artist smoking a pipe and pondering life. Another depicts him working *en plein air*, braving the elements in a ploughed field. His paint box lies on a clod of earth and the canvas rests precariously on a three-legged, home-made easel. Palette in hand, the artist stares into the distance, oblivious of the photographer and the paint dripping on his elegant, unpainterly clothes.

At this time Uys wrote to Bokkie, enthusiastically describing the improvements he perceived in François's work:

> *François se werk het verbasend verbeter. Dit lyk my bra, die rakker het 'genius'. So Sterk, so ferm. As hy so aangaan, keer niks op aarde hom nie. Ek het amper op my rug geval. Hy staan reeds ver bo meeste S. Afrikaanse skilders – tenminste, volgens my smaak … Franc [sic] sal groot opgang maak in die goudstad.*[7]

STYLISTIC EXPERIMENTATION

The art of this period, much of it done in Cathcart during protracted holidays (notably in the winter of 1929), reflects Krige's experimentation with various styles and media. Many of these new influences would have been acquired both from the work he came into contact with as a student in Cape Town and, more significantly, from his extensive reading of books on art. There are a number of bleak and expressionist Cathcart landscapes in pen and water-colour, but these tend to be over-worked with too much line and an abundance of unnecessary detail. They are rendered in a style that suggests Krige's close affinity with Van Gogh and the Cathcart garden's cypresses are derived straight from the Dutchman. There are some fine pencil sketches of figures, notably of his little sister, Xhosas in traditional dress, herd boys, dancers, and women cooking. The paintings of Xhosa heads and bare-breasted women are drawn in bold colour and in a style not dissimilar to Irma Stern's – small slit eyes, thick lips, large emphasised breasts, oval faces decorated with yellow clay – figures reminiscent of carved statuettes. These early clichéd renderings of the Other, of simplified and stylised figures, show no insight into the character of the subject, unlike his later portraiture. They are clearly products of contemporary artistic stereotypes and of one of his (and many other Cape artists of the time) current areas of interest, German Expressionism.

The earliest surviving oil painting is a garden scene painted at their home in February 1930 and signed with an unformed hand. It is painted with a thick, Van Gogh-like impasto, the oils often blended wet-in-wet on the board. Even at this early stage in his career, François shows his predilection for painting nature and gardens in particular. There are other oils of the local flour mill, the countryside and of Cathcart, showing the semi-rural character of the town with its small cultivated plots of land between the houses. He is already playing with colour and with Cézanne-like cubic houses, while the trees are painted unconvincingly as fuzzy green clouds of foliage. The bold outline so characteristic of much of his work is already there.

Let us consider in more detail the influence of Impressionism, Post-Impressionism and Expressionism on the young Krige. The 'Cape Impressionists', of which Hugo Naudé and Stratford Caldecott can be considered forerunners, adopted elements of the European Impressionists' technique. The bright South African light, landscape and colours in nature required a modified approach, however, and Caldecott was one of the first to adapt his palette to the African conditions, taking that which suited his subject matter, talent and temperament from the Impressionists, just as Krige was to do with the Post-Impressionists.

Impressionism began to gain a foothold in South Africa in the twenties. The exponents painted *alla prima*, direct from the subject *en plein air*. They preferred casual-looking compositions, realistic colour, sketchy brushwork and light that shimmered across the surface of the canvas. The medium was important and the means of paint application – the brushstroke or smear of the palette knife – became clearly visible. They also painted similar subjects to those of their European counterparts, such as unpretentiously rendered landscapes, still-lifes and figure studies.

Krige's early oil paintings picked up from European and South African Impressionism, although he was ultimately more interested in Post-Impressionist and Expressionist developments. Throughout his career, but especially in the thirties, Krige toyed with Impressionism and there are many works that employ all the techniques of his French forebears. But he did see its limitations. His colour preferences are more personal and his palette usually darker than the 'High' Impressionists. His application of paint is also more 'solid' than the Impressionists' short, staccato strokes and dashes. Impressionists tended to avoid continuous outline while the

Post-Impressionists often relied on it and the solidity and structure it provided. Krige certainly felt the need to go beyond the fleeting impression and give greater emphasis to construction and form.

Post-Impressionism is a label we could pin to much of Krige's oeuvre, but it must be stressed that he was no slave to any particular style and developed an individualistic and unmistakable technique that does not fit comfortably into any distinct category. At various times during his career he did pursue the stylistic avenues opened by the three great Post-Impressionists, Cézanne, Gauguin and Van Gogh. Cézanne's impact on Krige's landscape and still-life painting is particularly striking. We notice the characteristic distortions, parallel hatched strokes and 'architectural' approach to form (his influence will be dealt with at length in the Montagu chapter). From Gauguin and the Symbolists Krige learnt the value of heavy, dark outlines, curving contours and flat areas of smooth colour – the cloisonnist technique which eliminated the shimmering effects of Impressionism. In this, Krige would also have been inspired by Japanese prints, of which he had a fine collection as did many of the Symbolists. The third great Post-Impressionist, Van Gogh – who bridges the gap between Post-Impressionism and Expressionism – was, as we have seen, especially influential in the early stages of his career.

Indeed, in many of Krige's early oil paintings the young man paints in a slavish Van Gogh style, no doubt drawn like so many young artists to the passionate, bold and expressive qualities of his art. One bridge scene from the thirties, strongly reminiscent of Van Gogh's *The Drawbridge*, is flecked with thickly applied dabs of white, yellow and orange paint and attempts to capture both a fleeting light effect at sunrise and the emotions it inspired. Like Van Gogh's, we notice how Krige's brush draws as well as paints, often tracing strong silhouettes in coloured strokes. Lines are firmly accented and define large areas of colour. The dark outlines of objects establish their existence and autonomy, giving them an elevated status and rendering the humble significant. For a linear painter like François, this Japanese influence was an inspiring technique. Van Gogh was greatly drawn to Japanese art, particularly modern Japanese wood blocks, and François came to the Japanese via artists such as Van Gogh. The Dutchman sought 'Japanese' subjects during his time in Provence – pure blue skies, blossoming trees, landscapes cut by bridges, big flat areas of colour – and we see something similar happening in Krige's art. Much of the two artists' subject matter is similar: portraits of labourers, still-lifes, landscapes with labourers at work, fields and blossoming trees.

By the twenties German Expressionism had found its way to the Cape and its innovations could be seen in the works of Maggie Laubser and Irma Stern. Krige came into contact with Stern's Expressionist work in the early thirties and her approach rubbed off on him. 'Native studies', which had formerly served as detached ethnographic observations, or images of the archetypal 'noble savage', were now less stereotypical and François's early depictions of such subjects show the influence of Stern's approach. But his renderings were still exotic, the images clichéd and relying on stylistic conventions. He heeded brother Uys's condemnation of Stern's approach and style:

> *She knows less about natives ... than I do about that amiable old buffer on the top of the moon. She uses them ... only for their surface value, their decorative qualities. So she not only sentimentalises them but exploits them, artistically speaking.*[8]

François would, in time, bring his own humanist sensibility and the rigorous discipline and technique of Impressionist portraiture to the Expressionist 'native study' and forge a style that conveyed a compelling empathy for the sitter.

JOHANNESBURG

After completing his studies at UCT, François moved to Johannesburg, no doubt encouraged by Uys's enthusiastic letters describing the excitement of the city where he was working as a reporter on *The Rand Daily Mail*. Uys created a wonderful image of Johannesburg:

> *They all say here the place gets into one's blood ... Only 40 years ago bare veld – and so much has happened since then, discord and strife, Martial Law 4 or 5 times. Sniping. Bombing. Slaughter and fratricide ... The mine dumps look strangely fantastic. They have blasted the hills here to make some of our suburbs. Houghton Estate and Orange Grove are beautiful. This city has so many aspects. Chinatown where I can drink opium, Vrededorp, the Arab and Portuguese quarters.*[9]

François arrived in the Transvaal in the autumn of 1931, two months before Uys departed for Europe. He stepped off the train at Jo'burg Central with his hair over his eyes, his pyjamas in a paper bag and a set of canvases wrapped in blankets under his arm. Uys describes François's first experience of the city:

[8] Uys Krige, *The Cape Times*, 8 March 1938.
[9] Uys Krige, *Briewe I*, undated (1930?) letter to parents, pp. 3-4.

Almal het hom [François] somar [sic] dadelik ter harte geneem, en hy het honderde mense ontmoet en is baie uitgeneem. Levson[10] *het hom onder sy vlerk geneem. François het 'n vyftiental skilderye saamgebring en ons vertrou dat Levson vir hom 'n tentoonstelling kosteloos sal reël in sy ateljee. Natuurlik het die stad die sewentien-jarige verruk – die 'bohemian haunts' het hom baie aangetrek. Sy werk word by die dag sterker – een stillewe wat hy onlangs geskilder het is eenvoudig meesterlik – dit oortref enigiets wat ek ooit van 'n Suid-Afrikaanse skilder gesien het – dit slaan my dronk. Niks lyk my sal die jonkman van sy koers bring nie. Waar kry hy hierdie groot talent vandaan? En hy is so ongerinneweer, natuurlik en beskeie – almal hou van hom … Hy gaan skilder bo-op die dak van ons ag-verdieping gebou en Johannesburg het onderwerpe genoeg.*[11]

Uys introduced François to his circle of 'Bohemian' friends: communists, philosophers, artists and journalists. They frequented cafés together and watched talkies. Uys's flat was a popular meeting-place and friends and colleagues would drop in at all hours.

François spent much of the following three years based in the 'City of Gold', some of the time with Bokkie. He did a few works on commission and attended further art classes. In letters from Europe, Uys continued to give his youngest brother support, but also warned against laziness or complacency. He urged François to read widely and to keep sketching every spare minute of the day. When François felt discouraged by criticism – the struggling artist was trying to exhibit in Johannesburg during this period – the ebullient Uys was always there for his brother:

Hou moed, ou broer! Niks op Godsaarde – nie 'n tien duisend M L du Toits [a well-known critic] of tweegat-jakkalse of watter kakjasse ook al – geen teenspoed of troebel of trugslag [sic] gaan ons ooit stuit of van stryk bring nie, ons op ons mars voorwaarts trug [sic] hou nie.[12]

Uys even got his close friend, the poet Roy Campbell, to write a few words of encouragement to François. He was always scheming on his brother's behalf. For instance, he asked his mother and François to send examples of his work in order to promote it overseas; and after visiting Florence, Uys decided that it was the city best suited to François, the ideal place for him to further his education, as he told his parents:

Florence will be just the stimulus, the incentive, nay the intoxication he is in need of. It can't possibly do him any harm. He can attend the art school there, which I hear is extremely fine, or he can just study the masters – they are all there. Florence's galleries are perhaps the finest in the world. François should go mad with joy about them. The fees at the college are very moderate, I am told. I am writing to them for full particulars this evening … I think Mammie and Pappie you must absolutely give François this chance … François will be a fine if not a great artist. Let us, all of us, you who have bred this singular phenomenon – (I speak as if he were a species of plant) help him to the best of our ability.[13]

It was during this period that Uys began to urge François to draw subjects that could be used as illustrations or covers for his own books, thereby turning their respective artistic pursuits into a family industry like the small publishing business established by Ireland's Yeats clan. Eventually Bokkie and Sannie would also publish under Uys's encouragement, with François providing illustrations.

Sometimes Uys's constant advice became too much for the younger brother and he, albeit briefly, shut Uys up. Here is the poet's response:

Dit pynig my om te hoor dat al my advies en vermaninge François so verveel het. Het ek gepreek en gekatkiseer was dit werklik 'n predikasie en katkisasie meer tot myself gerig dan tot hom … Maar François is reg – advies op wit papier is nie die sous werd nie, het nooit die persoonlike stemklank nie, kan so maklik dor en dood of indringerig of oorbodig klink. Bly om te hoor hy's so vol vertroue. Vertroue, hoop ek meer om goeie werk te lewer dan sy duisende los te slaan.[14]

As is evident in the last sentence, even while apologising for dishing out unwanted advice, Uys just cannot resist slipping in more of the same.

After a few years François began slowly to be recognised in Johannesburg artistic circles and when he exhibited three works at the annual South African Exhibition in 1933, he received favourable criticism from the respected art historian, Dr AC Bouman. But he was not suited to life in Johannesburg and whenever the city got too much for him would escape to his parents who had been posted to Ladybrand, a pretty town in the eastern Free State. Their residence was, once again, a stone house with a large garden. François walked in the hills and the landscaped kloof, played tennis and relaxed, and it was from there that he began exploring the nearby Maluti Mountains which in later years were to become a particular passion. But first it was Europe and Uys's footsteps that beckoned …

Almal het hom … : Everybody just took to him immediately, and he has met hundreds of people and has been taken out many times. Levson has taken him under his wing. François has brought along some fifteen paintings and we trust that Levson will arrange a free exhibition in his studio. Of course the city amazed the seventeen-year-old – he's much attracted to the 'bohemian haunts'. His work is becoming stronger day by day – one still-life which he painted recently is simply masterly – it surpasses anything I've ever seen by a South African painter – I am dumbfounded. Nothing, it seems to me, will take this young man off course. Where does he get this great talent? And he is so unspoilt, natural and modest – everybody likes him … He gets onto the roof of our eight-storey building in order to paint and Johannesburg has enough subjects.

Hou moed, ou … : Courage, brother! Nothing on God's earth, not ten thousand ML du Toits [a well-known critic] or hypocrites or whichever shitbags – no adversities or setbacks will deter us or throw us off balance, will stop us on our forward march.

Dit pynig my … : It pains me to hear that François found all my advice and admonishments so boring. Had I preached and catechised, then it was a sermon and catechism directed more at myself than at him … But François is right – advice on white paper isn't worth the candle, always lacks the personal touch, can so easily sound dead and dry or intrusive. Glad to hear he has so much confidence. Confidence, I hope, to produce good work rather than make a lot of money.

---

[10] Levson was a documentary photographer who formed part of Alan Paton's liberal circle.
[11] Uys Krige, *Briewe I*, letter to Bokkie dated 6 May 1931, p. 39.
[12] Uys Krige, *Briewe II (Spanje)*: 1933-35 (unpublished letters, Stellenbosch University), letter to Bokkie and François dated 28 May (1934), p. 38.
[13] Uys Krige, *Briewe I*, letter to parents dated 11 January 1933, pp. 66d-e.
[14] Uys Krige, *Briewe I*, letter to Bokkie dated 10 October 1933, p. 194.

2. TRAVELS AND EARLY CAREER 1934-1940

A pony trek through the mountains of Lesotho in 1939 as described in Uys's book Na die Maluti's. From left: Setha (their guide), Uys, Mizzi, Terence McCaw and François.

EUROPE

For all the Krige children Europe had an allure which was cultivated by their mother and enhanced by the near-mythical status of their father's rugby tour to England. There was also a desire to trace their German, Dutch and French roots and to forge links with Europe. The values and aspirations of many enlightened Cape Afrikaners (as opposed to those who trekked into the interior) involved a very developed sense of Europe as a cultural centre and an emotional home.

> *Die woord 'Europa' is a sketter-klaroen wat roep tot onstuimige bloed. Een van die mooi dae breek ek los soos 'n jong bul wat in 'n hok vasgepen is en wat die vars geur van die weiland in sy trillende neus-vleuels nie langer kan duld nie.*[1]

The young Kriges broke the stockade one by one. Bokkie was awarded a Rhodes Scholarship from his school and sailed for Oxford in the spring of 1930 to read English at Wadham College. Uys resigned from *The Rand Daily Mail* and departed for Europe in June 1931. François followed in 1934 and three years later Mizzi left for Amsterdam to study drama.

For François, Europe was a natural and obligatory step in his education. Young local artists of the twenties and thirties were trying to break away from the conservative British academicism of Cape art and were primarily looking to trends in continental Europe for inspiration. With François's European roots and education, the desire to pursue his formal and informal studies in this environment and within this cultural tradition is understandable. He won a painting competition sponsored by Victor Kark, a prominent Johannesburg businessman interested in developing South African art, and the £450 prize money enabled him to spend three years travelling and learning his *métier* in Europe. He bade farewell to his family and set sail for England in the spring of 1934.

In a letter to Uys, Sannie expressed certain misgivings about François's stamina for such a long journey on his own. He had been a frail child in comparison with his sporty brothers. Uys misinterpreted her words and was drawn into an unnecessary, but for us enlightening, defence of his brother:

> *Your remarks, Mammie, about François surprise me. You say he is weak. Just the contrary, I think. He has a great security and confidence about him. Poise is the word. He lives entirely within himself, demands nothing from anybody, goes his own way, planning, watching, noticing things.*[2]

Uys's letter brought down his mother's long-distance wrath. She wrote to Bokkie:

> *Am indignant at Uys's remarks about François [sic] weakness. If ever anyone meant bodily weakness I did. I was so worried*

Die woord 'Europa' ... : The word 'Europe' is a clarion call, crying to tempestuous blood ... One of these days I am going to break loose like a young bull, trapped in a pen and unable any longer to endure inhaling the fresh smell of the grazing-land in his quivering nostrils.

---

[1] Uys Krige, *Briewe I*, letter to Bokkie dated August 1930, p. 16.
[2] Uys Krige, *Briewe II*, undated (1934?) letter to parents, p. 61.

WOMAN ON A DONKEY
WOODCUT

Hy was 'n ... : He was marvellous, a miracle of mobility, grace, lightning-like lightfootedness, incomparable elegance and swagger, and a godly, all-encompassing, stunning mastery. And all of this classical – no romantic bustle, no hey cockalorum jumping about – so cool, calm, classic, but as full of modest, veiled, warm tingling passion and emotion as any poem from the Greeks.

[3] Sannie Uys in Uys Krige, *Briewe II*, letter to Bokkie dated 14 January 1935, p. 60b.

[4] Uys Krige, *Briewe II*, undated (1934) letter to Bokkie, p. 14.

about François physically when he left here because he can stand no bodily stress and always caves in. François is the last person I would call weak.[3]

The young artist arrived in England and, no doubt with Bokkie's advice and the help of his many Oxford friends based in London, attended art classes for a short period before being enticed by Uys to flee the English weather and join him in Spain in November.

SPAIN

The Iberian Peninsula was to be a revelation for François, as it had been for Uys. When his youngest brother arrived, Uys plunged him into the Spanish way of life, giving him guided tours and infusing him with the love he felt for things Spanish. He took François to all his favourite restaurants and cafés where the older brother would engage anyone and everyone in conversation while the younger sat at the long rows of marble-topped tables and sketched the smoke-filled scene: intellectuals with round spectacles, befezzed Moors, peasants and labourers, sailors and fishermen. In their travels round Spain the brothers would get their daily meal in similar establishments amid anarchists, nihilists, political exiles, failed writers, prostitutes and gamblers. Dogs slept peacefully under the tables while the occasional chicken would strut about looking for crumbs.

The poet was reading voraciously in Spanish while writing for South African newspapers and magazines and he shared all he was doing with his brother. They would discuss the writers who captivated Uys, such as Cervantes, Calderon, Lope de Vega and Gongora. They also talked about art incessantly and Uys applauded François's interest in Goya, Velasquez and Ribera, encouraging him to travel to the towns where the originals were exhibited.

The Kriges saw Spain from slow rural trains which paused at every siding so that the driver could have a companionable drink with the stationmaster and where François captured the scenes in his sketchbook: quiet villages baking in the sun with donkeys flapping their ears in the shade, orchards of oranges and white blossoms and flowers to the horizon, donkeys harnessed to a treadmill at water holes, hauling dripping buckets out of the earth as they circled endlessly. The train would stop in the middle of nowhere and milk cans, cases of oranges and fruit would be loaded or unloaded, newspapers would thud onto the platform from the goods wagon. There would be glimpses from compartment windows of deep Mediterranean blue flecked with triangles of fishing boat canvas, of Moorish castles perched above whitewashed harbour villages.

An aspect of Spanish life that both attracted and repelled François was the bullfight. Sitting on the terraces surrounded by ecstatic fans, he sketched the many acts of the bloody drama: the *rejoneador* on his prancing stallion remaining just out of reach of the charging beast; the blood of the bull, the horse and sometimes the picador, *rejoneador* or matador staining the white arena sand. Uys was captivated by the scene and writes of Ortega, a famous contemporary matador, in effusive terms:

Hy was 'n wonder, 'n mirakel van beweeglikheid, grasie, blitssnellende veervoetigheid, onvergelyklike elegansie en swierigheid, en 'n godswonderlike alleroorheersende verbysterende meesterskap. En met dit alles kassiek [sic] – geen romantiese gewerskaf of bok-bok-staan-styf en hoeveel vingers op jou lyf rondspringery nie – so koel, kalm, klassiek, maar vol ingetoë bedekte warm-tintelende hartstog en ontroering soos enige gedig uit die Griekse Antologie [sic].[4]

François, more removed and analytical than his brother, tried to capture the grace and intensity of these encounters between man and bull in a series of economical matador drawings.

François moved in with Uys and his cousin Lance Krige in Valencia and the three young men enjoyed a carefree lifestyle in a house on the beach. The Valencians call themselves farmers and artists, and not without good reason: the Valencian school of the sixteenth and seventeenth centuries was famous. When François arrived, Uys gave him a tour of the city's galleries and dimly lit churches, pointing out the paintings of the native Ribera and his followers. The brothers debated the merits of the works and Uys's untutored, but insightful comments would have forced François to appraise the paintings in a perceptive way and compelled him to translate his observations into carefully considered theories, lest his quick-witted brother shoot him down in flames. The two must have given each other a formidable education in European art and literature in the months of their respective 'grand tours' that they spent together.

Soon the Kriges were integrating themselves into the community, adapting to the rhythms, and it was not long before François was getting by on his own in Spanish. They would take siestas like the locals and get to bed in the early hours of the morning. The laid-back attitude to time and the relaxed pace appealed strongly to the young artist. 'All haste is vulgar' was a saying François loved to use in later life and '*Mañana es otro dia*' (tomorrow is another day) was a code he always adhered to. In the mild evenings they would stroll leisurely along the promenades with the other citizens and marvel at the beauty of the Spanish women with their elegant veils and coloured fans. They found them incredibly attractive; as Uys writes: '*Hul is verdomp mooi met swart oë wat 'n Pous al sy papotiese [sic] bulle helder oordag skoon sal laat vergeet.*'[5]

François sketched the characters they met on the trams, in the parks, on the streets and beaches, always trying to capture something essentially Spanish in his drawings. There are priests robed in black reading their prayer books, farming women with baskets full of fruit and vegetables, young bucks in their pointed leather boots. The artist was also attracted to Valencia's harbour where he sketched the activities on the quays, the fishing boats and the fine lines of square-rigged coasters that crisscrossed the Mediterranean carrying their cargo of oranges.

The Kriges explored the surrounding area. On trips into the countryside they passed through orchards heavy with oranges and saw pomegranates hanging red from gnarled branches, farmers ploughing the red earth and hay carts making their way along country lanes. At springs or fountains groups of conversing women would be gathered to do the washing, wrestling the clothes with their sturdy arms. On the beaches brightly painted fishing boats were drawn up on the sand. They would go swimming and sunbathing along the coast and the young men were soon roasted brown as Spaniards. In the dunes they would find colourful 'Hottentot figs' and breathe in the strong 'fynbos' smell that reminded them of Onrus.

The notion of going to Almeria in southern Andalusia was François's; the thought of eating grapes in mid-winter – something he had read in a guide-book – captured his imagination. He suggested the idea to the other two: '*Dit gaan sneeu in Valencia vanjaar! Ek voel dit aan my murg! Waarvoor sit ons hier en verkluim? In Almeria dra die wingerde die hele winter deur …*'[6]

After making preparations they departed for Almeria and the later stages of the trip turned into a harrowing adventure. En route they initially spent three days in Altea with the poet Roy Campbell and his wife Mary. François greatly enjoyed the Campbells' company; he explored the beautiful village surrounded by mountains and was particularly struck by scenery which reminded him of the Boland. Uys wrote home concerning the Campbells' enthusiasm about François's work:

> *Roy en Mary Campbell was baie opgenome met hom [François]. Mary het gesê hy's effens 'inaccessible' maar met besondere 'poise'. Roy het uitgeroep: 'Eindelik het SA 'n goeie kans om 'n groot skilder voort te bring' en hy wou dadelik hê ons moet 'n kiekie laat neem van die drie van ons. Vir die verste nageslagte of waarom, weet ek eintlik nie. Hul dink ook dis baie goed dat François in sy nuutste werk hom inhou, hom betoom, probeer om in 'n besonder klein bestekkie en met geringe middele hom uit te druk, en so homself dissiplineer. Die tekeninge wat François in Engeland by die kunsskool gedoen het, het Mary wat self skilder is, verras. En Roy het soos gewoonlik baie opgewonde geraak om iemand wie se menings en opvattings omtrent die skilderkuns en skilderye in breë lyne met syne ooreenstem, te ontmoet.*[7]

After their visit to the Campbells, the caravan took to the road again. The young men did not travel light and their bags and suitcases were laden with books, papers and clothes. As Lance was also an artist, they were able to double up on canvases and other painting equipment. There were fourteen pieces of luggage and they had to make four or five changes at isolated stations during the night. A transfer on an unlit platform turned into a 'Marx Brothers' act:

> *Lance, met 'n kis boeke op sy skouers, struikel oor François se skildergereedskap. François, in sy angs om sy eiendom te red, word deur een van my reistassse gepootjie en slaan neer op die perron. Lance probeer manhaftig sy ewewig herwin, maar glip op iets papperigs ondervoet en hier kletter die kis grond-toe … Die twee skilders lê plat op hul rug langs mekaar en die taal wat hulle gebruik is so kleurryk as hul doeke.*

It was Uys's idea not to take the most direct coastal train to Almeria, but rather to follow the long route across half of Spain, much of this in the dark with no chance of his promised 'sightseeing opportunities'. The poet became less and less popular as the journey progressed but he, in his unique way, always tried to look on the bright side, claiming that at least they were seeing central Spain and were learning the customs of the locals (for instance their travelling companions' masterly ability to launch projectiles of saliva into the air and plant them on the only bare patch of compartment floor between their feet and the luggage). The trains they caught were jammed full of soldiers, policemen and farmers. The farmers were accompanied by chickens, ducks, pigs and dogs, and the dogs by fleas, which soon found a home on the young South Africans.

'*Hul is verdomp …*': 'They are damn pretty with black eyes which will make a Pope forget all his papist bulls in clear daylight.'

'*Dit gaan sneeu …*': 'There's going to be snow in Valencia this year! I feel it in my bones! Why do we sit here shivering? In Almeria the vines bear grapes throughout winter …'

Roy en Mary … : Roy and Mary Campbell were much taken with him [François]. Mary said he's a bit 'inaccessible', but with special 'poise'. Roy exclaimed: 'At last South Africa has a chance of producing a great painter', and immediately wanted a photo taken of the three of us. Whether for generations to come or what, I don't know. They also think that François's restraining himself in his latest work, his holding back, his trying to express himself in a tiny space and with limited means, is a good idea to discipline himself. The drawings which François did at the art school surprised Mary, who is a painter herself. And as usual, Roy got quite excited to meet someone whose views and opinions on painters and paintings coincide largely with his own.

Lance, met 'n … : Carrying a chest of books on his shoulders, Lance stumbles over François's painting gear. In his anxiety to save his property, François trips up over one of my suitcases and falls down on the railway platform. Bravely Lance tries to regain his balance, but slips on something mushy underfoot and the chest clanks down on the platform … The two painters are lying next to each other on their backs, their language as colourful as their canvases.

---

[5] Uys Krige, *Briewe II*, undated (1934) letter to Bokkie, p. 51.
[6] Quoted in Uys Krige, *Sol y Sombra (Spaanse Sketse)* (1948; Pretoria, 1975), p. 147. Much of the dialogue and many of the anecdotes that follow are derived from Uys's stories in this book of travel writing and will not be footnoted.
[7] Uys Krige, *Briewe II*, letter to parents dated 30 December (1934), p. 65b.

Needless to say, neither François nor Lance were as enthusiastic about the anthropological value of the 500-kilometre detour!

At midnight they changed trains at Alcázar de San Juan in the middle of La Mancha, Don Quixote country, the bare Great Karoo of Spain, dotted with silhouetted windmills. The handles on their suitcases were almost too icy to hold and they had to wait, shivering and hungry, on an open platform for five hours for the connection. At their Guadix change-over it first rained, then thinking better of it, hailed. At Moreda there was a thunderstorm and the little station building they were sheltering in felt as if it were about to break its moorings and sail into the sky. When they hammered past the towering, snow-covered Sierra Nevada, their wooden carriage was buffeted by gale-force winds. The train then crossed the dry coastal shale hills without a blade of green or any human habitation in sight. They took stock in the shuddering carriage. Items of clothing and luggage had disappeared into the Spanish night and the world outside looked exceptionally bleak. They considered returning to Valencia and by the time they reached the coast all three were nearing the end of their tether. What awaited them was a town they would grow to love and a period in their lives they would never forget.

The train slid through a rock portal and descended from the desert plateau into a warm and windless landscape adorned with vineyards and orchards of oranges. Villages clung to the mountain slopes and the Mediterranean lay stretched out before them, a deep, inviting blue.

In one of the very few letters to survive, François writes to his mother telling of their arrival, exhibiting his keen eye for detail in his description of Almeria:

Ons was moeg, vaak en vuil toe ons hier aanland; daarby het die dorpie in die verte maar bra verlate daar uitgesien, dus het ons nie te vrolik gevoel nie, maar was aangenaam verras met die hoofstraat vol lewe kleur en sang. My plan is om hier twee maande deur te bring en Spaans goed leer voor ek na Madrid vertrek. Die agterbuurte van hierdie stadjie is nog die interessantste wat ek gesien het. Die veelkleurige huisies wat opklim teen die kranse, baie van hul gebou in die mure van die berg onder die blakerende son. 'n Vry ongebonde lewe wat die mense daar ly [sic]. Die kinders loop half nakend rond en doen hul besigheid in die strate. Party vrouens voor hul huisies was besig om vlooie te soek in mekaar se hare. Die strate vol vuilis, selfs dooie katte en hoenders lê daar rond. Maar nieteenstande hierdie paar onaangenaamhede sien die mense daar heeltemal tevrede en gelukkig uit. 'n Paar van die grotbewoners besit selfs telefone en elektriese lig. Ek hoop om daardie wêreldjie nog op die doek te bring.[8]

It was December 1934 and they remained in Almeria until the spring. The boys were enchanted by the poor but peaceful town with its picturesque multi-coloured houses and golden-brown castle walls. They first stayed in a hotel overlooking the sea and then rented very cheaply a six-roomed house with high ceilings which they furnished with the essentials. The period in Almeria was a happy and productive one for the Kriges and the young men would look back on that peaceful time through Utopian eyes. Apart from Thursdays (when post from home was delivered) the rest of their days blended into one another. They shopped at the grocer on the corner and lived on a staple diet of fresh goat's milk cheese, tinned food, bread and wine. Milk was delivered at dawn by two characters who accompanied the 'milk van' – a white ewe – and milked the animal into a bucket which the Kriges left on their doorstep overnight. They settled into the slow rhythms of the town, grew to love the poor but generous townsfolk, dined in workers' restaurants, and attended plays and moving poetry recitals in the packed Cervantes Theatre. They went to bullfights, danced and wined at night, and at fiesta time turned out to watch the costumed peasants parading the streets.

The locals were so friendly and generous that the three *Boeros* (Boers) would frequently receive free meals and groceries, the Almerians' excuse being that they didn't want to chase visitors away with high prices. This non-materialistic attitude greatly appealed to François who himself shunned financial matters and was always content with only the basics.

The artist had a feel for languages and his Spanish, which he read and studied every day, was soon quite fluent. He was also disciplined about his sketching and thoroughly recorded aspects of the village that appealed to him: the tiled roofs and narrow cobbled streets, swaying palm trees, old fishermen mending their nets on the beach, donkeys bearing baskets of fruit and vegetables and the gentle sweep of the coastline. He worked out-of-doors, particularly around the market-place, which had a special attraction for him.

François made a series of detailed studies of donkeys with copper bells around their necks. As soon as he settled down to draw, a crowd of inquisitive locals would gather about him. There would be utter silence as the onlookers craned to follow

---

Ons was moeg … : We were tired, sleepy and dirty when we arrived here; also the town appeared rather desolate from afar, so we did not feel too cheerful, but were pleasantly surprised by the main street, full of colour and song. I am planning to stay here for two months and to learn Spanish well before departing for Madrid. The slum quarters of this little city are the most interesting I have ever seen. The colourful houses climbing up the rockface, many of them built into the mountain under the parching sun. A free, untrammeled life for the people living there. The children walk around half-naked and do their business in the streets. In front of their homes some of the women were busy picking fleas from each other's hair. The street full of rubbish, even dead cats and chickens lying about. But in spite of these few unpleasant things the people appear to be quite happy and content. Some of the cave-dwellers even have phones and electricity. I hope to depict this little world on canvas.

[8] François Krige in Uys Krige, *Briewe II*, undated (1934) letter to mother, p. 62.

the progress of the sketch. For the first time these Spaniards were seeing the old *burrico* through François's eyes as something special. Middle-aged gentlemen who spent their days on café sidewalks reading the newspaper would get up and sidle over to watch the metamorphosis of the donkey into crayon, pen or wash. If one of the assembled children exclaimed his appreciation for the drawing too loudly, a chorus of hushes would silence him. And if the donkey turned to see what all the fuss was about, one of the little boys would rush over, shove the *modelo* back into its former position and give it a cuff over the head for having disrupted the life class.

When François was sketching in the 'veld', an old goatherd would often leave his flock to come and greet the *maestro*. After offering him wine from a flask and coarse bread and chatting for a while, he would take up a position behind François. There he would remain, silently leaning on his staff, watching the progress of both the painting and his bleating children. At the end of the day when the light began to soften and the shadows stretch, he would put a hand on the artist's shoulder and say: '*Es muy bien, hijo, muy bien*' (it's very good, my boy, very good), and tramp home into the dusk behind his flock.

Krige also made sketching expeditions to nearby villages and places of interest. He visited hamlets like Aqua Dulce with its cliffs, bare veld, black sand, pepper trees and a few scattered houses. He sketched the ruined hill town of Sagunto and the mountains as viewed from Ronda. Krige's drawings of landscapes and particularly of towns are not simply picturesque stereotypes but give us a feeling for old Spain and for an urban way of life that has passed.

Having temporarily severed his links with South Africa, the young man was clearly becoming very serious about his art and focusing his mind in a way he was unable to do prior to leaving the country. This period of Krige's work shows an attempt to capture something of Spain every time he picked up a pen or brush. There are some fine works, such as delicate water-colours of farms and villages, the webs of masts and rigging in harbours and fishing boats drawn up on the beach at Almeria. The Spanish people themselves became the subjects of many of his studies: the matador, flamenco dancer, mounted soldier, the Moor sipping his coffee. There were also typical Spanish genre scenes of fishing, women at the well and café culture.

Stylistically, the artist was experimenting with economy of line and trying to capture everyday scenes instantly with a few deft strokes. He was training his eye and his hand to respond almost instinctively to the subject. The learning curve during his time in Spain was dramatic and, if we compare his drawings of this period with anything he had produced previously, the progress is remarkable. He moves from a sketching style that relies heavily on inexpert shading and the retouching of lines to a self-assured, delicate and autonomous line that conveys much more through its asceticism.

On 18 March 1935 Sannie joined the boys in Spain. She arrived by ship at Gibraltar where the three Kriges met her. She was elated to see her two sons again and wrote home to friends:

It is such a joy to be with François. He is a lovely boy still and has only one thought – his work.[9]

They travelled in southern Spain visiting towns such as Algeciras, Cadiz, Granada – where they saw the Alhambra Palace – and Seville, where they marvelled at the cathedral as well as the gardens of the Alcázar filled with the scent of wisteria, orange blossoms and the voices of flamenco singers.

By early April they had traversed the wide-open Castilian landscape and reached Madrid where they moved into a *posada*. In this city François took time to study the works in the galleries, particularly the Prado. He was in raptures over this temple of art and spent many hours studying Goya, Velasquez and El Greco. There are a number of pencil studies after Goya of dandies, matadors, soldiers and maidens, most likely done while visiting the Prado. He was so taken with Madrid that he stayed on in Spain to attend art classes under Daniel Vázquez Díaz,[10] before meeting up with his family again in Paris.

FRANCE AND THE LOW COUNTRIES

Uys and Sannie reached Paris first and waited for François, who arrived in June:

Ons wag op 'ou skraalbeen Fransie'. Weet nie waar hy is nie. Dwaal heel moontlik vanaand doelloos in hierdie wye wildernis van strate en boulevarde rond.[11]

When 'skraalbeen' arrived from Spain, Uys introduced him to his old haunts, particularly the cafés on the Boulevard Saint-Michel. From Paris Sannie split off and headed for home via Gibraltar and the boys proceeded to Belgium where they travelled widely in the Low Countries in July. During the summer, the brothers spent a few weeks together in Ghent in a cheap *pension* full of young eastern Europeans and found it a pic-

SETHA
CONTÉ

Ons wag op ... : We are waiting for 'old spindle-leg Fransie'. No idea where he could be. Possibly wandering about tonight in this wide wilderness of streets and boulevards.

[9] Sannie Uys in Uys Krige, *Briewe III: 1931-69* (unpublished letters, Stellenbosch University), letter to Howe-Browne dated 8 April 1935, p. 15.
[10] Daniel Vázquez Díaz (1882-1969) was a Spanish painter and etcher, and professor of mural painting at the Escuela de Bellas Artes de S Fernando in Madrid.
[11] Uys Krige, *Briewe II*, letter to Bokkie dated 20 June 1935, p. 70.

picturesque and appealing city. In July Uys wrote to his father describing how François was painting a series of portraits and how they were both speaking Dutch fluently: '*Dit klink nogal klankryk en kanselagtig in ons monde – en "de kleine Franske" wat 'n uitgesproke talent het vir tale, vorder net met die Frans.*'[12]

They admired the city's Gothic architecture and met a number of interesting artists, architects and writers with whom they gathered in the evenings in cafés or in their studios to talk about the arts. François's work was well received by this circle and they encouraged him to join in their activities and even to exhibit with them.

The Kriges then moved to Antwerp where François was keen to enrol at an art school. Uys found Ghent – in contrast with Antwerp – to have been friendlier and to have had a

> *geselliger, meer simpatieke omgewing … jong mense vol lewe en vreugde, idees, planne, geesdrif – God!, ek verstik en vrek hier [in Antwerp]! Ek mag hul 'n groot onreg aandoen, maar die mense lyk my hier pure Engelsmanne – net besig met 'beesmis' … ek meen 'beesnis' [business].*[13]

Uys returned to South Africa and François finally enrolled for an etching course at the Higher Institute for Fine Arts at Antwerp's Royal Academy (probably for the academic year September 1935 to June 1936), where he started to learn the laborious process of etching:

> *Jammer dat dit so 'n langsame proses is. Dit neem soms weke om een ets af te werk en klaar te druk. Mens kan daarmee mooi lig en toon effekte mee bekom. By my is dit maar nog in begin stadium dus experimenteer ek soveel moontlik.*[14]

François was probably attracted to etching by the works of the most famous etcher of them all, Rembrandt, whose work he greatly admired. There was also a long history of etching in South Africa with fine works by Pieter Wenning, Hugo Naudé and Frans Oerder that he would have been exposed to. In Antwerp François was to master the intaglio method of etching and in later life, when he eventually acquired an etching press, he was to produce some remarkable images. He spent eleven months in cold, grey Antwerp despite the rain and the '*swaar, stug en [swygsame]*'[15] locals to whom Uys could not relate. François's temperament was better suited to the reserve of the Belgians than his brother's and he felt quite at home there. With Afrikaans as his mother tongue he was comfortable in both Flemish and Dutch, and his French was improving all the time. Wanting his money to last, the impecunious artist took lodgings in a Seaman's House and lived largely on sugar beet and horseflesh for his year of study, spending his savings on building up a library of art books. He frequented the galleries and was interested in the old Flemish masters as well as Van Dyck, Rubens and the later Breugel.

But it was during his time in the Low Countries that Krige's love of Rembrandt's art matured – the Dutch master's painting and graphic work were to have a lasting influence on the young artist. Krige read avidly in art history and it is likely that he was inspired by Rembrandt's conception of the art of drawing as an immediate reaction to visual inspiration, an impulsive expression of an inner vision.

Krige studied Rembrandt's pen-and-wash sketches, noting how the brush was not only used for filling in the washes between the pen lines, but also as a drawing instrument and even partially to 'blend' the pen lines by dragging the moistened brush over the line-work. He learnt how to suggest light and shadow through the presence or absence of line by the way he held the drawing implement in his hand and by carefully regulating pressure on the support. The trait of Rembrandt's work that François studied and perfected, and is characteristic of almost all his drawing (both in graphic work and oils), is the 'breathing outline'. Instead of having an unbroken outline around a form, François usually drew with a light hand that created an intermittent line. This was in accordance with Rembrandt's principle of the silhouette opened by light and atmosphere, thus allowing the object to 'breathe' and forcing the viewer to participate in the image and use the imagination to 'complete' it. François was able to render extremely economical works and create a thing of beauty with a few deft strokes and with apparent ease and speed (a quality of those Japanese drawings that he so admired).

At art school he drew many nudes in life classes and there are a number of stiffly academic pieces of men standing in classical poses with spears in their hands, or strung out in crucifix positions (many of these were derived from the copies of classical statues that filled the corridors of the school). Figure drawing was a discipline he forced himself to master:

> *Die natuur is iets wat my haas begin vervreemd raak maar soo [sic] kan dit darem nie vir lang aangaan nie. Miskien is dit maar goed want ek het my uitsluitlik die laaste paar maande toegelê op die figuur en veral die kop en daarmee mooi vordering gemaak. My werk van ses maande gelede lyk nogal primitief …*[16]

'Dit klink nogal … ': 'It sounds rather melodious and sermonising in our mouths – and "de kleine Franske" with his obvious talent for languages, is getting along with French.'

geselliger, meer simpatieke … : convivial, more sympathetic environment – young people full of life and joy, ideas, plans, enthusiasm – God! I am suffocating, dying here [in Antwerp]! Perhaps I am doing them a great injustice, but the people here appear to me to be pure Englishmen – busy only with 'beesmis' [cow dung] … I mean 'beesnis' [business].

Jammer dat dit … : It's a pity it's such a slow process. Sometimes it takes weeks to complete a single etching and finish its printing. One can get pleasant results as regards lighting and tone. I am still much at a beginner's stage and therefore experiment as much as possible.

'swaar, stug en … ': 'heavy, dour and [taciturn]'.

---

[12] Uys Krige, *Briewe II*, letter to father dated 24 July (1935), p. 96.
[13] Uys Krige, *Briewe II*, letter to Bokkie dated 29 May (1935), p. 81a.
[14] François Krige in the Uys Krige Archive (Stellenbosch University), undated (1935?) letter to mother.
[15] Uys Krige, *Briewe II*, letter to Bokkie dated 29 May (1935), p. 81a.

His drawings developed a sureness of line and a stripping away of all superfluous elements in order to convey the essence of the subject. He learnt how each mark on the page is dependent upon, and a response to, other marks and how to set up contrasting or mutually enhancing forms and lines. But most importantly, drawing classes taught François the art of meticulous observation.

His palette in Belgium tends to be much more muted than in later life and he uses sombre colours and leaden skies to convey the atmosphere of the place. There is a view, perhaps from his Antwerp garret window, of roofs, chimneys and tiny backyards in a suburban part of the city, all in thickly applied dull hues. There is much we do not know about his protracted stay in Belgium. For instance, there are a number of fine images of an unidentified old man, perhaps a friend from the art school; there is also the painting of a pretty teenage girl with long blonde hair and blue eyes, marked '*vernietig*' on the back at the time of his death in 1994.

In Belgium, no doubt because of a dearth of models, François executed a large number of self-portraits in almost every medium, reworking his personal features again and again as if to probe his own identity. He closely analyses the image of the man staring back at him from the mirror. Most of the images are scrupulously honest; others are glamorous with softened features. In them we see a shy, sallow young man with concentrating – even piercing – eyes, full lips, a serious expression on his handsome but slightly gaunt face and a cow's lick of fine blonde hair. His pipe and his pen are trademark features. There are some unusual renderings of his own image in which he self-consciously poses with expressions of laughter or anger.

A contemporary oil self-portrait (1937) shows Krige's angular face looking up as he fills his pipe. The artist is conscious of his European education and the painting, from its chiaroscuro effects to the Bavarian-style hat with feather, pays homage to his time on the Continent and to its great artistic tradition. The landscape, seen through an open window, is distinctly northern European. Cattle graze on a green hill and mountains rise to a darkening sky in the distance. The rendering is academic with the face and hands carefully drawn and a full, dark tonal range employed in the flesh and shadows. Paint is applied in traditional thin glazes with brushstroke following form and, probably with Rembrandt in mind, the face is illuminated while the background dissolves into darker shadows.

It is in his contemporary etchings that the fruit of his learning is most apparent. Apart from works featuring local scenes of canals with barges and gabled façades, a number of the Antwerp etchings depict Spanish scenes and settings, and we can conclude that he was working from the many sketches he had done in Almeria in 1934. There are monumental Spanish peasant figures (often hooded), donkeys and images of the poor. We see Almeria's fishing harbour with the fortress walls behind and old men mending nets. In these images his training as a woodcarver is apparent in the heavy, 'sculpted' figures hatched in a web of dark lines. The scenes appear timeless, Rembrandtesque, the images consciously and nostalgically in contrast with the strife and change that were tearing Spain apart at the time of etching (1936). There is one particularly fine work of a family group on an open hillside with a few humble dwellings in the background; beside them stands a faithful donkey. The figures appear threatened by a stormy sky and lengthening shadows. The etching needle is deftly handled, revealing flowing mountains in parallel hatchings, sweeping gestures for the sky and densely cross-hatched shadows. The work has both political and Biblical connotations and from it emanates the artist's humanism.

François's concern for the political conditions in Spain grew as hostilities escalated. Although he was always reluctant to become involved in politics, it was in Spain, largely due to his brother's fascination for the current situation and socialist sympathies, that the artist had been drawn into discussing boiling issues for the first time. In the years leading up to the civil war Spanish cities were political hotbeds with regular party rallies, aggressive electioneering and bombing campaigns. François had been there during the general strikes when buildings were occupied by soldiers, bombs went off continually in city streets and cannons were deployed on main squares.

The two brothers saw the growing Spanish conflict through Afrikaner eyes and found themselves sympathising with the workers, the poor and the secessionists and comparing these Spaniards' plight to that of their republican relations during the Anglo-Boer War. Theirs was a complicated relationship with the English. On the one hand they were enlightened, SAP Afrikaners, yet on the other there was a residual resentment towards Britain stemming from the legacy of the Anglo-Boer War. Their Afrikaner allegiance, fuelled by the Spanish conflict and their feelings of homesickness, was tempered and

Die natuur is … : I am becoming estranged from nature, but it can't go on like this for long. Perhaps it's a good thing, because in the past couple of months I have concentrated exclusively on figures, especially heads, and I have come along quite well. My work of six months ago appears fairly primitive in comparison.

'*vernietig*': 'destroy'.

---

[16] François Krige in the Uys Krige Archive, undated (1935?) letter to mother.

complicated by a growing sympathy for the anarchist/communist cause and a hatred of fascist elements in Spain together with similar trends that they recognised in nationalist Afrikaner politics.

The growing uneasiness throughout Europe during the second half of the thirties worried François and he could see how South Africa was being dragged into another 'English' war. The Krige boys were torn between a resentment towards British imperialism and their loathing of that new form of imperialism raising its head in Spain, Italy and Germany. In September, Uys wrote from Spain to his brother in Belgium expressing his concern about the Italian invasion of Ethiopia:

> *Here, ou François, die nuus van die laaste paar dae ja my die skrik, die bewerasie en die hel op die lyf. Dit word elke dag duideliker. Duisende en tienduisende jong Afrikaners gaan weer op die vasteland van Europa onsterflike roem verwerf, in die slyk en modder die heldedood sterf ... Ons gaan weer Engeland se vuil werk vir haar doen.*[17]

Nevertheless, the Kriges were Smuts supporters and in the coming war all the brothers were to enlist on the side of 'England'.

GERMANY AND ITALY

During his time in Antwerp, François made frequent sketching expeditions to nearby cities. There are images of the barges, windmills and gables of pre-war Rotterdam, of street scenes and vendors in Low Country villages. He met up with the poet WEG Louw in Amsterdam where they drank beer and argued over politics, François strongly criticising Louw's interest in fascism. Although we have little evidence beyond his works, it appears that Krige left the Low Countries towards the end of 1936 for a slow tour to Florence via Germany and Austria. He spent some time in Bavaria in the Prien area, where he did a number of small oils, etchings and drawings of the undulating landscape. There are images of the Rhine flowing through green countryside, women harvesting, forests, the odd hamlet, and the Alps looming in the distance. Many of the drawings of this period show evidence of how the etching technique he had recently mastered influenced his style, and his pen is often used as if it were an etching needle, with short parallel and cross-hatched strokes predominating. There are water-colours of Rothenburg and the villages around Chiemsee where he was attracted by the architecture, by their spires, interlocking red roofs and the fretwork buildings. In the landscape sketches he shows how he is beginning to 'structure' the terrain to suit his own ends, using elements such as roads and selected areas of vegetation to lead the eye through the picture and towards the horizon.

In a letter from Rüdesheim he talks about the stimulating art collections and his own productivity, adding: '*Die lewe hier langs die Rhein is wonderlik. 'n gelag [sic], gesing en vrolikheid soos nergens nie en die noientjies [sic] net lieftallig.*'[18] Krige considered his time in Germany particularly fruitful and sent sketches back home to show his sponsor, Victor Kark, the kind of progress he was making. In that year, 1936, Krige's works survived the strict selection process and were exhibited at the Empire Exhibition in Johannesburg. This was a grand exposition which, prior to the Second World War, took place every four years, each time in a different city of the British Empire. The 1936 venue was the showground at Milner Park and the South African section of the art exhibition was the most important display of local art yet assembled (117 paintings and 63 sculptures). What was perhaps more important about the exhibit was the attention accorded by the judges to the 'modern' styles and contemporary attitudes, a first for South Africa.

Next it was Italy's turn and Krige headed south via Munich – meeting up again briefly with WEG Louw – to Venice where he spent a few days sketching St Mark's, gondolas and cathedral interiors, before pressing on to Florence and remaining there for some months. It was the heart of winter when he arrived in the quattrocento jewel, the city Uys had raved about, and François was not disappointed. He was astounded by the rich concentration of beautiful buildings, paintings and sculpture. Everywhere he looked there were works by Michelangelo, Cellini, da Vinci, Botticelli, Fra Angelico, Donatello and Titian.

We know that François studied mural painting and fresco in Florence, but little else about his time there. Only a handful of female nudes in 'academic' poses remain from his Florentine art classes. There are, however, a number of fine etchings featuring the Arno such as a dark image of the Ponte Vecchio and one of an Arno fisherman casting his huge net from a boat, with a Tuscan farmhouse on the far bank. He took time to get to know the town and sketched the piazzas, as well as locals drinking at street wine shops. He also made a number of drawings of statues, most notably some careful studies of the muscles of a dying Greek warrior in the Loggia dei Lanzi, and he frequented the Uffizi where he copied works by Andrea Mantegna.

Here, ou François ... : Good Lord, François, the news of the last few days scares me. It's becoming clearer from day to day. Thousands and tens of thousands of young Afrikaners will again earn fame on the continent of Europe, will again die heroes' deaths in the slime and mud ... We will again do England's dirty work for her.

'*Die lewe hier ... *': 'Life along the Rhine is wonderful, with laughter and singing as nowhere else, and the girls are sweet.'

[17] Uys Krige, *Briewe II*, letter to François dated 21 September (1935), p. 92.
[18] François Krige in the Uys Krige Archive, letter to Robbie (?) dated 15 July 1936.

TRAVELS AND EARLY CAREER

35

FISHERMEN (ALMEIRA)
ETCHING

By now François had been away from South Africa for nearly three years, his money was running short and he felt the need both to return to the wide open spaces and the landscape he loved and to see his family again. He came back to South Africa determined to launch his career and to dedicate his life to his art. He also had a burning desire to quench the homesickness he had felt for his country by travelling the length and breadth of the land.

SOUTH AFRICA

THE NEW GROUP

During the period of Krige's artistic education, British academic influence at the Cape was very strong. Victorian naturalism remained the fashion despite momentous events in the international art world. The Cape did have inspirational artists such as Hugo Naudé, Pieter Wenning, Ruth Prowse and Strat Caldecott, while modernist influences were being introduced in the expressionist work of artists like Irma Stern and Maggie Laubser. However, power and authority in the art world were represented by the influential Professor Edward Roworth, director of both the South African National Art Gallery and the Michaelis Art School and president of the South African Society of Artists. Roworth's followers were intolerant of modern art and determined to uphold traditional late nineteenth-century British academic art, or romantic realism.[19]

In the thirties many promising young artists like Krige had lived, travelled and studied in Europe and returned to South Africa with new and innovative ideas about the future of art. The New Group was formed by some of these artists who were exasperated by the inertia in the country and also by the conservative approach to art – particularly modernism – and sought to 'regenerate' and raise the standard of local art. Initially the prime movers behind the venture were Terence McCaw, Frieda Lock, Lippy Lipshitz, Gregoire Boonzaier, Walter Battiss and Alexis Preller who all pushed for a movement of younger artists which could promote and help to sell the works of those who did not receive due recognition from existing societies. Battiss was the chief organiser in the Transvaal and Boonzaier in the Cape.

The New Group was formed in February 1938 and Boonzaier, playing the *enfant terrible*, was reported in *The Cape Argus* of 14 April 1938 as saying: 'We shall have to limit our membership to about a dozen-and-a-half; there are not more young professional artists than that in South Africa, not artists whose work counts!'

The first, historic New Group exhibition was held in May 1938 in Cape Town and François, now Johannesburg-based, was a participant, exhibiting a number of etchings. A one-shilling entrance fee was charged, catalogues were on sale and about a thousand people attended the exhibition and its concurrent lunch-hour lecture series. This exhibition proved to be a turning point for South African art.

Soon there were regular New Group exhibits and members became involved in a 'proselytising' mission. However, the Group was not united by any shared aesthetic programme and, although Krige remained a member and exhibited with it until it was disbanded in 1954, his temperament was such that he seldom participated in its activities and before long he was only peripherally involved.[20]

BETHLEHEM

In 1937 Krige's family had moved to Bethlehem in the Free State, where they remained for the rest of the decade. Although Krige was again based in Johannesburg, he made frequent, lengthy trips to visit his parents and explore the region. He walked in the green summer hills to the reverberation of crashes of thunder, and returned in winter when the grass was bleached and red hot pokers pointed at the sky. François loved to hike in the mountains of what was then Basutoland (Lesotho) and to be in the presence of its dignified inhabitants.

In the spring of 1938, when the Malutis and Drakensberg were still covered in snow, Krige climbed these ranges on his own. Having recently returned from Europe, being alone in the mountains gave him an opportunity to reacquaint himself in a singular and romantic way with the land he loved. In Belgium's urbanised flatlands he had yearned for the wide expanses, the verticality of the mountains and, like so many South Africans abroad, resolved to make such a trip on his return.

There are many works from the artist's periods at Ladybrand, Bethlehem and Lesotho and the subjects he sketched while on his hikes recur in paintings as much as 40 years later. Even on the most arduous excursions he carried sketching equipment and water-colours in his rucksack and recorded all he saw. As in Spain, there are many domestic scenes: mountain villages with children playing, chickens and goats scattered between huts, old men drinking home-brewed

---

[19] Martin Bekker, *Gregoire Boonzaier* (Cape Town, 1990), p. 25.
[20] Despite his peripheral involvement, Krige did in fact serve as a committee member of the New Group for a short period. One other notable exception to his reticence in becoming involved in Group activities was over the issue of the proposed race resolution (aimed at excluding the black artist, Gérard Sekoto). In 1951 the Minister of Education offered the New Group £1 000 on condition that their exhibitions and functions would be for whites only. This proposal was rejected at a Group meeting by Ruth Prowse and seconded by Krige (Julia Kukard, *The Critical History of the New Group*, MA Thesis, University of Cape Town, 1992, p. 44).

beer, women crushing maize; also a few bright oils or pastels of women at the market. He executed dozens of figure studies of the Basotho: women with bracelets, armbands and bundles on their heads, men in battered *velskoene*, bright blankets and Basotho hats, goatherds with skins as well as the ubiquitous animal studies of goats, cattle and ponies. He also captured the mountain vistas with thorn trees, aloes, suspension bridges across streams and table-top koppies. Later, he turned some of his sketches into good figure etchings, most notably a group of Basotho holding down a struggling pony while a man tries to shoe the animal.

Two fine stylised oils were inspired by Krige's time in Lesotho. Both depict a group of Basotho women dancing in a circle and appear to be directly inspired by Henri Matisse's *The Dance* (1909). The composition and simplified use of monochromatic 'flat' colour is similar to that found in Matisse's work and in both Krige and Matisse the women dance on a green orb. This shape denotes the earth and the purple Drakensberg mountains in the background suggest that the dancers are performing on top of the world, their simplified rendering implying that their dance elevates them momentarily to a plane that is not part of this world. The stylised figures are archetypal and are an Africanised response not only to Matisse, but to similar archetypal renderings of dancing girls such as Botticelli's *Primavera* and Grecian urn figures. There is a snake-like rhythm enhanced by the positioning of their arms and heads, and the circular nature of the movement (as well as the loose circle the women form) adds to the cyclical, and hence timeless, quality of the piece.

NA DIE MALUTI'S
One of François's hikes in Lesotho was recorded in detail in a series of articles published by Uys in *Die Brandwag* from 9 June to 31 October 1939 and later collected in a book of travel sketches, *Na die Maluti's*.[21] As François was such a private person and wrote so seldom (and never about his work), this account of ten days with the young artist, in which we get to know him in an intimate way through his brother's eyes, is a valuable document.

In April 1939 a group of young Johannesburg-based artists, under François's instigation, decided to get away from the big city for the Easter break and head south to the Free State for a pony-trekking expedition. On a bright Saturday morning the four young men loaded their equipment into the back of a Ford V-8 and set off. Uys and François sat in front alongside Walter Battiss, who was at the wheel, while Terence McCaw sat alone in the back with a pile of baggage, paintboxes, easels, canvases and other painting equipment. Ahead of them lay ten days free of the city and rumours of war.

They sped south into open country patched with yellowing autumn colours, through farmlands, over a highveld covered in thorn bushes, cosmos flowers, bluegums and poplars, past farmstalls with boxes of apples and pears stacked outside. As their Ford growled towards the Orange Free State, the young men chatted and argued about art, literature, and politics, but most of all about art. They stopped along the road to buy braaied chicken for lunch and the seller, assuming that the young men's politics were somewhat different from his own, lambasted them with a party-political diatribe. The artists quickly retreated and François, always one to promote freedom of thought and expression, commented: '*Ja, daardie kêrel se gedagtes is so klaargekook soos sy hoender, net ek verkies die hoender.*' Between further mouthfuls of chicken he noted his disgust at politicians' use of clichés, slogans and battle cries: '*Hulle moor die gedagte, hulle's die dood van die gedagte … Ja lewe die onafhanklike denke, die eie vrye gedagte.*'

They stopped in Vereeniging where ox-wagons were drawn up on the broad main street, bought a few half-pint bottles of beer to have with their lunch, then motored down to the Vaal River, crossed its great steel bridge and parked on the bank among the willows to have their meal. In later life François was to perpetuate these rituals of leisurely travel: even a trip from Montagu to Cape Town – a distance of only 200 kilometres – would take all day with long pauses for lunch and for a swim in Du Toit's Kloof.

The group then headed further south over the flatlands of the Orange Free State with unstoppable Uys waxing lyrical about its beauty. Battiss was born and raised in this part of the world so he too sang its praises while leaning over the steering wheel in order to get a better look at his beautiful land, to admire the contrast between the plains and the soaring walls of rock to the south. The Ford shot past Viljoensdrif, blanketed in bluegums, and Wolwehoek and Gottenburg and Petrus Steyn, past tiny wayside stations comprising a couple of corrugated iron buildings, a few trees and little else. They passed sunflowers lifting their faces to the sky and deserted farmhouses with

---

velskoene: raw-hide shoes.

'*Ja, daardie kêrel …*': 'Yes, that guy's thoughts are as half-baked as his chicken, just I prefer the chicken.'

'*Hulle moor die …*': 'They murder all thought, they're the death of all thought … Yes, long live independent thinking, free thought.'

---

[21] Much of the following dialogue and descriptions of the artists' trip to the Malutis is derived from this book of travel sketches (Uys Krige, *Na die Maluti's* (Cape Town, 1990)).

'Waar ter wêreld … ': *'Where on earth can one find prettier towns than Ladybrand or Ficksburg, and where on earth lovelier mountains than the Malutis as they change continuously through a single summer's day, giving the shadows in their ravines or on their slopes a new appearance every half-hour, while their colours keep on changing through every variation of blue, grey and – towards evening – purple?'*

'Vat nou byvoorbeeld … ': *'Now take this obsession of yours [Uys] with the Free State landscape as an example … Your approach is like a surgeon starting to work on a patient on the operating table. And if you listen to me, you will notice that this image contains further criticism of you. You and your kind analyse a landscape – or anything for that matter – so minutely that the question occurs to me whether you haven't perhaps analysed it to death, and that you aren't able to love it any more.'*
To which Uys retorted: *'And a painter, does he not analyse a landscape?'*
'Yes, but possibly with his emotions rather than with his mind,' replied François. *'And what about Cézanne?'*
'That's precisely what I hold against some of his later work, or rather the work of his disciples who followed some of his doctrines and ideas to extreme conclusions. They were capable of stripping a clear southern landscape to such an extreme of nudity that it eventually looked almost like a surveyor's map, and then I start thinking that there is no real landscape here any longer, only the skeleton of a landscape.'

'rooinek': *'redneck'*, *'Englishman'*.

'Die Malutis! … ': *'The Malutis! Your first view of the mountains!'*

'En as julle … ': *'And if you look closely, you'll see where the Malutis join the Drakensberg.'*
'But you are city folk and I don't expect much from your eyes.'

'En wag maar … ': *'And just wait till you see the Le-Hong-Hong – the largest, barest, most desolate valley of Basutoland … if by this time you're not too tired and exhausted from sitting on the ponies all day to ride down into the valley!'*

the vanes of their windpumps creaking in the wind. The artist trio and the poet were enthralled by this bleak environment and its pale, cloudless skies. Like his brother, Uys looked at the landscape with a painter's eye for detail, colour and nuances of light: *'Waar ter wêreld kan mens mooier dorpe raakloop as Ladybrand of Ficksburg, en waar ter wêreld mooier berge as die Maluti's wanneer hulle in die loop van 'n enkele somersdag gedurig verander, die skaduwees in hul klowe of teen hul hange hulle dan elke halfuur heeltemal 'n nuwe voorkoms gee, terwyl hulle vir hul kleur of tint elke moontlike skakering van blou, grys – en teen die aand se kant – pers aanneem?'*

But François, interrupting his brother's eulogies about the landscape, was drawn into making a statement about his own romantic and perhaps naive opinion of the artistic profession, his affinity with expressionistic rather than formalist concerns:

'Vat nou byvoorbeeld hierdie obsessie van jou [Uys] met die Vrystaatse landskap … Jy gaan met hom te werke soos 'n snydokter met sy pasiënt op die operasietafel voor hom. En as jy goed oplet, sal jy merk dat hierdie beeld van my nog verdere kritiek op jou bevat. Jy, en jou soort mense, analiseer die landskap – of enigiets wat dit betref – só haarfyn dat die vraag by my opkom of jy dit nie miskien doodgeanaliseer het en jy dit dus nie meer lief kan hê nie.'

To which Uys retorted: *'En 'n skilder, analiseer hy nie die landskap nie?'*

'Ja maar miskien meer met sy gevoel as met sy verstand,' replied François.

'En wat van Cézanne?'

'Dis presies wat ek teen party van sy latere werke het, of liewer teen die werk van sy dissipels wat 'n paar van sy bevindings en leerstellings tot hul uiterste konsekwensies deurgevoer het. Hulle kon 'n helder suiderlike landskap só tot op sy been afstroop, dat dit naderhand byna gelyk het soos die kaart van 'n landmeter, en ek soms die gedagte kry dat dit hier geen werklike landskap meer is nie, maar net die geraamte van 'n landskap.'

And so the quarrelling band headed deeper into the Free State, with the Krige brothers debating the merits and failings of the visual arts over literature, Terence, the 'stubborn Irishman', adding a touch of dry humour to every exchange, and Battiss – fingering his pointed black beard – playing the older and wiser sage and trying to keep the arguments on track, but getting the brunt of being the *'rooinek'* whenever he stuck his head out with an unpopular opinion. François would often throw cold water on their intellectual flames and remind the others that they were too cerebral a bunch and that their problems arose from too much thinking and analysing and not enough feeling.

All of a sudden they came over a ridge and François asked Battiss to pull over. *'Die Maluti's!'* shouted François, making an excited gesture to the horizon, *'Jul eerste aanblik van die berge!'*

In the distant veil of heat haze the mountains floated grey like a battleship. *'En as julle mooi kyk, sal julle sien waar die Maluti's in die Drakensberge vasloop,'* said François. *'Maar julle is stadsmense en ek verwag nie veel van jul oë nie.'*

François saw himself as an experienced climber, a veteran of the Malutis and Drakensberg at their most inhospitable. He had much to tell of that mountain world and considered himself more or less the leader and guide of the group (Terence dryly noted, however, that they would still have to pay ten shillings and sixpence for a Basotho guide). When no one commented on the distant vista, François added: *'En wag maar net totdat julle die Le-Hong-Hong sien – die grootste, kaalste, mees verlate vallei van Basoetoland … as julle teen dié tyd nie al te moeg en gedaan is vir die heeldag op ponies sit om die vallei af te ry nie!'*

By late afternoon they were closer to the mountains which were starting to look increasingly impressive, their crests a deep blue, some of the faces catching the last rosiness of the day and the ravines wrinkling into black shadows.

It was already dark by the time the four entered Bethlehem and when they pulled up at the residence, Japie, Sannie, Mizzi and Suzanne were there to meet them at the door. There was port wine and a fully laden table to welcome the weary travellers. During the meal Mizzi insisted that she be included in the journey, but her two brothers strongly disagreed on the advisability of having a younger sister along on a men's expedition. The brothers cited safety reasons, their sister's 'rowdiness', the lack of space in the car and the hardship. François stressed how dangerous the mountains were, but Mizzi countered that she had recently spent six weeks in a working camp for women in Germany, that she wasn't frightened of the mountains and, besides, she would cook the meals. With the support of her parents, she was not to be dissuaded and even Battiss and McCaw were not averse to having a pretty young woman along. The brothers admitted defeat.

On Monday morning the party set off towards Harrismith. This time, with the addition of Mizzi and her baggage, the back of the car was stuffed to bursting point. François had disappeared under a mound of blankets, bags and camping equipment, but he bore his burden with tolerance and only once complained that he couldn't see his beloved mountains.

They passed dried-up Liebenbergsvlei with its carpets of cosmos, left Harrismith to the east and then began to wind up into the verdant foothills dotted with aloes. Soon the world of the white farmer was far behind as they climbed into the Basotho mountain realm. The Ford dragged a trail of dust through villages dotted with reed-roofed mud huts, angora goats and chickens wandering between them. Outside, bare-breasted women ground mealies and sorghum for *pap* and beer while old men sat and smoked. As they progressed, the roads grew worse and the luggage began to collapse on the Kriges trapped in the back.

Uys was fascinated by the Basotho names as they rolled off François's tongue: Boehabela, Machachaneng, Ntsannie Moplas, Mokhotlong, Thabana Tsuana. But he was equally intrigued by the names given by the Afrikaner settlers: Ararat Mountain and Woeste Arabië Valley. François had also memorised the names of farms in the vicinity such as Madrid, Noord-Brabant, Il Paradiso, Terre de Bourgogne, Friedrichsruhe, Louterbronne … The artist had excited his brother and the Krige boys were off, indulging each other's love of the geographic naming-game that conjured up images of their earlier roving years and of places still to be discovered in their wandering years to come.

Eventually they arrived at the Witzieshoek shop where the owner, Mr Rust, supplied them with ponies and a guide. A group of Basothos had assembled at the shop and turned their attention to the band of youngsters from the 'City of Gold'. The men were wrapped in red and dark brown blankets, the women wore bright headscarves and the children were naked except for a few loose skins. Mr Rust introduced them to one of the locals, Setha Mofolo, who was to be their guide for the coming week in the mountains. The middle-aged Basotho, who looked like a crow in his black coat, sat on his haunches sewing sacks of camping equipment together. His long face wore a sad expression and from his speech it was obvious that he was not entirely sober. François was at once drawn to the mountain-loving Setha, who considered '*goud-teng*' (Johannesburg) far more fearful and dangerous than a Maluti snowstorm, and the younger man learnt much from the elder in the coming days. It is clear from his art that François had an affinity with older, worldly-wise men such as Setha and frequently used them as subject matter. He made dozens of sketches and paintings of Setha, James Joubert (his tracker in the Cederberg), Bushman elders, Krisjan (a Montagu character) and others. So much of the hard lives of these men was evident in their faces that they formed perfect subjects; perhaps he was also looking to his own life and mortality in these sensitive studies. Following the introductions, Setha saddled up their ponies, loaded the provisions onto the pack animals, and after saying their goodbyes to Mr Rust, the little party set off. François slapped his riding crop hard against the saddle and his white pony trotted into the lead.

They coaxed their beasts through 2 500 metres. Far below them lay the Free State, its plains stretching into the gold and green distance. The road narrowed to a path next to sharp rocks and it began to drizzle. Setha's prediction that they would reach the climbers' huts at Mont-aux-Sources before dusk looked increasingly unlikely and François declared that their ponies would have to sprout wings like Pegasus in order to cover the 25 kilometres before the light failed.

As darkness began to fall, Setha guided them up an incline to the mouth of a large cave which, he announced, would be their dwelling for the night. They unpacked the blankets and provisions of dried fruit, eggs, butter, jam and rusks, all crushed together to leave an unappetising mush. Soon they got the fire going and began exploring the cave which was adorned with Bushman paintings (current anthropological opinion suggests a return to the word 'Bushman' rather than 'San')[22] which they could just make out in the dying light. They were in a 30-metre hollow below the crest of a mountain plateau with finch nests hanging like a curtain across the mouth and a herd of angora goats enclosed in the stomach of the cave behind a rough wall of stones. As a consequence the floor of their abode was not cold, bare rock, but a soft carpet of dried goat droppings.

Dinner round the fire was boerewors and braaivleis, salad and sandwiches, with oranges, raisins and almonds for dessert and coffee in abundance. Three silent shepherd boys dressed in skins appeared at the mouth of the cave and François called them to the warmth of the fire, offering them food. Once they had all eaten and the fire had begun to burn low, Battiss started to talk of his fascination for Bushman art: '*Ek wonder hoeveel mense besef watter skat van kuns so 'n, in die algemeen maar taamlik verguisde, ras soos die Boesmans ons nagelaat het … Dit is, na my mening, 'n kosbare erfenis.*'

---

pap: porridge.

'*Ek wonder hoeveel …* ': 'I wonder how many people realise what an artistic treasure an abused race like the Bushmen has bequeathed us … To my mind it is a priceless legacy.'

---

[22] I recognise that the word 'Bushmen' is often used simplistically to lump together various distinct groups, but the word 'San', frequently employed by academics, has arguably even more pejorative associations (see David Lewis-Williams and Thomas Dowson, *Images of Power: Understanding Bushman Rock Art* (Johannesburg, 1989), pp. 8-9). In this book I retain the better-known term 'Bushmen'.

Battiss went on to explain that the Bushmen no longer had a thriving art and that the few remaining members living in the Kalahari were considered 'living fossils'. François must have listened attentively and caught some of the older painter's enthusiasm for the Bushmen because he was to make repeated journeys to the Kalahari to record the fast-changing lifestyle of remaining clans after the war.

Battiss recounted how when still a boy he had discovered his first cave of Bushman art and told of his growing interest and current obsession with touring the country to discover new cave 'galleries' in isolated areas. He explained that until then it had only been scientists and anthropologists who had been interested in Bushman art, but that it was high time that artists began studying this indigenous art form for its unique aesthetic qualities. His hope was that young South African artists would learn from the minimalism of Bushman art, from their attention to the essentials in line, form and movement and their lack of gratuitous decorative elements. Krige would have been in accord with much of what Battiss had to say and the revelation of this African tradition fascinated the young artist.

His romanticised, colourful narrative thrilled Krige, newly returned from a post-industrial environment with its cerebral art: '*Daar het seker nog geen mens bestaan wat in so 'n innige verwantskap met die natuur geleef het nie, as die Boesman. In die lewe van die natuur het hy só opgegaan dat hy deel daarvan geword het, die geheime van lewe en dood vir hom geen geheime meer was nie … Sorgeloos soos die wind of die water het hulle gelewe in 'n vreedsaamheid wat niks verstoor nie, terwyl oor hul die komete kom en gaan. En toe kom die swart man en, later, die wit man. Nou het hulle almal verdwyn, net hul kuns bly staan.*'

Krige would have been particularly drawn to Battiss's description of the Bushman artist with his horn pots of clay-and-vegetable paints strapped to his belt, reed paintbrushes in hand, making his way into the mountains to find suitable rock 'canvases'.

When they were all wrapped in blankets and looking out of the cave mouth at the stars, Battiss continued his monologue, praising the Bushmen's appreciation of the grace and line of wild animals, particularly the eland, and their economical rendering of these creatures in rock art. He described the Valley of Art near Jamestown in the Eastern Cape where he had found hundreds of magnificent works. He had even come across paintings that featured Afrikaner ox-wagons, a study of a Boer woman and her daughter, and in one painting, which he called *Conversation Piece*, a group of Bushman women sat in a circle, chatting. During his periods in the Kalahari, Krige would draw many such 'conversation pieces', perhaps recording these threatened domestic scenes with the same intention as his Bushman forerunner.

The next morning the group was woken by the sound of mountain doves and of goats shuffling and bleating in the back of the cave. Setha served coffee from the fire in tin mugs. François soon retired to the back of the cave with his sketch book to draw the ewes with their newly born lambs. Peering over François's shoulder, Uys asked: '*Waarom is die bok daar onder tussen die mense soveel leliker as hierdie bergbok?*'

To which his animal-loving brother replied misanthropically: '*Miskien omdat hy so naby die mens is.*'

In the following days, François took the opportunity to record their journey in every spare moment, and his drawings of Setha, the ponies and of the Mokhotlong adorned the articles and travel anecdotes Uys published after their return to Johannesburg.

After breakfast, the ponies were saddled up and the party continued its ascent. They breathed the fresh mountain air as they wound along a track lined with nerinas, a rose-coloured mountain flower. François warned them against the autumn sun at this altitude and they all hauled out their hats. Mizzi sported a big beach hat, Terence a little green affair with a feather, Battiss a Basque beret, François a big Boer War commandant hat and Uys a little cap which his father had probably worn on his rugby tour of the British Isles.

At times, when the going got too steep, the party had to dismount and lead their ponies up the incline of the Machachaneng Pass. An eagle glided in circles above them on the updraught of the cliffs. Like young Romantics tramping the Alps, the group was struck by the sublime, feeling their spirits soar with the spectacle that unfurled before them. Soon they were on the roof of the Malutis and the Drakensberg splintered away to the southeast – a dragon's back serration dissolving into blue. In this eagle's nest the young trekkers felt the peace of the mountains. Wars, and rumours of war, seemed to belong to another world. Being removed from everyday life, temporarily and geographically isolated, gave them an objectivity about the inevitable destruction to come. Uys and François had watched the Spain they loved tear itself apart in civil carnage

---

BASOTHO ELDER
INK AND WASH
SANG COLLECTION

'Daar het seker … ': 'No human could have existed with such a profound relationship with nature as the Bushman. He was absorbed in nature to such an extent that he became part of it, the secrets of life and death were no secrets for him any more. As carefree as wind and water they lived in a peaceable state nothing could disturb, whilst the comets came and went above them. And then came black men, and later white men. Now all the Bushmen have disappeared, but their art endures.'

'Waarom is die … ': 'Why is the goat living down there with humans so much uglier than this mountain goat?' …

'Perhaps because he is so close to humans.'

and they knew that Europe would soon be plunged into another terrible conflict. This certainty lent a gravity to their current ascent, even a proleptic nostalgia for that which they were soon to lose.

François mused that if they wanted to form a little republic, cut off from the rest of the globe, they would be inviolate up here in the mountains. With a few machine guns to defend the passes they would be able to keep a huge army at bay and even enemy aeroplanes would have difficulty negotiating the treacherous weather and the dangers of the peaks. When Terence challenged him on his 'warmongering', he defended himself: '*Julle verstaan my nie … Ek teoretiseer maar net, sommerso op 'n abstrakte manier … Ek sit liewer agter 'n skilderspalet as agter 'n masjiengeweer, en ek sal dit aan die hele wêreld verkondig.*'

As they talked their ponies led them deeper into the Berg until suddenly a peak of giant proportions crowned with snow loomed before them under a leaden sky. '*Dit kan nie anders wees nie …*' said François. '*Dis Mont-aux-Sources, hoogste punt van Suid-Afrika!*'

But how to get to the top? Neither François nor Setha seemed to know the route from this angle of approach. The Krige boys, Mizzi and Terence rode on ahead, looking for the path, but soon realised that they would never be able to make it up the cliffs to the hut before nightfall. A maze of gorges and precipices unfolded before them and, to make matters worse, it began to snow on the rock face. As if that was not enough, a thick wall of mist began to flow into the valley. Uys's lively imagination retrieved the account of death that François had regaled them with a few nights earlier: '*Nie alleen in die donker nag nie, maar helder oordag dwaal die dood daar rond – die dood deur die sneeu, die koue, die grondstorting of die swart afgrond wat oral gaap. Ja, die dood … daar tussen die berge dool hy, soekende na die te vermetele Basoeto of die arme verdwaalde blanke wat vir hom bestem is. En hy gaan, in die vorm van 'n geraamte, op sy vleeslose hakskene, met die wind wat deur sy leë oogkasse blaas en droewig fluit deur sy ribbekas.*'

As there was clearly no way forward the four turned their ponies round and backtracked into the dying light until they found the slower Setha and Battiss. They immediately encamped on a windswept escarpment, knowing they had no chance of finding shelter before dark. Their accommodation was in starkest contrast to the cave of the night before. They gathered round the fire to eat a hasty meal and then curled up in their blankets on the grass. Nearby the earth fell away into a vast abyss and the group huddled together to generate warmth against the icy mountain wind. Somewhere in the dark a jackal began to yelp and mist closed in. Just as they dozed off it began to hail.

The completion of Uys's *Na die Maluti's* was interrupted by the outbreak of war and it was eventually published in its unfinished form. As a consequence, we have only a brief account of the rest of the journey. The climax of their ascent was when they peered over the edge of the highest point of the Amphitheatre and surveyed the dramatic Tugela Valley below. They also swam in the Orange River near its source and one evening, during a fiery sunset, they eventually led their ponies to the summit of Mont-aux-Sources where they spent three nights in a hut, crammed around a petrol stove for warmth while the mountain wind moaned between the cracks. During the day they rode out along the mountain's spine and at night they talked incessantly, Uys blazing the trail through every topic imaginable.

Finally the party descended to the valleys, winding down through rustling sorghum and khaki-bush, and approached the flickering lights of civilisation at dusk. It was late before they spied Mr Rust's shop and the ponies broke into a trot for home. Their first question concerned news from the outside world to which Mr Rust replied: '*Vandag was Goeie Vrydag en die Italiane het vanmôre Albanië binnegeval. So is nog 'n klein volkie na die maan … Ek wonder wie die volgende een gaan wees?*'

WAR CLOUDS

During the period 1938 to 1941 Krige lived largely in Johannesburg, spending part of the time with his mother's cousin, Sannie Pyper, in Hope Road, Orange Grove. She made a balcony room available for him in her lovely thatched home where he could paint undisturbed. Sannie was a flamboyant character who moved in art circles and with whom François got on very well. During this time he kept his head above water by doing illustrations for Afrikaans magazines (he recalled never having earned more than £100 a year until the war came).

Much of Krige's Johannesburg work from this period deals with sombre and disturbing subject matter. The artist tackled social issues and his treatment of city scenes betrayed his attitude towards living conditions. There are moving images which, although never overtly political, were motivated by what

'*Julle verstaan my …* ': 'You do not understand me … I am just theorising, in a sort of abstract way … I'd rather sit behind a painter's palette than behind a machine gun, and I will tell the whole world that.'

'*Dit kan nie …* ': 'It can't be otherwise,' said François, 'it's Mont-aux-Sources, the highest point in South Africa!'

'*Nie alleen in …* ': 'Not only in the dark of night but in full daylight death wanders there – death due to snow, cold, avalanche, or the gaping black chasms. Yes, death wanders in those mountains, waiting for the foolhardy Basotho or the poor lost white man who has a rendezvous with him. And he goes on his way, on his fleshless heels, with the wind blowing through his empty eye-sockets, whistling through his ribs.'

'*Vandag was Goeie …* ': 'It was Good Friday today and this morning the Italians invaded Albania. Another small nation down the drain … I wonder who's next.'

was happening abroad and by the situation in his own country. He riled against poverty, racism, squalor, disease and deprivation in the only way he could – through images. There are impressions of Fordsburg with bare trees, mine-dumps and smoke stacks, of horses out of place in the city, of locations and streets in the slums of Johannesburg. These are dark images sketched in pen, sometimes with a dull-toned or black wash. The artist's sympathy for the inhabitants of the 'City of Gold' and his own depression at the coming strife are disturbingly conveyed.

There are also images of poor people trying to make a living on the Rand, of black men warming their hands over a brazier, a poor woman peeling potatoes, a black beggar with his upturned hat, old men sitting or sleeping on park benches, a cripple pulling himself through the streets on hands and knees, workers bent double hauling cocopans away from a mine shaft or sleeping fully clothed on the ground. Powerful, moody charcoal drawings show miners drilling at the rock face, their bare torsos straining in the dim light of their lamps. These are not social realist or futurist celebrations of honest labour, but rather François's form of protest: an expressive and humanist portrayal of the dehumanising effects of that labour.

There were trips to Cape Town and Durban during these years, as well as many journeys to the Orange Free State. But Krige looked at these places with eyes tainted by war and depression. A 1941 Lesotho landscape scene is reminiscent of Chagall in its use of a range of non-naturalistic colours and is disturbing, almost science-fictional. There are strange-looking cacti and aloes; a moon rises over lunar mountains and the *memento mori* goat skull draws the eye to the foreground. During holidays in the Cape even his genre scenes are tinged with hopelessness: fishermen are shown inebriated, bottles of alcohol in their hands. An Onrus series of paintings from 1940 depicts a dead bird, probably a seagull, with its desiccated wings mangled in the sand and its skull showing through the feathers. Another portrays a hauntingly thin and crippled boy, rendered in an expressionist style borrowed from Irma Stern, and there is one of a woman begging in Hermanus. There are Karoo scenes which feature ghostly, almost skeletal figures. *Funeral in the Karoo* (1940), a dark, ink and water-colour piece, is a moving portrayal of a group of Coloured mourners gathered round a grave on an arid plain. It is François's humble, platteland response to Gustave Courbet's monumental *A Burial at Ornans* (1850) which he would no doubt have admired at the Louvre. The French painting was unusual in its subject matter – a Realist, unheroic depiction of a rural bourgeois funeral. François takes this one step further, producing a sympathetic portrayal of a burial in a poverty-stricken, farm-labourer community. A sombre sky and darkened landscape convey the atmosphere of mourning. Men in black hold their hats and bow their heads. In the centre of the composition stands an old, barefoot woman with a face that resembles a skull, looking more like the Grim Reaper than a mourner.

His *Merry-go-round* (1940), painted at a carnival in Cape Town, is one apparent exception to the sombre works of this period. It is a vibrant, night-time scene full of drama and motion in which a group of Coloureds and Malays share in their children's fun as they swirl around on a carousel's painted horses. Bold outlines surround the figures and the bright colours of the machine are set against the dark blue of the night, reminiscent of the Expressionist paintings of Georges Rouault who used glowing colours encased in thick, dark outlines that recalled stained-glass windows. There are, however, disturbing elements to this seemingly happy scene. The viewer finds himself excluded from the activity as the onlookers all have their backs turned. Furthermore, the faces of the merry-makers are completely depersonalised, suggested in a dash or two of paint. This expressionist device is used to convey the artist's feeling of isolation, his inability to join in the festivities. Even the title of the work, *Merry-go-round*, suggests a wheel of fortune where merriment is soon swung into the darkness and replaced by despair, an idea reinforced in two of the three theatrical masks attached to the top of the carousel which depict exaggerated frowning faces. These catch reflections of the red and yellow lights, giving the faces a sinister look. Examining the masks more carefully one notices that the face on the right is smiling, but as the carousel is turning anti-clockwise, it is being replaced by a frowning mask which will in turn give way to a satanic face with pointed ears. Even more interesting are the two scenes painted on the rim of the carousel between the masks. On the right is a ship gliding on an orange sea, followed by an Egyptian image of pyramids and palm trees. Could these be allusions to the troopship journey and North African campaign in which so many South African soldiers were then involved? And could the raised arms of the child against the fence in the foreground allude to the raised hands of surrender?

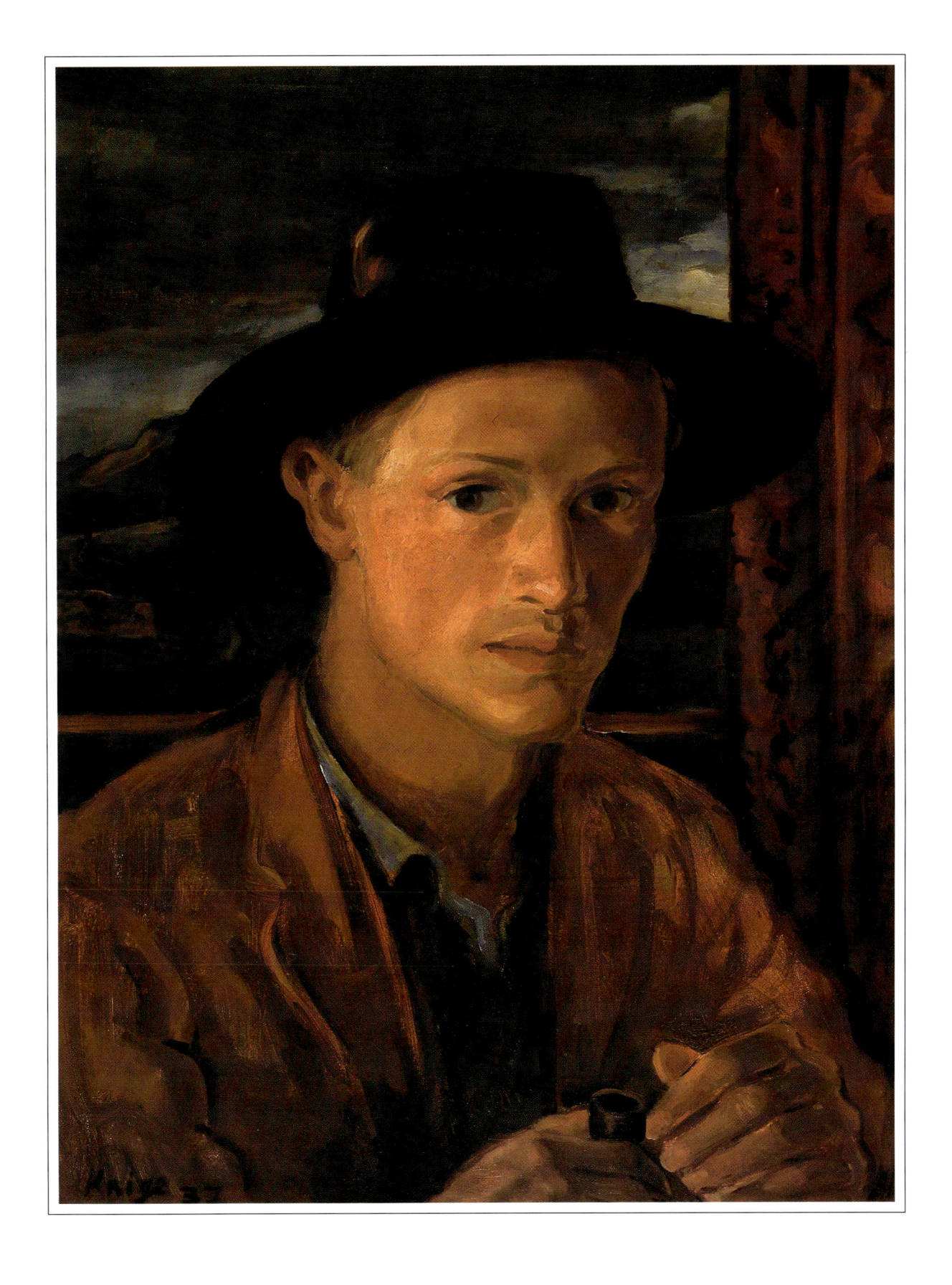

SELF-PORTRAIT WITH HAT,
ANTWERP, 1937
OIL ON BOARD
49,5 x 36,5 CM
PRIVATE COLLECTION

FRANÇOIS KRIGE

44

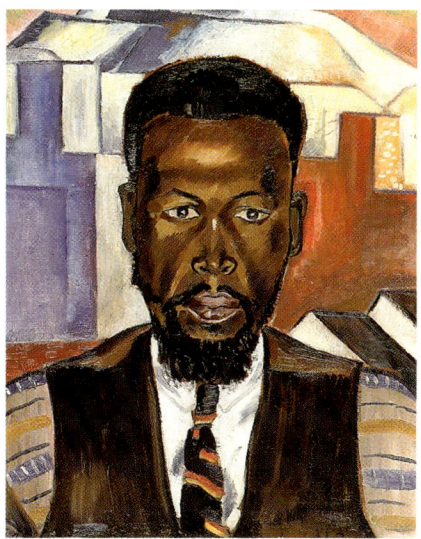

1
MERRY-GO-ROUND, 1940
OIL ON CANVAS
60 x 80 CM
PRIVATE COLLECTION

2
OLD WOMAN READING
INK AND WASH

3
MINERS
CHARCOAL

4
PORTRAIT OF A MAN, 1930s
OIL ON CANVAS
60 x 70 CM
MTN COLLECTION

5
BASOTHO STORE, C. 1930s
OIL ON CANVAS
36 x 46 CM
SANG COLLECTION

FRANÇOIS KRIGE

46

1
NUDE
PEN AND INK

2
BASOTHO WOMEN DANCING
(A LATER PAINTING INSPIRED
BY SKETCHES DONE IN
THE 1930S)
OIL ON BOARD
56 x 70 CM
PRIVATE COLLECTION

3
STILL-LIFE WITH SPRING FLOWERS
IN A TERRACOTTA VASE
OIL ON CANVAS BOARD C. 1930S
40 x 32 CM
WELZ COLLECTION

4
SUZANNE, 1939
OIL ON CANVAS
42,3 x 32,2 CM
PRIVATE COLLECTION

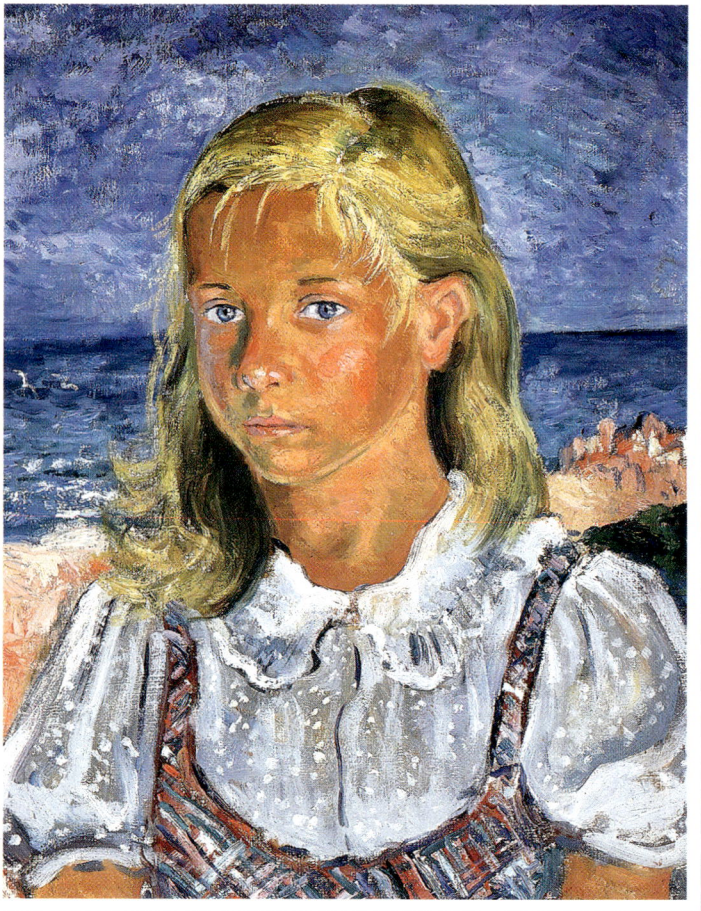

3. WAR 1941-1945

Lieutenant Krige sketching at a railway siding in Egypt.

By 1941 all four Krige brothers had signed up. Bokkie became an air force colonel, Uys a war correspondent, Arnold an intelligence officer and François a war artist. Their sister, Mizzi, and Uys's wife, Lydia, were also present at the front as part of a touring company of actors sent to North Africa to entertain the troops. The position that François and Uys took, as Afrikaner artists actively involved in the conflict, was an unusual one. François was the only Afrikaner war artist and Uys one of only three Afrikaans authors to declare themselves unambiguously against Hitler (the others were Jan van Melle and C Louis Leipoldt). Indeed their involvement in anti-Nazi propaganda drew strong criticism from nationalist quarters. Right-wing newspapers poured abuse particularly on Uys and – under the leadership of the architect of apartheid, Hendrik Verwoerd – instituted a systematic programme of discrimination and character assassination, labelling the 'traitorous' writer a '*Kakieridder*' (knight in khaki).

WAR ARTISTS

Soon after the outbreak of the Second World War the Union Defence Forces created a War Art Section to which a group of South African artists were appointed whose job it was to record various aspects of the conflict for posterity. It was felt that artists as well as journalists could make a valuable contribution to the war effort:

> *Their record could not compare in factual detail with photography … The artist's viewpoint is one of involvement, and this very subjectivity makes it possible for us to get an insight into not only what it looked like to be there in the front line but what it felt like.*[1]

There were eventually seven official war artists in all, but the initial three who formed the core in the early stages of the war and paved the way for the others were Neville Lewis, Geoffrey Long and François Krige. These artists became instant officers in the Intelligence Corps (without formal military training) and were instructed to follow the progress of the war wherever South Africans were involved. Today much of the art of these paintbrush soldiers (François produced 124 official works) is housed in the South African National Museum of Military History in Johannesburg.

During the war years these artists' works met with considerable acclaim and were shipped back to South Africa and exhibited as part of the propaganda war effort. Some of the images were even shown in war-time London in the summer of 1943 and were well received, Krige's fine draughtsmanship and use of colour particularly impressing the London critics. And in the

[1] André Verster quoted in C Kruger, *South African Images of War* (Pretoria, 1990), p. 51.

1943 New Group exhibition Krige's *Dryfsand Bo-op Halfaya Pass* was hailed as one of the outstanding works on view.

François signed up as an official war artist in the spring of 1941 and Second Lieutenant Krige spent the last months of that year painting military subjects in South Africa and selling them to the War Art Committee for prices ranging between about 18 and 40 guineas. There are images of soldiers guarding South African armoured cars, of pilots in training and mechanics working on aircraft, of young men with rucksacks enduring the hardships of basic training and of Roberts Heights (Voortrekkerhoogte) where he depicted soldiers receiving Vickers machine-gun instruction.

By the end of the year Defence Headquarters decided that an artist should be sent 'up north' to record the action of South African soldiers in the war zone. On 3 December Krige boarded a troopship in a convoy bound for the Middle East and his experience of convoy life is well recorded in his sketchbooks. An oil shows an embarkation with uniformed figures swarming up gangplanks and ladders onto the troopships, lifeboats and seagulls hanging in the gap of sky between the vessels. The bustling scene is offset by the disinterested gaze of two Indian soldiers in the foreground who have already settled aboard the ship.

At sea Krige re-creates the atmosphere in a series of sketches and oils depicting the long lazy days through the tropics in which boredom is the main enemy. Shirtless soldiers stand at the rail watching the other ships in the convoy heave up and down on the Indian Ocean swell. They sleep or write letters in deck chairs and play ball games on the wooden decks. A game of blind man's buff is organised among the black soldiers and everyone gathers round to watch the antics of the blindfolded men staggering about on the rolling deck. A painting from a later convoy (probably when he crossed the Mediterranean from North Africa to Italy in 1944) shows their ship under attack. Sailors man a Vickers Quadruple machine gun which spits fire into the sky at aircraft, the spray and smoke suggested in quick, gestural brushstrokes.

ART IN THE DESERT

When he arrived in Egypt the artist was immediately sent to the 'forward areas' where he set to work diligently recording scenes at the front. Pen and wash and pencil were his main armaments, particularly when on the move. When he reached a forward area, Krige reported to the Public Relations Office – a branch of Military Intelligence – which was the mobile, temporary headquarters of the press (war correspondents, photographers and war artists). Here Krige was fed, and received messages, rations, petrol and pay. It was a busy environment filled with journalists hammering at typewriters and scrawling notes as news came in from the front.

The nomadic conditions in the forward areas were harsh and certainly not conducive to painting. A gust of wind could easily knock a canvas from an easel set up in the desert face down in the sand and put paid to a day's work. Fierce khamsin gales and sandstorms reduced daylight to twilight and dust penetrated everywhere. The heat was searing and squadrons of flies snared their undercarriages in wet paint, while at night blackouts made it impossible to do any work at all.

Krige was uninterested in trying to paint battle pieces or celebrate the 'glory' of war. Instead, he became a master at capturing the daily genre scenes of life in the desert, the non-heroic chores and boredom, the workman-like jobs behind the lines. There are images of troops trying to push their jeep out of the sand, a tank recovery crew working on a Crusader, and a field-gun repair shop. There is even the amusing sight of a soldier, trousers around his ankles, sitting reading on a box-toilet with the panoramic view of a battle taking place in the distance. If there is heroism, it is in the face of the common soldier enduring years of harsh conditions and tragic losses.

Many of Krige's desert images are overworked and the use of oil colour is often unsure, probably because he was supposed to be a quasi-journalist recording facts and was not at all enthusiastic about the kind of images of destruction he was compelled to record. Tanks and trucks were not his chosen material. War art foregrounds the subject, tending to demand stark realism for the sake of the record and these constraints and prescriptions did not suit him. In keeping with his practice as an artist before the war, Krige was often more interested in the landscape and in depicting characters rather than battle scenes or portraits of heroes. He was a 'symbolist' rather than a social realist, and it is thus hardly surprising that (with the exception of some emotionally charged scenes) he struggled to deliver what was required of him. As Krige's war art is often inferior, in this chapter I will suggest the breadth of his subject matter rather than go into detailed discussions of works that were mostly meant to record the South African army at war.

When approaching unfamiliar subjects Krige gets his proportions wrong and colours are often muddy, particularly in the earlier war works. Figures are awkwardly rendered and when the brushstrokes fail to follow form, the effect can be unconvincing. The paintings are too fussy and abundant details make for confusing compositions. In graphic work he uses a mass of lines, a 'scribbling' effect, reworking the shape repeatedly until it hits the right note. This is a shorthand that does not require the precision of thought and line that his economical pen-work does.

But with time his line drawing became more refined and the desert story he has left us is a valuable one. Most of the images were drawn in pencil, charcoal or pen and wash and later used as *aide-mémoires* for bigger oils. As a nomadic war artist capturing fleeting desert scenes, more than ever before Krige had to produce images in a short space of time, seeking only the essentials – it was an invaluable education. In a sense François was picking up from where his POW brother had left off (Uys had been captured by the Germans at the battle of Sidi Rezegh). The poet had written impressionistic, sketch-like anecdotes of conditions at the front, often jotted down in slit trenches or while under air attack; François translates these into visual images captured in sketched note form with a similar vividness and spontaneity.

A letter dated 15 January 1942 from the Deputy Chief of Staff in Pretoria to the Headquarters in Cairo reads:

> *It would be appreciated if you would ask Lieut. Krige to forward by air to DDMI [Military Intelligence] as soon as possible any drawings or paintings which he has completed. In addition to our being anxious to see how he is shaping, we are keen to utilise his material for propaganda purposes in the Union.*[2]

Krige duly sent his first of many batches of drawings and paintings, but it is unlikely that the war office would have found his work particularly suitable for 'propaganda' purposes as the artist was more keen to depict behind-the-line scenes and when he did produce images of war, he invariably tried to capture the alienation of battle. Indeed there were high-ranking officers who were not impressed with Krige's work (no doubt wanting to see action scenes such as those of Geoffrey Long) and what with ill health and a long delay in his promotion, it looked as though he would soon be returning to the Union. This would have suited him perfectly as the brutality of war became increasingly disturbing to his sensitive nature.

BEHIND THE LINES

Creating art on a swift-moving battle front such as that of the Western Desert was a difficult task. Krige thus sought areas and operations of the forces where his subject matter was more static. Behind the lines he sketched fixed gun emplacements and the activities on airfields, painted portraits of soldiers waiting to go into action and recorded the work of the medical corps.

Bofors anti-aircraft gun emplacements were fairly immobile and Krige produced a number of works featuring these weapons and their crews. In one he shows the weapon firing at a squadron of enemy bombers; six figures, shirtless and helmeted, fire continuously, scattering cotton-wool flashes among the aircraft. The gunners, however, appear motionless and there is no drama or plasticity of form. The oil entitled *El Alamein A/A Gun and Crew* is far more successful. It shows two gunners relaxing near their weapon which has been dug into a sand dune. Beyond them and to the right is the sea, offset against the lively white brushstrokes of the sand. The more static scene is confidently handled with deft, broad brush work, often wet-in-wet.

Krige also spent time with the air force in order to record the activities of that arm of the service. We see Spitfires taking off from makeshift runways in the middle of nowhere, while *At Home, SAAF* depicts a group of pilots relaxing in their Bedouin-looking tent or 'mess' after a mission. The artist plays on the Arab theme, showing how the pilots have all the creature comforts that their foot-soldier comrades lack, suggested in the Renoir-like soft focus, the 'luxurious' drapes of the tent and the presence of a dog and a piano in the officers' quarters. Outside through the tent flaps, however, we glimpse the real world where fighters stand ready for take-off. It is not certain whether the artist went on a bombing raid (it seems unlikely that he did) and it is more probable that his oil painting of South African Martin Maryland medium bombers (1943) is derived from photographs. The two aircraft are seen from above, flying with the pink earth of Halfaya Pass and the blue of the Mediterranean far below them.

Krige painted and sketched a number of portraits of officers and particularly troops which serve as a valuable record of the personalities of those at war. There are the faces of flying aces such as Major Derrick Moodie, distinguished commander of two squadrons of Spitfires, and Captain Doug Rogan (Tunisia,

[2] François Krige File at the archive of the South African National Museum of Military History.

1943) who was back in the cockpit of his Tomahawk once more after his leg had been severed by flak during a ground-strafing operation. A quick oil sketch shows an Australian lad with a big bush hat, smoking a cigarette; there is one of an Indian soldier in a turban and of a Senussi guard standing with his rifle at the ready. A good-looking young ack-ack gunner with his shirt off and helmet pushed back nonchalantly appears as though he is suntanning on the beach without a care in the world. His faraway look and the presence of a Bofors gunner scanning the sky with binoculars suggest otherwise. There is a superb charcoal study (1942) of Philoman Mougi, the batman of Brigadier Armstrong, Officer Commanding 5 SA Infantry Brigade, who had been captured at Sidi Rezegh. The handsome black man – bundled against the cold of the Libyan Desert night in a wool cap, jersey and greatcoat – stands beside a tent at dusk. The charcoal is used expressionistically and is smudged in places, creating a strikingly sombre effect.

These are small, quick portraits that are successful in giving us a sense of the multinational flavour of the armies ranged against Rommel. Each man has a determined expression and the slightly romanticised rendering is appropriate to the ideals of these young soldiers. They stare past the viewer to the desert sands, focusing on the job at hand. As is apparent in Uys's writing, there is a conscious inclusion of black soldiers involved in the war effort and an implied condemnation of a system which prohibited them from carrying weapons.[3]

In the summer of 1942 François was taken ill and hospitalised for a long period. Although I can find no direct reference to his illness, a letter from the following year complains of a chronic inflammation of the mucous membrane of the nose and throat, probably caused by the constant irritation of desert sand and dust. He was also not coping well with the destruction around him and probably had a dose of 'sand-happiness', an artistic temperament up against forces it was not capable of dealing with. It was during this period that he began drawing scenes from his hospital bed, an activity he pursued once he was back on his feet, sketching round the Middle East Base Hospital and in other field hospitals. By the end of the war he had created a unique collection of art works – mostly pen and wash – dealing with the military medical corps. There are tender images of soldiers visiting wounded friends, of patients reading in their beds under a web of mosquito netting, of advance dressing stations, their white tents emblazoned with red crosses, of ambulances and of nurses trying to work in difficult conditions.

CHASING ROMMEL WEST

The road to the west which Krige traced and retraced many times during his stint in North Africa led from the cities of Cairo and Alexandria along the coast of Egypt via El Alamein, Mersa Matruh and Halfaya Pass to Sollum Bay. It then hugged the Libyan shore through Bardia, Sidi Rezegh, Tobruk, Benghazi and on to Tripoli. It was a journey into the unknown and each desert sortie would present new horrors for the artist. Those soldiers, like fellow war artist Philip Bawcombe, who were with François in the desert, say he was a loner who kept very much apart from the others, the artist turning in upon himself in an attempt to deal with the nightmare. Each convoy journey into the desert was an apocalyptic one for him and the deep-thinking artist was forced to confront aspects of humanity and of himself that he could hardly bear. For François the drive to the west was not a push to chase Field Marshal Rommel into the sea; it became a quest to exorcise the spectre of death and to deal with the fears he felt for his combatant brothers, particularly Uys. He did not rise to the horror and produce great art. Instead, working within the system and trying to do his duty inhibited him and rendered him unable to paint the defiant gesture. The South African *Guernica*, we shall see, was to come 45 years later when he revisited the emotional space of 1942 and painted his anti-war statement.

On each journey west he left Cairo in convoy and crossed the island of Gezira. Where the highway ended and the desert began stood the three pyramids of Giza like a symbolic portal. Once he had passed the pyramids he entered a world of rock and sand. Going west was a journey into an Armageddon-like landscape, scorched of vegetation and waterless, with burnt-out vehicles and the beached carcasses of ships the only landmarks on a bare horizon.

EL ALAMEIN

First stop along the coast road was El Alamein. Krige made this his desert base and spent much of the summer of 1942 there sketching the camp – a city of tents and trenches – and the vast military build-up round the place where his brother, Arnold, was to be wounded in the decisive battle to come. We see little Honey tanks taking up position, trucks and anti-tank guns dug

---

PHILOMAN MOUGI
CHARCOAL
SANMMH COLLECTION

---

[3] This opinion is made explicit in Uys's short story 'Two Daumiers' in *The Dream and the Desert* (London, 1953).

into the landscape, miles of barbed wire and mine fields, Ford and Bedford trucks ferrying troops and provisions up and down the Springbok Road (so named because it ran through South African positions). There are images of soldiers waiting for something to happen, playing cards next to their Bofors guns, lounging in tents, smoking and drinking. There is drama too. Krige was in El Alamein on 13 July 1942 during one of Rommel's assaults on the position and he sketched South African tanks advancing on the powerful German armoured force. He also experienced air attacks and made quick pen sketches of figures running for cover as ack-ack guns are brought into action and bombs lance down.

Axis (German and Italian) prisoners of war were assembled at El Alamein and Krige painted them being escorted away by Indian troops along Springbok Road towards the railway station, the only prominent landmark in the area. The verticality of the column of humans bisects with a train that steams across the flat horizon. The image of prisoners being led away at sunset is a disturbing one and recalls Uys's long march to captivity. Anxious about his brother's fate in an Italian POW camp, François was naturally interested in the fate of Axis prisoners. At El Alamein he also painted the 'cage' (a guarded area surrounded by coiled barbed wire) where prisoners were collected before being removed for interrogation or sent to POW camps. Some of the Italian soldiers carry small bundles of their possessions and wait around in groups, disorientated by the fear and shock of capture. Their bandaged wounds, motley green uniforms and the odd red hat show that they are no longer a disciplined fighting unit. The barbed wire that hems them in is well drawn in free, calligraphic swirls and the Mediterranean blue behind is employed as a contrasting symbol of freedom. It is clear from the depiction that François's sympathy goes out to these prisoners and, by extension, to his brother across the sea in Italy.

MERSA MATRUH TO BARDIA

West of El Alamein there was evidence of heavy fighting and at Daba the artist came across an abandoned Italian field hospital. The verges were littered with broken-down vehicles and fingers of smoke pointed skyward. The road turned into a string of supply points, some just a few fuel drums on an endless dirt track. His convoy halted at one such desert point, Bir El Thalatha, where there were a few broken-down vehicles, a tent, and a gruesome skull and cross-bones lest anyone venture deeper into the desert unprepared. A sign read: 'Going West? You must carry 3 days' rations, water and petrol for 200 miles. This is your last chance.'

At night they pulled off the road and Krige would pitch his bivouac or simply dig a slit trench in the sand, making sure it was far from vehicles or gun emplacements in case of air attack. He would huddle against the cold in a heavy greatcoat and balaclava (it was too cold to wash and water was scarce) and eat his bully beef or occasionally enjoy the treat of tinned yellow peaches from the Boland. He brewed his tea over a petrol-soaked rag in a jam tin to hide the telltale glimmer of fire; even cigarettes had to be shielded. The only light would come from the looping colours of tracer shells, arcing like fireworks through the darkness. Sometimes he sheltered with others in the cellars of bombed desert buildings, drank beer, listened to Italian opera on the enemy airwaves and to the anti-aircraft guns firing into the night.

He spent days in the dusty cab of a truck, shuddering along the supply lines, cut off by the roaring of the engines, the clouds of dust and his thoughts. The convoy would have been constantly on the lookout for low-flying Messerschmitts which skimmed over the Allied convoys and emplacements. Occasionally they came across Roman ruins or nomad caravans moving silently and gracefully through the desert, the camels in stark contrast with their machinery of war. Dust devils swirled out of mirages as the furnace-like khamsin wind kept blasting them.

A further 230 kilometres up the line Krige came to Mersa Matruh. The town had recently suffered a naval bombardment from Italian warships and very little was left undamaged. At night the Allied troops burrowed into the ground like moles in anticipation of attack from the air and a total blackout was enforced. Here Krige sketched the body of a German infantryman lying in a machine-gun post by the side of the road. The soldier's means of protection – helmet, grenades and ammunition rounds – are scattered beside him. He lies crumpled behind sandbags, limbs twisted in an awkward pose, his body riddled with bullet holes.

At Mersa Matruh Krige met up with the next two war artists to be sent into the Western Desert, Geoffrey Long and Philip Bawcombe. The latter remembers that Krige was painting scenes with fairly lurid 'fried egg' sunsets at the time. They sketched together and bathed naked in the Mediterranean with the troops (Bawcombe recalls that he and Krige had to dive under the water during afternoon Stuka bombing attacks). Krige painted a number of oils of the bay and town, its mosque and palm trees. His landscapes of the beach, rocks and ancient settlement, in which there is hardly a hint of war, are good. The stone structures in the foreground could be contemporary defences or ancient ruins, and the ambiguity is intended. He painted with confidence, using fine colour harmonies and allowing the unifying ground hue of grey canvas to show through. The images capture the atmosphere of these coastal desert towns. It is North Africa that reigns, not the European powers passing like itinerants across its expanse. Although less successful and more topical, *First View of Mersa Matruh* (1942) shows the town under attack and anti-aircraft shells bursting above figures darting for cover.

From Mersa Matruh the road stretched further west over Halfaya Pass on the border of Libya and Egypt – or the 'Hell-Fire' gap as it was known to the troops – where the artist sketched a sea of graves, turretless tanks beside the road and a scene of total destruction with not a building, vehicle or ship left intact.

Further up the line and just across the border was Bardia. In January 1942 the town was the site of a major South African victory in which more than 7 000 German and Italian soldiers had been captured after four days of heavy fighting. When Krige first arrived there, it was something of a ghost town with many houses reduced to rubble and the church peppered with shell holes, a few surviving bluegums and fig trees providing the only dashes of green. He paints a lone soldier walking up a main street lined with bombed-out buildings and a mosque. The image is rendered in thick, buttery paint and the blue-grey roadway which sweeps up to meet the sky dominates the image.

As his convoy approached Tobruk the horizon became littered with burnt-out tanks and trucks, and signposts began appearing in German and Italian. François stopped beside a Leichter Messtruppkraftwagen, or German staff car, which had fallen victim to a strafing from the South African Air Force, its two Afrika Korps occupants slumped dead beside the vehicle. The stench of carrion and hosts of carcass flies demanded a response from him and as always his sketchbook provided the only answer.

SIDI REZEGH

Krige arrived at Sidi Rezegh on the outskirts of Tobruk not long after the dreadful three-day assault on the South African 5th Brigade which culminated in the fateful Sunday of 23 November 1941. The losses were so heavy on that day that the participating German panzer-division soldiers referred to it as *Totensonntag* or 'Sunday of the Dead' (it fell on the Lutheran All Souls' Day). Uys had been trapped by the German encirclement of Sidi Rezegh and was captured on the last day of the battle. After being pinned down in a shell crater and subjected to hours of non-stop fire, Uys and his companions surrendered to a group of German Mark IV tanks prowling through the South African lines.

During the battle the South African armour had been outgunned by the faster and better-armed German tanks. All that remained on the open plain when François arrived were the bodies of soldiers and the skeletons of vehicles of war. Uys's description of the battlefield as he was marched to captivity in a column of South African troops was a scene that François would find a few weeks later and one he would sketch, the absent presence of his POW brother haunting the images:

The desert was one golden glow; the sky above scarlet, crimson and purple, with streaks of mother-of-pearl blue and green; and against those distant stately horizons the smoke from burning trucks, tanks or armoured cars stood up like slim ebony columns in the still air.

A scene of great static dignity and grandeur, quite unrelated to these first aimless steps we were taking on the long road to captivity. That wide incandescence, that sombre as if consecrated splendour, all that magnificence of light and colour, and those towering black pillars ... it seemed against that majestic arch of sky Vikings were being burned on their funeral pyres.[4]

In a short story, 'Two Daumiers', Uys describes the aftermath of one of the skirmishes at Sidi Rezegh, the kind of scene François was to paint repeatedly:

They stopped beside what remained of the South African twenty-pounder. The tank-shell had scored a direct hit; gun and pit seemed as useless as a match box on which someone had stamped a nailed boot ... About five hundred yards away the four Italian tanks lay almost in a straight line at irregular intervals from one another, with the deep criss-cross tracks they had cut into the moist earth plainly visible. One tank lay on its side, another was embedded in a patch of yellow churned-up mud like some

---

[4] Uys Krige, 'Totensonntag' in *Orphan of the Desert* (1967; Cape Town, 1983), p. 70.

monstrous grey fly stuck in flypaper, the third, a dull black, had been burnt out, and the turret of the fourth tank had been blown off and was lying ten yards from the tank, its long slim gun still slanted towards the sky.[5]

Upon investigating one of the Italian tanks the narrator paints the reader a picture that mirrors François's most haunting portrait series:

The shell had taken off the turret as neatly as with a knife; and they had a detailed view of the tank's interior. With his hands firmly grasping the steering-wheel, the driver sat erect in his seat, straining backwards as if, in that final moment, he had wanted to jerk his stationary tank into sudden action. A taut figure, pitch-black since it had been completely carbonised, but perfectly preserved except that it had contracted to about two-thirds of an ordinary man's size; and naked with the black penis as rigid as the rest of the body.[6]

Is it possible that both brothers stumbled upon the same gruesome scene? Unlikely. What is significant is that each of them tried to convey the same kind of horror, grappling with words and paint to express in meticulous detail what was too big to comprehend fully and too awful to process.

One of the characters in Uys's story suggests that the only way to 'get rid of the scene' and to 'preserve self-respect' is to write it down, and it is clear from the number of times the brothers 'wrote down' this image that it was never fully 'got rid of'. The protagonists, both war correspondents, talk of trying to capture the scene. Mostert says to Johnstone:

'I don't think even Tolstoy could have done it. Words can't do it. You need the drawing pencil or the etching needle of a great artist. Do you know Goya's series of etchings, The Disasters of War? … Yes, Goya, with his love of the common people, his passion for democracy and his Spanish genius for contrasts. He would have slashed that tank scene out of steel and acid as if he were cutting snake-poison from his arm.' …

'Not Goya,' said Johnstone, 'Daumier … He is more classical in that he uses less detail, he filters all that emotion very carefully through his brain, he stands at some distance from what he paints or draws. And he never wallows in his disgust or pity.'[7]

This surely is where François stands: carefully recording all he sees as dispassionately as possible. Forty-five years after making the preliminary sketches and taking photographs, the artist returned to this horrifying image and painted his most disturbing work. It is rendered in a sombre range of browns, the eye

DEAD TANK DRIVER, 1987
OIL ON CANVAS
65 x 55 CM
PRIVATE COLLECTION

---

[5] Uys Krige, 'Two Daumiers' in *The Dream and the Desert* (London, 1953), pp. 122-3.
[6] Ibid. p. 125.
[7] Ibid. p. 129.

trapped by the metal interior of the burnt-out tank – there is no tonal or spatial relief from the claustrophobic, coffin-like square of canvas. The radio headset still hangs round the driver's neck, while his hand rests on the gear lever. The carbonised face has slit eyes and pinched features, its lips burnt away to reveal a terrifying grimace. In the short story Uys draws the analogy between the cindered man – with his high brow and long straight nose – and an image of Pharaoh Akhenaten in the Cairo Museum. In François's painting the metaphor is also apparent and appropriate to the setting. A second charred figure sits behind the driver, a 'doppelgänger', dark as the shadows of this metal tomb. The painting is an old man's powerful condemnation of war, the exorcism of a haunting image from his youth.

The battlefield at Sidi Rezegh left an indelible impression on François and from the number of sketches we have (most of them done in January 1942), it appears that he spent quite some time recording the scene of destruction. He was riveted by the mangled vehicles and repeatedly sketched the 'still-life' carcasses of burnt-out German tanks, 88 millimetre guns and half-tracks, armoured cars and trucks with their debris scattered across the desert. Among this battlefield flotsam and jetsam Krige included reminders – helmets, boots, gas masks – of the soldiers who had been consumed in the explosions. One gets the sense that he was drawing rapidly without taking in the full horror of the scene – a numbed and automatic initial response.

At Sidi Rezegh, Krige came upon an unusual field kitchen which he sketched and then painted. It was made out of a derelict German Mark IV tank which provided shelter from the wind and a firm base for some of the tent's guy ropes. This transformation of the war machine, with the draped canvas over its barrel softening its angular contours, appealed to his pacifist nature. Soldiers sit at trellis tables enjoying warm food or a cup of coffee, oblivious of the enemy panzer in their midst.

When Krige came to the burial grounds of the Sidi Rezegh fatalities laid out near an ancient sandstone tomb, he was deeply moved and the scene is reworked in almost every medium. There are images of simple crosses on a flaming horizon and the wounded bodies of tanks in the foreground. In many there is a 'fried egg' sunset softening the scene of grave-diggers with their picks and shovels raised rhythmically against the sky. More corpses wrapped in canvas bags arrive on stretchers to await burial, while white crosses stretch into the distance. In one oil, *Grave-diggers, Sidi Rezegh* (1943), a shirtless black soldier rests on his pick and stares at the terrible work at hand. In this 'democratic' picture, François tries to convey with an image what his brother writes in short-story form – a protest against the discrimination towards blacks, particularly those who had signed up to fight alongside their white compatriots. A well-built young man is momentarily equal to his fellow South Africans as they battle against the hard ground with their picks and lay their countrymen to rest.

There is also a series of *nature morte* images of a group of four body bags rendered as though they were butterfly cocoons waiting to unfold new life – a brilliant visual metaphor to convey his sense of the tragedy. An upside-down wooden crucifix lies to one side in an indefinite foreground area, echoing the shapes of the pick-axes. A full moon rises over a plain where diggers toil to get all the corpses buried. In the oil versions each body bag is a subtly different combination of greys, blues and mauves pointing to the unique character of each of its contents. Pairs of army boots jut out of the bottom of the bags – the butterflies trying to awake.

TOBRUK TO TRIPOLI

Krige arrived at Tobruk in November 1942 soon after the German evacuation to find the area severely bombed, the town square full of troops and armour and the bay where Nelson's fleet had once anchored strewn with wrecks. Tobruk had changed hands a number of times during the campaign and was the place where 11 000 South Africans had surrendered five months previously. The area was honeycombed with dugouts and trenches and festooned with miles of barbed wire.

Moving west through Libya, Krige passed the Italian settlements of Mussolini's African colonisation scheme, with deserted farmhouses, overgrown gardens, roaming herds of cattle and packs of starving cats and dogs. He kept on the move with the armour by day, pursuing Rommel across the coastal plains, and camped in the dunes at night, eating the NAAFI food from dixies with the troops.

Out in the desert the artist came across a weird-looking German glider. The aircraft had landed behind enemy lines and his painting shows it squatting menacingly over its dark shadow like some prehistoric bird. Its tail fin points a swastika to the pink sky where Allied aircraft clear the air of enemy. The effect

1 Krige sketching nomads in the Sahara during the war.

2 Sketching in the Western Desert.

3 Krige painting a battle scene from the desert in his hotel room at the Continental Savoy in Cairo.

is almost Miltonic: a flight of angels passing over a vanquished, Satanic bird.

By 1943 Krige was venturing further into Libya close on the heels of the Allied advance. He pulled into the strategic harbour town of Benghazi, where barrage balloons hung eerily above the town and apartment buildings were split open, displaying their shattered interiors to the street. Then onward past the lonely fort at El Agheila to Tripoli, his final destination on the desert trek. It was a relief to be at the end of the road and he must have felt an affinity for the other nomads with camels 'outspanned' at the end of their own caravan journeys. On the Garab (Tripoli) market square he duly hauled out his pen and sketchbook, his old instinct preventing him from leaving a Mediterranean market-place without capturing it on paper.

LEAVE FROM THE FRONT
CAIRO

While on leave, Krige visited Alexandria where he sketched bombed buildings, Free French sailors in the gharri-filled streets, as well as the promenade along the sweep of the bay. But it was Cairo that he made his temporary home and which held a particular allure. Cairo meant an escape from the harsh conditions of the front – comparative luxury, hot baths, clean clothes – as well as the opportunity to get to know this other, northern African culture. He set himself up in a temporary studio where he could take his time over the paintings whose preparatory sketches he had made in the desert. Oil colours and other painting utensils were not high on the war office list of equipment destined for the front and so he had to make do with improvised materials and scrounge in the back streets for what he needed.

His headquarters and official gathering place was the South African Bureau of Information situated in a building at the corner of Sharia Champollion and El Malika Farida. He would occasionally visit the Press Club Bar and the South African Officers' Club but spent much of his time in the Continental Savoy Hotel where he was billeted and where he made a number of studies of the guests and visitors. A sophisticated, colonial atmosphere reigns with officers, stylish-looking women and wealthy Egyptians passing the time of day chatting and drinking in cane chairs while waiters hover in attendance. Outside is a pretty terrace with palm trees and a lovely garden beyond.

But Krige was predictably more drawn to the local inhabitants and culture, and was captivated by the everyday scenes of Cairo: women in black wearing yashmaks with bundles on their heads, long-suffering babies shrouded in clouds of flies, loaded donkeys, hooting taxis and military trucks muscling through the throng, pavements packed with beggars and vendors accosting the khaki-clad troops on leave from the front. He strolled the streets and bazaars in the evenings when the cool breeze blew off the Nile or sat sketching in street cafés alongside men smoking hookah. He made detailed studies of locals he came into contact with, even recording their names, subjects that could not possibly have been in his war brief. Here he was indulging his personal interest and sketching subjects he related to. His style loosened up and the drawings are more accomplished. There is something of the Krige *joie de vivre* in his sketches of Egyptian market-places, donkeys and feluccas. This bustling African/European/Middle Eastern world came as a relief after the desert and his pen celebrates the release.

At night in the smoky Cabaret Bardia he made a series of drawings and water-colours of belly dancers and the wide-eyed audience of befezzed locals and soldiers, along with musicians playing guitars and tambourines. The new dimension of air-raids was added to the thriving night-life of the Egyptian city, and the eerie sound of sirens would wail like deranged muezzins across the rooftops. From his hotel room he would listen to the ack-ack guns, watch the groping searchlight columns and webs of tracer fire arcing up to meet the parachute flares dropped by the enemy above; then came the terrifying thud of German bombs.

There are two good paintings of Cairo viewed from a balcony window (probably the Savoy) overlooking the gardens and streets of the town. In the better version a big grey and pink sky fills half the canvas and presses on a city of minarets, domes and public gardens. The dirty board colour is used as a dull ground, the oils are dry and their application sketchy, with a minimal suggestion of buildings, foliage and wheeling birds.

In Cairo, Krige had regular contact with his superiors, received news from the Union and could meet up with his fellow war artists. It was at one of these gatherings that Geoffrey Long, Major RN Lindsay and François got together to discuss how to improve the war artist programme. Major Lindsay, their immediate superior, then submitted a report suggesting some changes to the scheme. Krige also wrote to Colonel EG

Malherbe at Defence Headquarters giving his opinions and offering his endorsement of the report. He suggested strengthening the powers of the Arts Committee and also the continued support and even retention of these artists after the war in order to record the peace-time activities of various arms of the service:

> *Ek sien egter nie waarom hierdie ondersteuning na die oorlog moet wegval nie en indien dit kon voortgaan sou dit oneindig veel bydra om kuns in Suid Afrika te help en aan te moedig. Ek is seker elke kunstenaar hetsy musikant, beeldhouer of digter wat al die moeilikhede wat sy professie meebring deurgemaak het; sal so 'n materiele ondersteuning verwelkom.*[8]

Given military priorities and budget constraints, however, this was not to be.

DOWN THE NILE

Journeys from Cairo took Krige all over the Nile Delta and into the desert to palm-fringed oases, mud-walled towns, pyramids, tombs, Arab markets and camel halts. One excursion brought him as far as Lebanon and Syria (1943) where he sketched members of the South African Mines Engineering Brigade and their tunnelling efforts for the Haifa to Tripoli railway line at Ras Bayada.[9]

Like most servicemen, Krige made a number of voyages down the Nile, a pleasant way for soldiers and convalescents to relax when on leave from the front. He sketched a romantic night-time cruise with officers and Wrens seated under the sail and a band of minstrels serenading them from the prow, their 'clarinet' and tambourine music echoing across the water to other sailing craft merging into the darkness.

There are many photographs and pen-and-wash sketches done while gliding along under the lateen sail of feluccas with their blunt, upturned bows. In the almost wind-free conditions the squat vessels with their huge triangles of patched canvas coast along silently. François was fascinated by the graceful bow shape of the flexible yard and its feather of canvas against the horizontality of river and flood plain. Block and tackle, young Arab boys limbering up the masts, the trimming of yards and tacking through the current – this was a world far removed from the blood and dust of desert warfare and his repeated portrayal of this riverine lifestyle is a testament to his relief at being away from the front. For Krige the Nile existence was rooted in a time frame that dwarfed his era – similar vessels had been cruising the Nile since long before Moses floated downstream in his reed basket – and he found this particularly comforting.

The Egyptian felucca crew became his travelling companions on longer voyages, pulling at the oars when the wind died and leading him to ruins. With camera and pen he recorded the passing vessels, water buffalo knee-deep in the stream, the off-loading of passengers on the banks of the stream and beautiful women in black robes hitching a ride in the bows. He passed picturesque Nile villages that reminded him of Spain with their flat-roofed mud houses and groves of swaying dom palms. The style in these sketches is economical, a deft use of pen and wash conveying the 'exotic' riverine scenes. Relieved of war duty, he captured this passing world for the pleasure it gave him and revealed the North African sights that truly interested him.

LUXOR

Krige made a long journey south with an Indian officer friend to visit Luxor and the Valley of the Kings. He explored the City of the Dead on the right bank of the Nile and the mortuary temples overlooking the river and was struck by the largest of them, that of Queen Hatshepsut at Deir el Bahri. Its stark 'Modernism' and dramatic setting below the cliffs made a strong impression on him. As he approached the ramped entrance to the temple he was accosted by the many scarab sellers and baksheesh hunters and later sketched the robed merchants as they surrounded luckless soldiers on leave. The sellers trail loudly after troops who try to take photographs and explore the temple in peace.

François wandered among the giant columns of the Temple of Amun-Re at Luxor and through its processional sequence of colonnaded courts and halls. He marvelled at the obelisks and the avenue of sphinxes, at the palm-leaf capitals atop columns simulating bundles of papyrus stems, their horizontal bands of hieroglyphs and bas-relief carvings, at the sheer scale of it all. His camera never stopped snapping and with his pen and sketchbook he recorded what must have seemed so timeless and permanent compared to the mayhem of the desert fight.

SOUTH AFRICA

In about September 1943, Krige returned to South Africa on leave and it appears from military correspondence that he was keen to paint naval and coastal defence subjects around Cape Town, such as the crash boats based at Gordon's Bay. A letter

ALLIED SOLDIER
MIXED MEDIA

Ek sien egter … : I don't see why this support must end after the war; if it could continue it would contribute immensely to help and encourage art in South Africa. I am sure that every artist, whether musician, sculptor or poet who has endured the vicissitudes of his profession, will welcome such material support.

[8] François Krige File at the archive of the South African National Museum of Military History, letter to Colonel Malherbe dated 2 April 1943.
[9] There are two photographs showing him sketching in Baalbek, Lebanon.

Sketching on the move in Egypt.

dated September that year suggests that he was staying at his parents' home in the leafy Cape Town suburb of Newlands and spending his days out sketching military installations. He also set himself up in a studio near the family home where he completed some of his desert oils. It appears that at this time he painted a portrait for the newly formed women's section of the South African Navy, the Swans. He also talked of a sea trip up to Saldanha and the possibility of painting war-time activities in Cape Town docks. He returned to Pretoria in November and from there was sent back to North Africa where he prepared to join the South African forces in Italy, a country vastly changed from the one he had visited seven years earlier.

ITALY
FOGGIA

The Allied invasion of southern Italy took place in the summer of 1943, but it was not until the following year that Krige embarked for Europe. He joined a convoy from Alexandria early in 1944, probably with the 6th South African Armoured Division, and crossed the Mediterranean. In North Africa the artist had found the battle front bad enough, but at least most of the fighting had remained far from civilians. In Europe war was in the suburbs and villages. It was devastating the old-world Italy that François had grown to love and was to shock and disturb him profoundly.

Krige reported to the South African Public Relations Office at Foggia, situated in a second-floor flat in a dilapidated building. Foggia, a strategic town which was to be his base for much of his time in Italy, is in the southeast of the country and was the centre of a complex of airfields and railroads. As such, the town and its environs had come under repeated attack from both sides which left the area badly scarred. Krige was moved by the residents' plight and painted a series of works featuring the devastation wrought by air raids and shelling. By now he was bitter about the violence and had little interest in recording the troops' activities – it was the civilians that concerned him and his Italian images are a commemoration of their struggle and hardship. His Foggia works, done in the winter of 1944, show labourers trying to clear the debris from shattered apartment blocks as furniture spills from buildings sliced open by bombs. The images feature mountains of rubble, damaged red-and-ochre buildings and frail figures toiling at the job of reconstruction. Horse-drawn carts clear the wreckage – petrol rationing was in full force. In some paintings the structural building supports are exposed like great ribs, creating a powerful skeletal metaphor. Destitute Italians dressed in rags rummage through the remains of their homes while the futurist shapes of bombers streak beneath leaden skies. Many of these images were painted long after the war and speak of the lasting impression the scenes of destruction made on the artist.

In the countryside the peasants tried to conduct a normal life and continued to bring in the olive crops and sell their wares at the market. But many had been made homeless and the roads were full of peasants clutching their belongings, pulling carts as they fled the fighting. There are images of hill towns seemingly untouched by war except for army trucks winding up the narrow streets, and there are medieval villages under bombardment. In one small, fine oil a family group of refugees pause by the side of the road, their hill town under attack in the background, while flak smoke peppers the sky above. Women in shawls cast their eyes to the ground. The work's muted colours are contrasted with the red of one of the women's scarves and the crimson flames of her home behind. The little group has a few bundles of goods and the image convincingly portrays the suffering of civilians in times of war.

Perhaps his most accomplished and poignant painting of the war period is the portrait of a child, *Italian Girl* (1944), whose tragic expression suggests far more than any battle piece could. It is a small, humble picture and hangs in the artist's home, not in a war museum. The child is a victim of the conflict, perhaps a refugee. Her pale face is in soft focus and Krige's characteristic bold outline is omitted. She looks *up* at the viewer (enhancing the pathos) with sad eyes and a world-weary expression that belies her pigtails, ribbons and blue dress with baubles. An offset 'frame' within the picture frame is created by a curtain and dado line and this decentring device, combined with the look in her knowing hazel-brown eyes, further conveys her emotional 'decentring' and displacement.

François escaped the scenes of suffering and destruction in Foggia and retreated to the nearby town of Vasto where he could rest his nerves. Here was the Europe he remembered, a fishing village largely untouched by war. It was a typical Mediterranean coastal town and he made water-colours of the winding coast road and colourful lateen-rigged boats – with intricate woodwork and prominent bow sprits – drawn up on the sand. He depicts the multihued vessels festooned with nets and fishermen wading their Italian 'feluccas' into the surf. Here, as elsewhere, the artist celebrates the unity of Mediterranean civilisation, drawing visual analogies between Egyptian and Italian fishing craft.

VESUVIUS

In early spring Krige found himself on the western side of the Apennines near Naples and it was here that he again met up with his friend, Philip Bawcombe. He was in fact staying with Bawcombe at La Favorita, in a grand villa turned transit camp, when Vesuvius erupted on 17 March 1944. The following day they awoke to see the cone hurling cinders 10 000 metres into the air and red lava pouring down its slopes. The countryside was showered with pink pumice dust and locals groped through the choking ash-fog trying to protect themselves with raincoats and umbrellas.

Both artists were excited by the phenomenon and anxious to record it up close. When a war correspondent with a jeep joined them, they were able to reach San Sebastiano on the northern slope, where they watched a wave of lava descend towards the town and pour over walls and into gardens, filling rooms and crushing homes. Having survived destruction by bombing and artillery, the inhabitants had to watch their village being destroyed by natural forces. Krige sketched the column of ash and the ruined villas, his charcoal stick (here medium truly matches subject!) used to good effect to suggest cinders and rubble. The two intrepid artists then decided to hike up to the rim of the crater. At first they walked on a carpet of warm ash but soon the going got rough. They soaked their handkerchiefs in water and tied them round their faces, trying not to inhale the sulphurous fumes. It became increasingly uncomfortable underfoot and when they neared the crater the cinders became too hot and they were forced to descend, thrilled by their close encounter.

PUSH TO ROME

After the winter stalemate, during which the Germans had dug themselves in, the Allied troops and tank columns began pushing north again in the spring of 1944. As the Germans retreated they mined the routes through the mountains and destroyed the bridges. One such strategic bridge was the railway crossing at the Sangro River near Monte Cassino. The Allied response to the destruction of crossing points was the Bailey bridge, a device made up from standard steel and timber components which could be bolted and locked together in a number of different ways. In the spring François made an 'official' (and hence fairly unsuccessful) war painting of the South African Engineer Corps completing work on the Sangro River Bailey Bridge, the snow-covered Apennines rising out of the valley in the background. A train waits on one side of the stream while engineers make finishing touches.

While in this part of Italy he also paid a visit to the Italian farmer, Vincenzo Pedrella, who had helped Uys escape from the Germans across the mountains to Allied lines. When François got to the Abruzzi farm, Vincenzo handed over a large watertight flask containing Uys's papers and POW writings which the brave Italian had concealed at the bottom of the local well.

Once Monte Cassino had fallen, the road to Rome was open and Krige reported to his new Public Relations office shortly after the take-over of the city. Rome, despite the dearth of electricity and water and its war-time drabness, had escaped the conflict relatively unscathed and was a revelation to François. He explored the streets and frequented a restaurant at the Spanish Steps where he watched the bustle of flower sellers, pimps, pickpockets and lovers. In an almost normal environment once again, the artist realised the extent of the stress he had been living under. But by this stage not even the Eternal City could alleviate the emotional strain that the war in Italy had exerted on him and he decided to request a discharge. In June he wrote a remarkable letter from the Advance Press Camp to Colonel Malherbe, Director of Military Intelligence, asking for a discharge from the army:

Ek is nou reeds 33 maande in die Verdedigingsmag as oorlogskunstenaar en het in die afgelope drie jaar 'n geweldige ondervinding gehad, maar het lank reeds 'n toestand bereik waarin ek al die indrukke nie meer verteer nie. Indien ek voortgaan kan dit alleen die gevolg hê dat my werk in kwaliteit vinnig sal afneem en voel dus dat ek my posisie as oorlogskunstenaar nie langer regverdig nie. Ek het 'n groot behoefte aan 'n rustige normale lewenswyse en wil u dus graag vra om my aansoek om ontslag uit die leër in aanmerking te neem.

Ons het in Rome 'n dag na sy val aangeland en dit was 'n groot verligting om 'n stad binne te kom wat ongeskonde is deur die oorlog, om weer glimlaggende gesigte te sien en die burgerlike bevolking aan te tref in 'n taamlike normale toestand. In die Suide

---

Ek is nou … : I have been in the Defence Force as a war artist for 33 months now and in the past three years I have had a tremendous experience, but I long ago reached a stage where I cannot assimilate my experiences any longer. Should I continue, it could only result in a reduction in the quality of my work, and I therefore feel that I cannot justify my position as a war artist. I have great need of a quiet and normal life and I therefore ask you to consider my application for a discharge from the army.

We arrived in Rome the day after it surrendered and it was a great relief to enter a city untouched by war, to see smiling faces again and to find the civilian population in a fairly normal state. Where the war had passed through the South the villages and countryside were mostly in ruins and the people in a desperate situation.

Rome has a great wealth of art museums and monuments; indeed it is possibly the richest in the world in this respect. If possible, I would like to stay here for a while – it would help my development as a painter and would be an experience which might not come along again in my lifetime.

waar die oorlog deur getrek het was die dorpies en land meesal in puin en die mense in 'n benarde toestand.

Rome het 'n groot rykdom aan kunsmuseums en monumente; trouens seker die rykste van enige stad in die wêreld en as dit moontlik is sou ek graag hier wil stilstaan vir 'n tydlang – dit sou baie help in my ontwikkeling as skilder en 'n ondervinding wat hom in my leeftyd miskien nie weer sal voordoen nie.[10]

And here is the equally intriguing endorsement from Krige's immediate superior, Major Lindsay:

The strain of painting in a war area is considerable in the case of an artist who is probably inclined to be rather temperamental, and I would strongly recommend that Krige be given an opportunity immediately to return to the Union.[11]

François's letter is remarkable for a number of reasons. To have an officer (by this stage he was a captain) requesting discharge from an army during a major offensive is unusual, to say the least. And then his naivety in asking whether he could not perhaps stay on in Rome to further his artistic education at military expense is preposterous. What is even more staggering is that the South African Defence Force more or less acceded to his requests. He remained in Rome for a while and his superiors agreed to 'respect the artist's mentality',[12] having him recalled to South Africa!

HOME FRONT

Captain Krige duly returned home in September 1944 and spent the South African summer living with his parents in Newlands, working on the Italian pictures and executing paintings for the South African Railways and Harbours to which he was seconded. These works depict convoy activity in Table Bay and industry in the docks. He writes: 'They are all big jobs especially the one of the graving dock: a gigantic concrete hole in the earth with minuscule lorrys [*sic*], trucks & little human busy bodies milling around to the accompaniment of shattering noise of riveting, flashing and creaking cranes & the usual raging South Easter does not ease matters.'[13] Krige remained in Cape Town throughout the summer trying to organise a personal exhibition of his recent works and enlisting support for what turned out to be a very successful exhibition of war art in Cape Town in February 1945.

Later that year in Pretoria he painted his largest and most ambitious war work, a monumental image depicting the homecoming of South African POWs. It is realistically and naively drawn and is an unsuccessful piece although it is of historical interest. In the background a Dakota stands on the Swartkops Air Base runway while the foreground is filled with a tableau of family members greeting their loved ones. Krige is careful to record the various emotions, the excited children and dogs running between the adults' legs, a melancholy note struck in the figures of an old man and a crying woman who turn away from the crowd, their boy not having returned.

In August the War Advisory Committee suggested that artists be sent to theatres of war which had not been covered during the fighting and Captain Krige was assigned to Madagascar. By the end of the year, however, authority had still not been given for this purpose and François was finally discharged.

EL ALAMEIN A/A GUN AND CREW, C. 1942
OIL ON CANVAS
31 x 61,5 CM
SANNMH COLLECTION

---

[10] François Krige File at the archive of the South African National Museum of Military History, letter to Colonel Malherbe dated 17 June 1944.
[11] François Krige File at the archive of the South African National Museum of Military History, letter to Defence Headquarters dated 27 July 1944.
[12] Ibid. Note added to this letter by Colonel Malherbe.
[13] François Krige File at the archive of the South African National Museum of Military History, letter to Tony (?) dated 17 January 1945.

WAR
61

ON BOARD SHIP, 1980S
OIL ON CANVAS
71,3 x 86,5 CM
PRIVATE COLLECTION

FRANÇOIS KRIGE

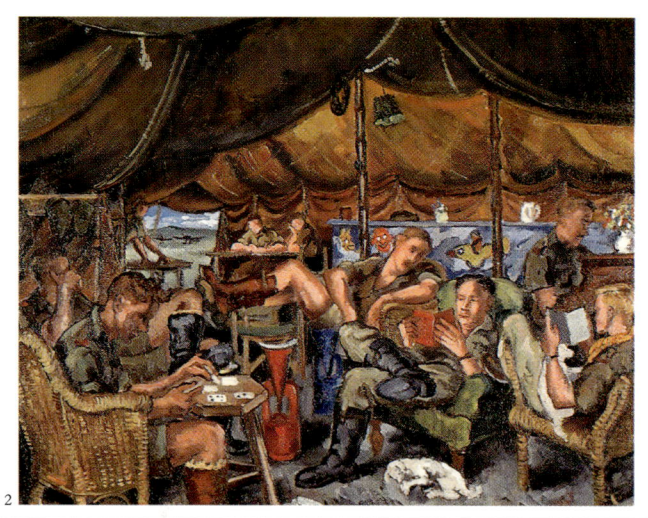

62

1
ITALIAN GIRL, 1944
OIL ON CANVAS
32,5 x 27,5 CM
PRIVATE COLLECTION

2
AT HOME, SAAF, C. 1942
OIL ON CANVAS
65 x 83,5 CM
SANMMH COLLECTION

3
FOGGIA, WINTER, 1944
OIL ON CANVAS
48,5 x 59 CM
SANMMH COLLECTION

1
NATURE MORTE, C. 1943
OIL ON CANVAS
45,5 x 60,5 CM
SANMMH COLLECTION

2
GRAVE-DIGGERS, SIDI REZEGH, 1943
OIL ON CANVAS
71,5 x 86 CM
SANMMH COLLECTION

3
IN CONVOY (SOUTH AFRICAN SAILORS IN ACTION), 1940s
OIL ON CANVAS
46 x 49 CM
SANMMH COLLECTION

4
STURROCK GRAVING DOCK, 1945
OIL ON CANVAS
80,7 x 94 CM
TRANSNET COLLECTION

4. CAPE TOWN 1946-1966

Sylvia at work in the office of her gallery in Parliament Street, Gallery Shear, in the sixties.

POST-WAR

After the war Krige found it difficult to settle down and again travelled widely in South Africa, drifting from place to place on his war savings. He returned to his beloved Lesotho where he sketched extensively at Cathedral Peak and undertook long hikes with a young Basotho guide in the Mokhotlong area. After years at war he was thrilled to be back in a place where he felt at home, 'purified' by mountain air. He slept in kraals high in the hills at night, went out walking the tracks with locals during the day, and on one expedition in 1946 he spent sixteen days pony-trekking in the Malutis.

The artist returned to Cape Town and held his first post-war exhibition of paintings there in September 1946, a potpourri of work done in Europe and the Union. During this time he stayed with his parents who were living in Constantia from where he made sketching excursions – sometimes by bicycle – round the Peninsula, up the west coast and into the Boland. He could not settle down and was soon on the road again with his paintings, exhibiting in Worcester and then Bloemfontein. Later, he stayed with Sannie Pyper in Johannesburg and exhibited there and in Pretoria. In his letters home Krige described how he was finishing works and having them framed for exhibition. It was an uncertain time for him:

Word nou moeg vir die rondvallery en ontwrigting en moet nou eenmaal die probleem van 'n verblyf en werkplaas oplos as ek weer terug [in die Kaap] is.[1]

The solution to his '*rondvallery*' was a decisive one. He returned and settled in Cape Town, married a widow and acquired two unruly stepsons in the process. Not much is known of Poppie Plantinga, other than that she was a German whose Belgian husband had died and left her with a wrought-iron factory. She had originally been a nurse and is remembered by the family as a colourful character with a lively personality.

Krige moved into her home at 35 Bergvliet Road, Heathfield, and Poppie rented a studio for him nearby. Based in Cape Town's southern suburbs in the late forties and early fifties he painted vignettes of the area. An interesting contemporary painting, reminiscent of Van Gogh in its vibrant use of thick impasto colour, shows the patchwork greens of the fields in Constantia Valley rising to purple mountains, while the sky is rendered in multicoloured, pastel hues which evoke the colours of late autumn in the valley. The composition is cut by a foreground diagonal slope on which three labourers prune the vines.

In 1949 he was awarded the medal of honour for painting and graphic art by the South African Academy for Science and Arts. With his reputation now firmly established, Krige again

---

Word nou moeg … : Am getting tired of the floundering and dislocation and will simply have to solve the problem of a home and work-place once I'm back [in Cape Town].

[1] François Krige in the Uys Krige Archive, undated letter to mother.

exhibited in Cape Town the following year; his range stretching from the thirties to his latest works showed a maturation and growth from sombre colour (*Self-portrait with Hat, Antwerp, 1937*) and a tentative style, to the bolder and more expressive colour of his Constantia works. In an interview with a friend, Lawrence Green, after the exhibition, Krige hinted at his approach to painting. He said that he only worked when he felt like it: 'I believe you should enjoy what you are doing, even if you are doing nothing.'[2] Krige was certainly never prolific and his art acquired something of a scarcity value. He went on to talk about his method of working:

> *All my life I have been filling sketchbooks, so that now I have many more than I shall ever use for my paintings. I have been a rolling stone – it is a family failing – and that is why I have never achieved a large output.*
>
> *I am not a specialist. If you concentrate too much on one subject you narrow the field, and that detracts from the interest. The great masters painted anything that appealed to them.*

Family life made heavier financial demands on him and he started to eke out a small supplementary income by providing illustrations for newspapers and magazines, and from book illustration. In 1948 his drawings for Uys's book of travel sketches, *Sol y Sombra,* were published and in 1952 his most ambitious project to date appeared, illustrations for Francis Brett Young's *In South Africa*. He provided a large number of water-colours of various parts of the subcontinent for this 'imperial' travel book, such as delicate, highly coloured paintings of animals in the Kruger National Park, city scenes in Johannesburg, Pretoria, Durban and Cape Town and images from rural southern Africa ranging from the Knysna forest to Great Zimbabwe. The following year Eitemal's unusual novel, *Jaffie*, about the lives of two donkeys, was published. Krige furnished the illustrations, which comprised a large series of fine pen drawings of animals, mostly of the faithful creature he so loved to draw, the donkey. In 1960 a collection of bushveld stories, *Their Secret Ways*, written by Victor Pohl and charmingly illustrated by Krige, was published. The tales concern the animals of the veld and the author's childhood on the Lesotho border. Both themes were close to Krige's heart and his drawings of the ordinary animals of the veld – including hares, field mice, ants, mongooses and guinea fowl – show a tenderness and a conviction of the importance of even the most humble creature. In 1963 he provided illustrations for two Jan J van der Post novels about the Bushmen, *Agarop: Kind van die Duine* and *Gaub: Vlugteling van die Duine*. These images derive from the artist's sketchbook during his periods of living with the Bushmen in the Kalahari Desert which will be discussed more fully further on.

Most of these books presented a conservative and at times colonial notion of 'old Africa' and, although Krige would probably not have agreed with all their implicit views, he would have been in accord with the conservationist sentiments and their celebration of nature.

Krige's first marriage did not last more than a few years. The couple had little in common and François could not live up to the expectations of a family which needed security, a provider and a father figure. His mother-in-law, who lived with them, suggested that in order to make a better living, François should go to Blouberg, plant his easel in the sand and paint Table Mountain, as such works were easily saleable. This was just the kind of interference that Krige could not abide.

CAPE FISHERMEN

While he lived on the Cape Peninsula, particularly during the decade following the war, Krige returned to the kind of fishing villages he had loved to frequent as a child growing up along the Onrus coast. Hundreds of his studies of fishing boats, hamlets and the traditional life style of Coloured fishermen from all over the Western Cape abound. We see old sailing craft, genre scenes of men repairing their nets, boat-builders at work on vessels and the wrecked carcasses of others washed up on the beach. Trek fishermen surf their boats home and drag in nets shimmering with fish; some sleep off the early morning voyage on the sand beside their craft, while others celebrate a good catch in the dingy local bar. We see the ubiquitous whitewashed cottages on high ground overlooking the ocean and shacks down at the waterline with *bokkems* (dried mullet) strung up to dry.

Krige would often spend so much time in a fishing community that his presence went unnoticed and he was able to move among the locals recording their daily tasks in a uniquely insightful way, unmatched by any other South African artist. He was consciously capturing a lifestyle that he felt was threatened; indeed his beloved fishing harbour at Hermanus was soon to become extinct, replaced by a modern harbour and power-driven boats.

[2] Lawrence G Green, 'He Paints Only When It Pleases Him' in *The Cape Argus*, 2 December 1950.

Both Uys and François were drawn to Cape Coloured culture and sought to incorporate aspects of it into their art. It is interesting that during the fifties, a period when apartheid legislation was biting into the fabric of this community, both brothers took to interpreting, recording and celebrating it in their own unique way. There is an assertion of South Africanness in this act, an acknowledgement of what is good and admirable in our heritage, and an attempt to stress points of contact across the colour line at a time when the line was being starkly drawn. While François captured the visual images, Uys was busy writing his celebrated book of poems, *Ballade van die Groot Begeer* (Ballad of the Great Desiring), much of it written with a vibrant and humorous use of the Coloured idiom. The artist's fisherman pictures bring to mind images from contemporary poems by his brother, such as those in 'Ken jy die See':

> *Was jy al van jou bootjie soos 'n veer gevee*
> *deur 'n grys golf hoog soos 'n tronk se muur.*
> *Wat help dit om te spartel en te skree: 'Nee! Nee!'*
> *sluk eers daardie waters sout en suur?*
> *Dan sê jy nog, Meneer, die vis is duur.*

François travelled the length of the Western Cape coast, recording the littoral villages, from Arniston in the southeast to Lambert's Bay in the northwest. There are images of simple fishermen's cottages with white-washed stone walls and thatched roofs, huddled on the bluff overlooking the ocean at Arniston, and of the great sea cave booming with surf. He continued to spend holidays at the summer home in Onrus from where he could visit the old fishing harbour at Hermanus. Here he sketched and later painted the activities of the fishermen as they negotiated the promontory. There is the bustle of activity as the oars of a little flotilla dip and heave around the point from Skulphoek before running the boats up the rocky slipway. We see the craft being borne out of the water on poles hauled by fishermen and the catch loaded into baskets, biblical-style.

From Heathfield and later from his studio in Cape Town he made daily visits to Hout Bay where he drew the harbour, fishermen drinking wine round their boats, waiting for shoals to enter the bay, and women hard at work cleaning fish. Chapman's Peak towers above rigging and the jetty is strewn with nets. Boats are being overhauled on the slipway and Krige's fascination with detail is evident in the manner in which he notes the busy shapes of rigging, hulls and nets. He found the shipwreck of a fishing trawler in Hout Bay and returned to the spot repeatedly to make a series of sketches, and later paintings, of the vessel. Holes in the hull offer vignettes of the bay and cliffs behind while the shattered vessel is juxtaposed with operational fishing craft that hover around it.

The barren west coast had a particular allure for Krige and he undertook numerous sketching expeditions along these shores. Here he experimented with a quill pen made from a Cape gannet's feather and learnt to use the uneven line and unusual quality it created to his advantage. It was again indigenous fishing communities, so similar to those he had been drawn to in Europe, that attracted the attention of his painting eye in Saldanha Bay, Paternoster, Lambert's Bay, Hoedjiesbaai and Donkergat.

Saldanha Bay and Langebaan with its pale green lagoon were regular destinations. On one sketching trip he wrote to his parents enthusing about the inspiring subject matter:

> *Saldanha wemel met onderwerpe – ongelukkig is hul besig om die volkshuisies af te breek en natuurlik moderne abominasies in hul plek op te rig dus is ek bly dat ek die geleentheid het om 'n rekord te maak voordat die dorpie totaal kapot is. Ek skilder tenminste een skildery met 'n paar tekeninge ingesluit per dag en as dit so aangaan sal ek 'n mooi versameling hê.*[3]

He drew the cottages with the sails of fishing boats in the background. A series of water-colours shows Langebaan beach, houses and boats, the luminous green-blue water stretching from Sandy Bay across to the Postberg Peninsula. The horizontality of the compositions and ground-hugging scrub convey something of the windswept west coast atmosphere.

In 1951 Krige visited Paternoster and was so enchanted by this tiny community that he decided to remain there for some time, producing a large number of sketches. Boat-builders hammer at the ribs of a graceful vessel webbed in scaffolding up on the hard; indeed, Krige loved the shape and lines of old Cape fishing boats, stocky and seaworthy craft built to weather the storms off this treacherous coast. He also took his sketchpad to the well in Paternoster where he found constant material. Women come and go with containers on their heads and haul a bucket by hand from the depths while children clamber about the social meeting place. He sketched and painted the cottages, the lighthouse, children with wire toys, and donkey carts on the gravel roads. Here style certainly matches subject

---

'Ken jy die see ... ': (literal translation)
'Do you know the sea?'
Have you ever been swept from your skiff like a feather
By a big grey wave high as a prison wall.
What use to flounder and shout: 'No! No!'
when you've swallowed water, salty and sour?
Then you still say, Sir, the fish is expensive.

Saldanha wemel met ... : Saldanha teems with subjects – unfortunately they are demolishing the fishermen's cottages and of course putting up modern abominations in their place, therefore I am glad I have the opportunity of creating a record before the village has totally gone to pot. I paint at least one painting a day with a couple of drawings and if it continues like this I'll have a good collection.

---

[3] François Krige in the Uys Krige Archive, undated letter to parents. At this time Krige was staying in a Saldanha Bay hotel and paying for his board and lodging with paintings.

matter. These are simple, economical images that reflect the humble nature of the fisherfolk and also Krige's own austerity and asceticism.

Three important oils derive from Krige's time at Paternoster and Saldanha in the early fifties. In *Fetching Water, Paternoster* – two simplified figures in the foreground with fishermen's cottages behind – a limited and 'whitened' palette of cool, non-naturalistic hues gives a strange atmosphere. The forms are roughly and expressionistically painted in dry, chalky applications. A white sun hangs above the fishing village as if in a mist or haze, casting no shadow. It is one of his more abstract pieces and gives the impression of being an étude, roughly sketched in bold strokes and with a loaded palette knife.

The second painting depicts three fishermen mending their nets (1955) in which the grounds of colour only loosely match the sketched outlines, not unlike a Raoul Dufy. Even the roughly worked underpainting – which does not entirely match the final pose of the seated fisherman – has not been erased. This creates an interesting, 'uncompleted' feeling in the composition and also implies movement. The colour and line mismatch brings about a certain visual tension between painting and drawing (and as a result focuses attention on both) as though the lines actually shimmer above the colour fields. The net is suggested by the barest of means and the area of netting on which the two background figures are working has been painted over. Only the seated fisherman's hands – like those of an artist, the 'tools' of his trade – are drawn in detail as they weave a needle through the nylon web. The composition is carefully worked out, a 'cyclical' ellipse being formed by the basket, net and figures, offset by the horizontal bands of beach, sea, flotation corks and sky.

The third oil, *Hoedjiesbaai* (1955), features a basket and three snoek lying in the foreground, a simple cottage and *bokkems* on a line in the middle distance and a fishing boat making for shore under sail in the background. These form three narrowing spatial bands, all cleverly united by the *bokkem* pole; greater unity is achieved by the repetition of forms – the shape of the beached boat echoes those of the fresh fish and *bokkems* – an inspired visual metaphor. The flat-roofed buildings look classically 'Mediterranean' and the image is so archetypal that it could be a scene from the shores of Galilee. Indeed, the artist has simplified his elements and reduced his palette, and the bold, dark outlines give the features an iconic, timeless feeling.

On his journeys along the coast Krige was also intrigued by sea-life, particularly the creatures living in the shallows and intertidal zone. He explored Langebaan Lagoon by boat, renting a small 'pram' dinghy and rowing out to Schaapen Island. Here he sketched sea darters, cormorants, sacred ibises and seals with a sinuous style, capturing the mass of creatures with a few deft lines. Every time he went out rowing he encountered an old fisherman, Jacob Bleeker, anchored opposite Donkergat whaling station with his tame seagull perched in the prow.

Krige also began painting underwater scenes. Peering into rockpools he depicted the world he saw: *klipvissies*, *perlemoen* shells, sea snails, anemones, sea urchins and their green egg carcasses, starfish and swaying weeds. He was fascinated by these microcosms. It was a colourful realm far removed from his normal subject matter, a strange, decorative world in which to lose himself. The most unusual of his underwater scenes is a series of paintings done many years later (1972) of colourful jellyfish in a blue-black ocean. The images were inspired by

FISHERMEN
LITHOGRAPH
SANG COLLECTION

perlemoen: abalone, mother-of-pearl.

photographs he came across in a Smithsonian science journal and mark a departure – both stylistically and in terms of subject matter – from his usual work, a curious exercise in stark scientific realism. The creatures glow from within in an array of pinks, oranges and greens and approach the viewer out of the depths with heads of swaying 'hair'. The transparent spheres of jelly make the water look pale blue and in the dark middle distance we see other such creatures arcing their trails of light like underwater comets.

ONRUS

Krige returned regularly to Onrus where he stayed in his brother Arnold's summer house (later sold to Uys) and it was here at Swartdakkies, which had been designed by his brother-in-law, Revel Fox, that he painted the places of his idyllic childhood holidays. From the *stoep* of the open-plan beach house with its commanding views, he painted the lagoon where he had swum and boated as a child. The family would sit outside sipping their evening '*drankies*' and watch the egrets coming home to nest and the Onrus mountain changing hue.

His *Onrus Lagoon* is an interesting *contre-jour* work painted at Swartdakkies and evokes the atmosphere of the view from this magical spot (now destroyed by holiday development). It is a morning scene with the sunlight sparkling white on the water and the reeds, which are drawn in short, bright parallel hatches *à la* Gauguin. Two old milkwood trees stand in the foreground. The dark mauve of the lagoon is picked up in the shadows and on the slopes of the mountain and is juxtaposed with luminous expanses of green, appropriate to the *contre-jour* effect. Houses, foliage and lawns make up a patchwork of colours on the far bank. Forms are difficult to discern here and this draws one's eye in as one tries to understand the spatial relationships between water, reeds and bank. The carefully controlled blue-green-mauve colour range and the lack of recession make for a compelling landscape.

Like Monet at Étretat, Krige took to painting the Onrus shore-line and there are many studies of rocks, seaweed and breaking waves, some done with quill pen and wash in a 'Japanese' manner. A series of oils depicts the coast along the road to Vermont and captures the midday light on a summer's day. Krige introduces pinks, greens and violets into his sky, colours which reflect the hues of the rocks and vegetation. Spiky rocks rear up as if to break on the shore and echo the shape of waves crashing on a distant reef. The forms are drawn with a lively and assured calligraphic handling of the brush. Line is used economically to accent the knife edges of the rock and these occur in a whole range of flesh hues, umbers, yellows, blues, greens and greys, yet the illusion of rock is never lost. Distant breakers are painted wet-in-wet in touches of pale green and white over Prussian blue, an effect which enhances the suggestion of movement and is repeated in the wet-in-wet calligraphy of the rock edges. Krige has revelled in the surface texture of paint, banishing chiaroscuro in an almost Abstract Expressionist celebration of the painted surface. Influences of Abstract Expressionism can be seen in a number of paintings from the fifties and early sixties, particularly in the Onrus works.

THE DORP STREET STUDIO

In the mid-fifties, after his divorce, Krige moved into a rented first floor studio apartment at 19 Dorp Street, Cape Town. It was a comfortable place that suited his needs. Everything in the city was within walking distance and he could have a five shilling lunch at the local pub with other impecunious artists. Contemporary paintings show the interior of his studio and views through French doors onto the balcony with the street below. Many have a simplified, Matisse-like rendering of the interior with areas of flat colour and the carpet and curtain patterning foregrounded. We glimpse the pub across the road and the façades of Long Street and Signal Hill in the distance, while interlocking building forms are reflected in the window panes.

At this time most of Krige's family were living in the city. His sister Suzanne and parents were in Greenham Terrace in Annandale Street, his sister Mizzi in Oranjezicht, Uys in a bungalow on Clifton Beach and Arnold in Wandel Street. It was an intimate time for the family. Sannie would gather the extended clan at her home on Sunday evenings for dinner and these were important family-bonding occasions where the elderly matriarch would hold court. François's sister, Mizzi Baumann, would sometimes drop her twin sons off at Dorp Street where she hoped her brother would teach his nephews the basics of painting. The twins remember that instead of providing an art class their quiet uncle simply continued working and they would sit in the corner watching and breathing oil paint fumes, Krige probably hoping they would learn by osmosis.

Financially, François – never one for self-promotion – remained in a precarious situation. As always, Uys tried to help

SANNIE UYS
ETCHING

---

drankies: drinks, sundowners.

and encouraged friends and family to arrange private exhibitions in their homes. He even contacted his journalist friends asking them to review François's work:

> *Ek was juis van plan om van F. se skilderye wat nou-die-dag uit Bloemfontein in 'n groot kas hier aangekom het, hier in ons huis [in Cape Town] aan vriende te wys en so van hulle aan 'n paar van my vriende van die hand te sit. Ek voel ons moet nou rêrig vir hom in die bres spring – om, as openbare tentoonstellings dan windeiers en volslae misoeste bly, die man of koper self op eie houtjie aan die doek te [sic] bring.*[4]

A couple of months later Uys wrote again about François's lack of sales and recognition:

> *Rupert Shephard (hoof van die Michaelisskool) sê nou-die-dag vir my: 'François mustn't worry ... He'll be appreciated ... (lang pouse) perhaps only after his death.' En toe sê ek: 'that'll be cold comfort to him ...' En voeg ook by, dinkende aan my eie geval en ook Mammie se verhale: 'You mean the only good Krige is a dead Krige.' ... Rupert het ook gesê: 'The trouble about François is that he's too good for S. A. ... too sensitive.'*[5]

Despite his financial difficulties, Cape Town excited the artist and he recorded life in and around the city with enthusiasm. The subject matter during this period gives a sense of nostalgia for the traditional life, culture and architecture of old Cape Town. He sought images and locations that depicted timeless aspects of the city, shunning the modern, industrial sphere. Indeed, when painting street scenes he would leave out cars, telephone lines and modern lampposts. There are many joyous images of the inhabitants at play: the circus and its animals, and a number of colourful oils of Coons (minstrels) moving through town playing banjos and twirling umbrellas as they travel in a wave up Wale Street.

From Krige's studio he could hear the muezzin's daily summons wailing across the city which took him back to his time in Cairo. It was a short walk from his studio up to the Bo-Kaap (Malay Quarter) and he spent much time sketching there. Many painters before him had been drawn to this picturesque part of the city, including Wenning, Ruth Prowse, Florence Zerffi and later Boonzaier. In his article, 'A Painter in the Malay Quarter', Caldecott speaks of his own excitement when working in the Bo-Kaap:

> *Here all seems good, all solicits, with silent urgency, projection [sic] into the unreality of the painted universe. Parallel and wavering-straight, mouldings cap the bulging walls, giving sharp perspectives underlined in horizontal shadow ... chimneys lean outwards, inwards, standing drunken but undaunted, whitewashed, black-lipped, generously broad, massive for the houses that bear them. Here and again, painted turrets topping a mosque make a circumflex accent of dull brown on the blue sky.*[6]

Krige would settle down to sketch in the street and his presence would attract the attention of urchins who took to calling him 'Mr Van Gogh'. He painted street scenes with mosques, minarets, flat-roofed Bo-Kaap houses, Signal Hill rising behind and Table Bay in the background. Out beyond the harbour wall we see a Union Castle liner gliding past the stacks of the old power station. One excellent painting – a typical 'Cape Impressionist' work – offers a narrowing view down a cobbled street towards the city with the dockyard cranes beyond and the green slopes of Blouberg across the bay. The eye is drawn through the painting from building to building and led to the minaret with its dome merging with the horizon and its tower marrying the spatial bands. The verticals of the foreground buildings and the middle distance minaret contrast with the horizontals of the background giving the image depth, while the multihued walls and roofs form a pattern-like flattening and hence 'contradicting' effect which creates an interesting visual tension between picture plane and depth. The idea of a close-knit Cape Malay community is suggested in the figures going about their chores in the street or simply sitting on their stoeps, chatting and watching the activities of their neighbours.

STILL-LIFE

Still-life is the genre in which Krige was to make his most important contribution to South African painting. The term *nature morte* (still-life) means dead nature, but what Krige does is to try to imbue matter with life. His numerous vegetable and fruit studies hark back to the seventeenth-century Dutch stilleven of foodstuffs, but more importantly to the Modernist formalism of Cézanne's still-life masterpieces. Krige's still-lifes done in his studio were careful experiments: he was a scientist in a laboratory, an environment where he could exert complete control over his subject matter. He enjoyed the challenge of setting up his components in compelling sculptural arrangements. Then came the arranging of planes and colours on the canvas so that the pictorial space would be balanced and harmonious. Although he concentrated on fruit and flower studies, he sometimes used strange combinations of items, such as a skull, a

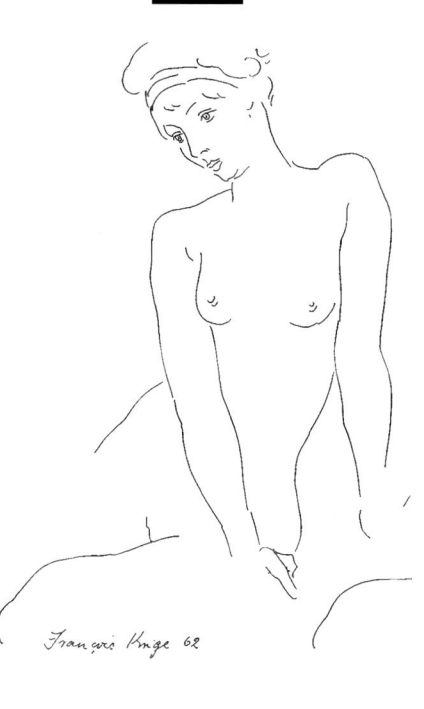

NUDE
PEN AND INK

Ek was juis ... : Indeed I had planned to show some of F's paintings, which arrived here in a large crate from Bloemfontein the other day, to friends in our home [in Cape Town] and to sell a few to some of my friends. I feel we should now really come to his rescue – if public exhibitions fail and turn out total flops, to bring the buyer to the canvas by our own efforts.

Rupert Shephard (hoof) ... : Rupert Shephard (head of the Michaelis School) told me the other day: 'François mustn't worry ... He'll be appreciated ... (long pause) perhaps only after his death.' And then I said: 'that'll be cold comfort to him ...' And added, thinking of my and Mammie's stories: 'You mean the only good Krige is a dead Krige.' Rupert also said: 'The trouble with François is that he's too good for SA ... too sensitive.'

---

[4] Uys Krige, *Briewe III*, letter to Bokkie dated 22 June 1955, p. 83.
[5] Uys Krige, *Briewe III*, letter to Bokkie dated 25 August 1955, p. 85.
[6] Quoted in J du P Scholtz, *Strat Caldecott* (Cape Town, 1970), p. 45.

François sketching with a quill pen in a 'pram' dinghy on Langebaan Lagoon in the early fifties.

waterblommetjies: water hawthorn, Cape pondweed.

pineapple and a Greek pot, and also did still-lifes of Bushman artefacts.

Pomegranates is an impressive fruit piece from the Cape Town period. Iconic pomegranates are encased in their own dark shadows, brilliant saturated reds resonating with a yellow-gold background. The solidity of the work and the broad, confident brushstrokes are reminiscent of Wenning. Foliage is placed in three corners to balance and anchor the dynamic composition while the keynote red of the fruit remains the subject of the piece and even the greens of the vine leaves are bled into by the pomegranate's red.

Krige also experimented with still-lifes of countless varieties of flowers, from dried fynbos to rioting tropical plants, from humble *waterblommetjies* to rare proteas picked on friends' farms. *Still-Life with Veld Flowers* (1948) is a successful early study which depicts an array of indigenous plants in a blue-and-white porcelain vase. It is roughly and confidently drawn and the palette is dark. The foliage – much of it dried – is rendered in quick strokes, often wet-in-wet. The table on which the vase is placed is 'tipped up', Cézanne-like, creating a foreshortening effect. The background is broken up into areas of colour that give no sense of depth and force the eye to remain on the picture plane where the foliage sprays like fireworks.

Sunflower (1955) is an exceptional, expressionistic flower study (actually a 'landscape' series) of a sunflower bending its head towards the earth. There is certainly dialogue here with Van Gogh's sunflower, but Krige has made his image a distinctly southern African one. A golden, end-of-summer haze fills the canvas; a koppie rises in the background and a Basotho village nestles in the valley below. There is the suggestion of nature's seasonal cycle in the organic, circular shapes echoing through the image: in the flower, sky forms, leaves and the shape of the Basotho kraal; even the landscape traces part of a circle. The round form in the sky alludes not only to the previous position of the sunflower before it began to droop, but also suggests the sun – nourisher and name-giver to the plant – now descending towards the horizon. Dried leaves curl like hands in the heat and the flower's orange petals resemble tongues of flame. The earth and autumn colours that pattern the canvas – cool blues tempering the play of yellows, reds and browns – do not fully correspond to the forms as they are drawn (as in Dufy), creating a certain dynamism.

FIGURE STUDIES AND PORTRAITS

In order to improve his rendering of the human figure, Krige attended life-drawing classes in Green Point for many years and produced hundreds of sketches of nudes, most of them practice pieces of academic poses. There are, however, certain nudes that are worth noting. His broken-line pen studies, done with the barest of means and only vaguely suggesting some features of the anatomy, are very fine indeed. There are a number of Matisse-like nudes where outline predominates – these are often the most arresting – but he also experiments extensively with shading and line. The oil nudes are less successful in that they say too much, as his realist method combined with the exigencies of the medium leads him to render the whole figure without the intriguing obfuscation that the broken-line drawing allows.

Portraiture traditionally deals with status, with depicting the patron or client in a pleasing likeness or even in a flattering light. For the Impressionists, by contrast, parents, siblings, wives and friends became the category of sitter most frequently portrayed and the artist endowed *personality* with greater importance. Most of these Impressionist portraits were not commissions, but rather personal meditations concerning loved ones. Workers and labourers also found a place in Impressionist portraiture. In traditional European or South African art these folk would have been rendered as types, their names never recorded, but the Impressionists saw the humble as worthy of great art.

Krige studied the portrait tradition from Rembrandt to the Post-Impressionists, seeking techniques with which to portray an essential likeness. Less interested in Modernist distortions and abstractions, he too wanted to render the personality of the individuals he loved and the characters of his country and, as with the Impressionists, no one was too insignificant.

During the Cape Town period the artist continued to struggle with the human figure: '*Die portretkuns bly vir my maar altyd 'n probleem; nie alleen om goeie skilderye te maak nie, maar tegelyk jou kliënt tevrede te stel – en al die klein anatomiese verskille wat die een mens van die ander onderskei (die gelykenis) word so belangrik.*'[7] It is thus not surprising that so many of his portraits, like those of the Impressionists and Post-Impressionists, are not for clients, but images of labourers and vagrants who were prepared to sit for him – and these are also some of his most successful works. It was important for the artist not to have the pressure of a client's expectations. It is perhaps also for this reason that he did such a large number of self-portraits as well as portraits of family members, especially during the fifties when he painted a number of images of his parents, particularly Japie, seen in characteristic pose reading *Die Burger* in dressing-gown or Springbok rugby blazer.

Anna-Magrieta, a portrait of his young cousin, is an étude in which the unfinished-looking red, green and yellow background is drawn in broad, 'scribbled' strokes and the bare, canvas-board background becomes an integral cohesive element. The girl's face is rendered with thin, pale applications of paint and the effect of spontaneous execution is further conveyed by scratch marks in her hair from the reverse end of the brush.

Krige's portraits of children are serious pieces in which little of the joy of childhood is revealed. Rather, he imbues his child sitters with an adult awareness and avoids sentimentality, making for compelling works. These children stare back at the viewer with knowing eyes and demand to have their world taken on its own terms. They are not simply good likenesses, but express character and emotion in the subtle manipulation of formal elements and achieve a remarkable distillation of the child's personality.

There is an unfinished oil of a black boy sitting on a swing in which the large head and 'disproportionate' body are dwarfed by the swing to which he clings and the child locks our gaze with big brown eyes. A little girl with blonde hair in Renoiresque style has big staring blue eyes and fat cheeks. The many engaging images of little girls become confusing as quite a number feature his three nieces, Eulalia, Melanie and Grethe, who all fit the wide-faced, blonde Krige type.

Revie (circa 1959) is a particularly fine portrait – just a sketch really – of his nephew, Revel Fox Junior, painted when the child was six. It is executed on untreated plywood and the brown wood is allowed to stand out in places as a unifying element. The image was completed in one sitting and the rough, unfinished result adds to the charming quality of the painting. The background and clothing are considered totally subordinate and painted in a few rough, but deft, brushstrokes, the colour of the boy's jersey picking up the grey of his eyes.

Revel Junior was a shy, quiet and introverted boy and François captures this quality in his tiny (27 by 23 cm) portrait. This idea is conveyed through a number of judiciously employed formal devices: the boy's melancholy expression is given a poignant and even disturbing dimension by a lowering of features on the left side of his face. Thus the child's left ear and eye are slightly dropped, while the left side of his mouth is skewed. The wide, rosy cheeks and pale hair are a Krige phenomenon, but the extreme whitening of Revel's hair is also suggestive of an old man and implies a world-weary sitter, enhanced by the boy's sad, staring eyes. At this time François was doing a number of portraits of his aged father and it is interesting to note that the portrait of this child could easily be mistaken for a childhood image of the boy's Springbok grandfather – certainly the idea of the '*witkoppie*' (as Japie was known) is perpetuated. Indeed there is something of the childless François in the boy too. (As we know, portraits are never simply an objective record; they are a response to the human tendency to consider oneself in relation to others and to include personal elements in the image.) Thus the artist alludes to three generations of Kriges, and their salient characteristics of sensitivity and even vulnerability, in the image of a small boy (Revel Junior is the nephew who most resembles his late uncle in looks and temperament).

CAPESCAPES

Landscape has long been the central tradition in South African painting, pioneered by white settlers wishing to describe their African environment. In Europe, landscape painting was the chief nineteenth-century genre, and the approach pioneered by the French plein-airists and Impressionists had a lasting effect

---

'Die portretkuns bly … ': 'Portraiture always remains a problem for me; not only to make a good painting, but to please your client at the same time – and all the little anatomical differences which distinguish one person from another (the likeness) become so important.'

'witkoppie': 'blondie'.

---

[7] François Krige in the Uys Krige Archive, letter to parents dated 2 December 1952.

on subsequent landscape artists throughout the world. South African painters of Krige's generation married these innovations with the more conservative traditions of the 'academic' landscapes they were exposed to in the Union and experimented with new techniques. The challenge was to create a uniquely African vision to capture local topography.

Krige's vision of his Cape environment, particularly in the later Montagu works, was influenced by his artistic forebears' nineteenth-century portrayal of Provence. In the representation of light, atmosphere, relationship with natural surroundings and subject matter we are dealing with a similar approach and sensibility. By aligning himself with a late nineteenth-century bourgeois genre, Krige identifies himself with a feeling of comfort within a nature that no longer holds the threat it did for pioneers. Painting a landscape, like the act of naming, carries with it the notion of appropriation, even possession. In South Africa it also brought with it the baggage of patriotism and nationalism, a celebration of the white man's conquest of the land. Krige's art reveals a love of the land seemingly uncomplicated by the act of possession or the later struggle to maintain control. He appears to 'read' the landscape with an eye that is half European and half African. The contradictions and problems with this stance are diminished by the sincerity and 'truth' of his vision. His images speak of someone completely at home in the veld and of a strong identification with nature.

His approach to the depiction of the South African landscape was a personal and emotional one. He shunned the idea of painting nature decoratively and when Uys once lauded the decorative qualities of a certain tree for a painter, François was quick to correct him and stress his holistic approach:

> *Ek het reeds die landskap geskilder en die garingboom is daar. Nie as dekorasie nie, hoop ek, maar as integrale deel van die landskap, heeltemal opgegaan in die innerlike eenheid van die geheel.*[8]

Krige loved the Cape countryside in all its forms and he painted local scenes with a perceptive eye, depicting combinations of landscapes with humans, animals and buildings. It is interesting to note that in these images Krige, like the French Realists of the mid-nineteenth century, recalls a former, more rural existence in a nostalgic manner. We never see technically advanced farming equipment, telephone poles or tarred roads. When he depicts ploughing, sowing or reaping it is always being done by traditional means, by hand or horse. Indeed, nostalgia is a central concern in much of Krige's art. His vision is often based on the tragic reality of the impermanence of life: places, people and things change, disappear and die. This would have been driven home to him most emphatically during his war experience.

His oil *Small Town in the Karoo* of Victoria West is one of the exceptional works of the post-war decade. It evokes the old-world platteland atmosphere with not a hint of the twentieth century in the townscape. We look from a koppie as a descending shepherd and flock lead the viewer's eye down into the village, while a snaking road draws the vision out of the far side of town and up into the hills. In fact the painting's structure is even more complicated than this. Our gaze is led from left to right along the line of the ridge where the sheep stand to a lone house on the far right. It is then drawn back into town along the nearby line of red- and blue-roofed houses; a road guides us from the red-and-white *afdak* to the church (our gaze actually turns at the transept) and then out of town and through the hills, a distant farm breaking the eye's headlong rush to the horizon. The scene is an archetypal Karoo village with dominating spire and gabled houses with corrugated iron roofs. The spire and cypress trees are echoed by aloes and cacti and repeated in the horizon's pointed koppies. The densely packed cluster of buildings is contrasted with the Chagall-like, colourful expanse of hills, the shadows of passing clouds playing across their slopes – the 'indefinite' dry and chalky application of paint employed to good effect. The use of ochres, pinks and reds provides an appealing colour harmony, while the cooling influence of blue is everywhere apparent in the sky, roofs and even in the vegetation and earth, making for a compelling balance of hue. Perhaps the only discordant note is the naive realism of the plants in the foreground and the tortoise struggling off stage, bottom right.

In the mid-sixties the artist was commissioned by KWV to provide illustrations for a book on viticulture, *Die Witwyne van Suid-Afrika* (1967) by WA de Klerk. Krige already had a lot of appropriate material available in his sketchbooks, but also spent time travelling the Western Cape producing works specifically for the book. There are many images of old Cape Dutch houses such as his excellent series of Schoongezicht, Groot Constantia and the old Krige farm of Boschendal in which he displays a particularly sensitive eye for architecture and envi-

---

BARAKWENA MUSICIAN
PEN AND INK

Ek het reeds ... : I have already painted the landscape and the aloe is there. Not as a decoration, I hope, but as an integral part of the landscape, completely absorbed in the inner unity of the whole.

afdak: shed, lean-to.

[8] François Krige in Uys Krige, *Na die Maluti's*, p. 50.

ronment, for the depiction of buildings in a landscape. The horse-drawn plough studies of Groot Constantia (the house rendered in a few deft touches of charcoal) and those of the oak avenue, the Jonkershuis and the baroque pediment of the winery are superb. The book required drawings of wine-growing districts and to this end he made sketches of the Land van Waveren farms hugging the foothills of the Witsenberg. There are also images, some in water-colour, of labourers harvesting, details of vines, of farms in the Groot Drakenstein and Franschhoek valleys and a whole series in many media of Malay coopers working on barrels.

THE BUSHMEN

Krige's interest in Bushmen was sparked early in life by enthusiasts such as Walter Battiss and Uys's friend, Laurens van der Post, and his curiosity was rekindled after reading Elizabeth Marshall Thomas's *The Harmless People*. Krige's was a romantic, nostalgic and idealised vision: he was drawn to the apparent simplicity of Bushman life, unencumbered as it was by many of the things he despised about modern, urban existence. Together, Krige's collections of Bushman drawings, etchings and paintings form a significant body of work which can be viewed as a separate, 'anthropological' entity.

Battiss explored Bushman customs and art and contributed to our knowledge of these, but his involvement became self-serving and even questionable at times. For instance, he went so far as to conduct experiments on jailed Bushmen in which he gave them paper and crayons to see whether their ancestors had 'passed on' their iconography and drawing ability in some mumbo-jumbo Lamarckian way. Krige on the other hand was not interested in appropriating their imagery or conducting any spurious experiments with them; indeed, most of his paintings of Bushmen were never shown to anyone, not even friends and family. He was motivated by a personal quest and an empathy which shines through his drawings (in the oils, painted later, his position is more complicated – see Montagu chapter).

Most of Krige's journeys took him to the !Kung Bushmen in northeastern Namibia, to an isolated and government-restricted area where he could find clans gathered at waterholes during the dry season. The !Kung called themselves *zhu twa si* – the harmless people – and Krige was certainly struck by their modest nature and peaceful communal way of life where everything was shared and violence was extremely rare. Theirs was a culture of mutual dependency in which property and possessions were alien concepts and this struck a chord with Krige's own non-materialist outlook on life. The !Kung had no calendar and did not count years, living essentially for the present – this too would have appealed to a man who despised rushed metropolitan life.

Krige was fascinated by their material existence and how they survived in an unforgiving terrain: their small utilitarian camps, the makeshift dwellings with the branches of trees serving as cupboards in which to hang quivers, skin bags and garments. He was also impressed by their vast knowledge of the fauna and flora, of animal behaviour and edible plants, and their uncanny sense of topography in an apparently featureless land.

Krige made long expeditions to Namibia and Botswana in order to sketch the Bushmen in 1957, 1960, 1962 and 1968. His desire to record their fast-disappearing life style dovetailed with his 'anthropological' quest to capture traditional indigenous cultures that he revered. In his youth it was the Xhosa and Basotho; in Europe he was interested in Spain's peasant culture; North African and nomadic traditions occupied him during the war, and then there were his studies of Cape fishermen. His work concerning the Bushmen fits into this continuum, but is more significant from a cultural and historical perspective, given the near extinction of the hunter-gatherer communities today.

In 1957 Krige became the travelling companion of Jens Bjerre, a Danish adventurer and ethnographer, on a seven-month Danish expedition to the Kalahari under the patronage of the Royal Geographical Society in London. Krige's task was to draw and paint the Bushmen, to copy their rock art and also to be Bjerre's Afrikaans interpreter. One of the main aims of the expedition was to make two documentary films, one on the Bushmen and the other on the geographical phenomena of Namibia. Another objective was to collect ethnographic material for the Danish National Museum, among others. (Bjerre also wrote a book, *Kalahari*, about the journey.)[9]

A specially built camping trailer had been shipped from Denmark and was towed behind their Land Rover during much of the 11 000-kilometre journey. Although scientists and ethnographers joined the expedition at various times, it was Bjerre and Krige who spent the winter months of 1957 alone with !Kung Bushmen in a remote part of the Kalahari.

BUSHMAN BOY WITH PLAYING STICK
PEN AND INK

[9] Some of the following account of the expedition is derived from Bjerre's book (London, 1960).

The pair set off from Cape Town heading north via the Augrabies Falls and Fish River Canyon to the Brandberg, home of the famous and enigmatic Bushman painting, the 'White Lady' (the figure is neither white nor female), where they camped for a week near the rock paintings. Plagued by swarms of mopani flies which crawled into their eyes and nostrils in search of moisture, they stuck it out to experience the mountain and record the wealth of cave art.

Next they made for Tsumeb and Grootfontein, driving through wide plains filled with springbok. At Okaukuejo they found that although the vast Etosha National Park had been a blessing for the preservation of game, a ban on hunting with bow and arrow had had dire consequences for the local clan of Heikum Bushmen. Only a handful remained, living on government rations in a corrugated-iron camp where they danced for tourists on Saturdays in exchange for a few cigarettes. Krige was distressed that the clan was being kept as a tourist attraction. He found their dances too 'ersatz' and ascribed this to the fact that they could not conduct their lives as normal: '*[Hul het] 'n apatetese [sic], lustelose indruk geskep, soos iets wat besig is om weg te kwyn en self daarvan nie bewus is nie.*'[10]

When the pair arrived in Grootfontein, the town was all abuzz with news of a policeman who had been wounded by a Bushman's poisoned arrow at Karakuwisa. Krige and Bjerre were apprehensive that permission to travel into the Kalahari would be withdrawn as Karakuwisa lay on their proposed route. After some discussion, however, they were allowed to proceed and left their trailer behind at Maroelaboom, the last police outpost before the desert sands. They piled as much as they could into the Land Rover, discarding cases of tinned food in place of drums of water. 'Water is the most important thing,' said the sergeant at Maroelaboom. 'Food the Bushmen will no doubt get for you.'

They headed north via Karakuwisa where the artist encountered his first fairly 'authentic' Bushmen who had little contact with white men. They were

> *'n lustige, vrolike opgewekte groepie en ek kon my verkyk aan die amper legendariese klein mensies van wie ek al soveel gehoor en gelees het. Baie van hul met fyn gelaatstrekke die meide en kinders almal versier [met] krale van volstruisdoppe ringe om die arms en bene, skilpaddoppies vir poeier om die nek en die enigste kleredrag 'n bokvel om die een skouer en 'n tweede om die heupe tot onderkant die knie.*[11]

But Krige and Bjerre wanted to find Bushmen who had no contact with the outside world and who were living exactly as they had been for millennia. At Rundu they were advised to make for Saman Geigei, a waterhole deep in the Kalahari, and set off into the wilderness using their compass to guide them.

When they reached Saman Geigei, Bjerre and Krige encamped for a four-month stay with a clan of about 50 Bushmen who lived in three separate settlements situated a kilometre from the waterhole so as not to scare away the game coming to drink. The two men set up camp near the largest of the three settlements where 20 Bushmen lived in rough shelters made of branches and grass. They exchanged rolls of tobacco, beads, and salt and gradually made friends with their hosts. Bjerre made recordings of the language and they had soon built up a small vocabulary and could communicate in a rudimentary way.

The clan provided the two foreigners with nicknames: Bjerre was known as 'leather on legs' because of his long boots, while the artist – a pipe smoker – became 'tobacco man'. Bjerre shot footage for his documentary while Krige spent his days sketching the Bushmen. There was old Kau, the story teller, who features in many drawings, and the hunters, Tsonoma, Keigei, Narni and Samgau. We see group portraits of the young women, Nau, Ngum and Nusi, while the old wrinkled grandmother, Gausje, is the focus of numerous studies.

After a successful gemsbok hunt – recorded by Bjerre on film – there was dancing which lasted through the night. The women sat by the fire singing and clapping the beat while the men snaked around them stamping the earth until dust blurred their movements. At one point during the gemsbok dance Samgau leapt into the ring stretching his arms to simulate the horns of the prey. Then Tsonoma and Narni grabbed their bows and pursued him, feet pounding the rhythm ever faster. When Samgau had finally been 'killed' they launched into first the ostrich and then the grasshopper dance and even old Gausje ventured a few steps. When Bjerre and Krige finally retired to their sleeping bags, the sound of clapping and high-pitched monotone singing pursued them into the night. Later, after the singing had stopped and their Bushman hosts had wrapped themselves in karosses (leather capes made from whole animal hides) in shallow holes, they listened to the jackals yelping and hares and buck scuffling in the long grass. In the ensuing days Krige sketched the preparation and curing of the

---

[Hul het] 'n …': 'They made an impression of apathy, of listlessness, like something pining away and not knowing it.'

'n lustige, vrolike … : a merry, cheerful group and I could hardly stop staring at the almost legendary 'little people' of whom I had heard and read so much. Many of them fine-featured, the women and children adorned with strings of ostrich eggshell, bracelets on their arms and legs, tortoiseshells for powder around their necks, and their only clothing a buckskin slung over one shoulder and another around the hips, extending to below the knees.

---

[10] François Krige in the Uys Krige Archive, letter to unknown addressee dated 11 September 1957.
[11] Ibid.

gemsbok skin which was first stretched out on the ground with wooden pegs and then treated with resin.

As the winter progressed water became increasingly scarce. So as not to reduce the Bushmen's small supply, the two visitors rationed themselves to half a cup a day each for washing and it was soon impossible to keep fleas and lice at bay. As the water shortage became more acute, it became apparent that the four cases of Danish beer would have to keep them alive during the last month of drought. In the final days before the rains they had almost run out of food and tobacco (their only currency) and when the beer supply came to an end they had to make do with a sparse and muddy water ration. Both men lost several kilograms and even the Bushmen were becoming despondent.

When the rain eventually came, there was rejoicing and the desert was quickly transformed into an expanse of colour. But now it was time for the travellers to depart as their four months were up and they were expected back in Grootfontein. On their return journey to South Africa they visited places of interest in Namibia for Bjerre's natural history documentary, such as a great subterranean lake in a cave large enough to contain an eight-storey building. Consolidated Diamond Mines gave them permission to pass through their vast concession and they explored the bleak Namibian coastline. They came upon shipwrecks, seal colonies and sun-bleached skeletons as they travelled the length of this desolate shore. Krige was impressed by picturesque Lüderitz with its pre-war German feel and the contrast of Kaiser-style buildings and Namib topography.

In the winter of 1960, Krige was back in Botswana and Namibia in search of Bushmen. After driving through the Kalahari he had to wait two weeks in Windhoek for a permit to travel to the restricted areas. Eventually, with the personal intervention of the administrator, a place was found for him in one of the vehicles of a convoy making a 1 000-kilometre journey through northern Namibia. The group was busy organising camp accommodation and facilities for the Minister of 'Naturelle Sake' whose entourage, accompanied by journalists, was about to make a tour of that vast region.

Krige wrote to his parents from Rundu and the evocative description of his surroundings conveys something of this man's love of nature and being in the wilds of Namibia:

Die gefluit van voëls, die harde grond … het my vanoggend vroeg uit die vere gehaal. 'n Honderd voet bokant die gelykte het

BUSHMAN GIRL GRINDING WHEAT
CONTÉ

'Naturelle Sake': 'Native Affairs'.

Die gefluit van … : Birdsong, the hard ground … got me out of bed this morning. From a hundred feet above the flats one had a vista over the yellow grass plains of Angola and South West with the meandering Okavango River. … From time to time you hear the shrill call of fish eagles.

BUSHMAN BOY WITH BOW AND ARROW
CONTÉ

'*besondere primitiewe stam ... *': '*very primitive tribal life*'.

[12] François Krige in the Uys Krige Archive, letter to parents dated 8 August 1960.
[13] Ibid.

mens 'n vergesig oor die geel gras vlaktes van Angola en Suidwes met die kronkelgang van die Okavongo [sic] rivier. ... Af en toe hoor 'n mens die skril geskreeu van vis arende.[12]

His group journeyed for weeks in the Caprivi Strip and on one occasion they came upon an isolated clan which Krige decided to return to and sketch. Thus, loner that he was, soon after arriving at Rundu he set off on his own in a borrowed WNLA (Witwatersrand Native Labour Association) vehicle and headed back to Andara in the mouth of the Caprivi to rejoin these Bushmen who had a '*besondere primitiewe stam lewe*'.[13]

During his extensive travels Krige was not only interested in recording images of Bushman lifestyle, but also in capturing anthropological details. In his sketchbooks he jotted down the names of his Bushman friends as well the words they taught him for the objects he was drawing: mouth bow (*gaeing*), five-string harp (*guashi*), wooden bowl (*neu*), ostrich eggshell (*nsho*), a container for powder made from a tortoise shell (*xora*).

His travels took him back to Saman Geigei and Karakuwisa where he made extensive studies. In his images we see little boys learning to use bows and arrows, women drilling holes in ostrich eggshells, musicians playing their instruments and girls grinding corn. He shows men preparing hides by scraping off fat, then tanning and rubbing them until they are like suede before sewing them together into leather bags and garments. His drawings are executed with an extreme economy of line, often without shading, and are works of great beauty and sensitivity which have left an important record. They are simple sketches, often almost exclusively in silhouette, and convey an empathy and love for the Other that is rare in South African art.

The idea of Bushmen as harmless people did not match the centuries-old, racist myth of them as wild and thieving 'vermin'. Krige's sketches and paintings reveal a very different concept of Bushmen (one that dates from the thirties when artists like Pierneef and Battiss had begun generating an appreciation of Bushman art based on a comparatively positive perception of the hunter-gatherers) and in particular scenes such as the joyous domestic gatherings serve to discredit the stereotypes. In these images, groups are rendered with fine, broken lines, capturing the grace of their postures and movements. He sat with them in the hot afternoons when they were resting and this gave him the opportunity to make many figure studies and group portraits. In these drawings plastic figures move in different directions looking this way and that, children playing between them. He draws old people with their wrinkled bodies rendered in a web of fine lines, men wearing only a loincloth and women clad in leather aprons and big karosses belted at the waist with a sinew cord forming a pouch behind, in which a baby can ride and where the woman carries her blown ostrich-egg water containers. White ornaments made from eggshell beads dangle from tufts of hair and are strung in bands around neck, arms and knees.

Krige was especially adept at capturing the details of domestic scenes. It is common for the women to sit close together, often touching one another, and the young men do this too. Their physical closeness speaks of an emotional bond and a mutual dependency in an unforgiving environment where inhabitants must live at peace with one another in order to survive. This is conveyed in the tight-knit groups and overlapping forms of his compositions; colour harmonies (earth colours predominate in the figures and landscapes) reinforce this idea in the later oils. Krige records life around the tiny encampment: women sharpen digging sticks, crack shive nuts or do beadwork. We see them with the produce of their gathering expeditions: *tsama* melons, roots, bulbs, berries and nuts. Folk relax and enjoy a smoke from a big home-made pipe. Men prepare for the hunt, tipping their arrows with deadly poison extracted from grubs. People sit talking or singing, playing tirelessly with the babies, delousing each other's heads or resting in the shade of trees.

There are many images of a beautiful Bushman woman, whom François called the 'princess'. She sits or stands in various attitudes, decorated in her finery, holding a calabash or ostrich-egg container while a tortoise shell containing a sweet-smelling cosmetic powder hangs between her breasts.

He also captures the dance: raised buttocks and shimmering cocoon rattles, figures taking small pounding steps and moving in a circle, imitating animal movements. He sketches their intricate rhythms: strange, minimalist, ink-silhouette figures reminiscent of Bushman rock art. These black images of dance and movement are drawn in an 'animated' continuum recording each footstep, almost like one of Eadweard Muybridge's studies of motion.

Images from his final, abortive expedition to the Bushmen in 1968 show a disturbing trend. We see women clad in rag clothing with scarves covering their hair. Western civilisation had already hunted down some of the last of the nomads. Many had become pastoralists and owned livestock or worked on farms. Their hunter-gatherer existence was dying out and Krige could not bear seeing the annual decay of their traditional way of life. He never physically returned to the Bushmen, except in his imagination many years later, in flights of creative energy resulting in a series of remarkable paintings.

SYLVIA

From his home in Dorp Street, François used to visit Uys and his writer friend, Jack Cope, at their bungalow, Sea Girt, on Clifton Second Beach. When the writers had visitors – a frequent occurrence – he would wander about on the beach, reluctant to spend much time at the house. François would seat himself on rocks and sketch the scene: cottages perched above the white sand, people playing beach bats or diving into the icy water, dogs chasing each other between sunbathers.

It was on one such afternoon, a Sunday, while out sketching on the beach, that François was approached by an attractive, petite brunette who introduced herself as one of Uys's friends. Sylvia Shear recalls that she was looking her best that summer of 1960, fit, tanned and wearing a new bathing suit. She struck up a conversation with the shy artist and then suggested that he come up to her flat on Kloof Road overlooking the beach. Krige declined, saying he had to attend the weekly family gathering at his mother's house. A determined Sylvia objected, suggesting he phone and tell his mother he could not make it that week. After some persuasion he consented. 'And that was the end of the story,' contends Sylvia with a knowing smile.

Sylvia loved art and although she only dabbled in pottery, mosaic-work and later naive oils, she had a shrewd eye for what was good – and Krige's work had long attracted her attention. This keen eye for art led her to try her hand at the business side of the profession. She became an entrepreneurial art dealer who, in the early sixties, opened her own gallery, Gallery Shear, first in Parliament Street and then in Long Street. Sylvia had no capital (she had to sell her beloved Pierneef landscape of the Eastern Transvaal to raise the initial funds) but plenty of enthusiasm and determination. She wanted her gallery to be a meeting place for painters, buyers and art lovers. She had tea and coffee constantly brewing and visitors were encouraged to relax and enjoy the paintings, which included works by well-known artists such as Boonzaier and Stanley Pinker, in the old-world atmosphere of her gallery. Born in the Free State to a Jewish family[14] that was not particularly art conscious, Sylvia had no formal education in the subject, but her childhood interest in art was re-stimulated in Palestine where she met a number of artists while serving as a nurse with the South African surgical team in the 1948 Israeli War of Independence. Thereafter she became a frequent gallery visitor both in South Africa and on her travels abroad (in England she became friendly with Jacob Epstein and the Viennese sculptor, George Erhlich).

Krige began seeing her regularly during the summer of 1960 and would walk over Kloof Nek to Clifton from Dorp Street to visit her. On one of his first visits he arrived with a rather dull-looking bunch of flowers which Sylvia politely placed in a vase on the table. It took some time before François ventured a suggestion: perhaps the flowers would be better in a stew than in a vase; they were, after all, *waterblommetjies*.

There were other awkward moments in their courtship. For instance, another adamant suitor, a renowned Cape Town doctor, would not take Sylvia's 'no' for an answer. One night he climbed up the drainpipe of the four-storey building and started hammering at the bathroom window. An incredulous Krige, not understanding what all the fuss was about, helped the man in, asking him why on earth he hadn't simply used the front door, unaware that this means of access had been barred to him. To Sylvia's exasperation François politely led him through to the living room where the two of them sat drinking until midnight, at which point Sylvia, wishing to appear even-handed, asked them both to leave. Krige took Sylvia's car and drove home only to receive a phone call summoning him to return immediately as the inebriated suitor was now banging on her door. Krige arrived, 'some sort of tussle' took place (wholly out of character for Krige), and the man was not heard from again.

At an early stage in their relationship Krige painted an image of Sylvia (the simplified face of the sitter is kept anonymous) seated in her flat with the sweep of Clifton's beaches below. It is a colourful, 'flattened' image in which the saturated hues, particularly those of the orange cushions and the sitter's yellow gown, lend a certain resonance. Blue outlines, walls and light blue shadows are cooling elements juxtaposed with the hot cushions and gown. There are interesting formal issues at play. Elements in the picture create the illusion that the image has been 'tipped up': the bowl's shape is 'wrong' for the angle, while the female form and the couch on which it is poised appear to be sliding towards us and even the view through the window has a raised and flattened perspective. Despite these distortions the picture's structure is kept tight by strict formal divisions into a number of verticals and three horizontal bands described by the windowsill, dado line and curtain.

Before long the couple were seeing each other on a serious basis. It was a good match for François as Sylvia took over the business aspect of his profession – something he had never been good at – and her gallery provided an outlet for his work. Sylvia was an astute businesswoman and it was not long before she was able to sell Kriges for over R800, a considerable sum for a living South African artist at that time.[15]

François and Sylvia at the time of their marriage in the mid-sixties.

---

[14] When Sylvia's father met François he was not perturbed by the fact that his daughter's suitor was not Jewish, saying in mitigation, 'But he's such a genteel Gentile!'

[15] *The Sisters* went for R850 in 1964 and in his 1967 exhibition, Sylvia's acumen brought in over R2 000.

EUROPE

In 1961, the deaths of François's father and sister Mizzi left him shattered; soon after, he resolved to take to the road again, feeling that he needed to spend time away from the country and his family. His plan was to embark on a year-long sketching journey through Europe and to return to his haunts of two decades previously. Money was, as always, the problem. In September 1963, thanks to Sylvia, he held a relatively successful exhibition of paintings and drawings at Grosvenor House in Stellenbosch and the remuneration allowed him to undertake the much-delayed trip.

Krige set sail for Europe and, apart from a pilgrimage to London to see the British Museum, was to spend most of his time on the shores of the Mediterranean in Egypt, Greece and Italy. Greece was a new experience for him and he was immediately drawn to the islanders and their congenial lifestyle. His sketchbook shows the churches, farmhouses and windmills of Mykonos; we see fishing boats crowded into the circular harbour at Hydra, tiled houses climbing the hill behind.

François was also overjoyed to be back in Italy and spent months in the countryside sketching typical village scenes with stepped streets, cypresses, donkeys, chickens and the ubiquitous bell tower commanding the town. A series of drawings and paintings was inspired by a network of caves, perhaps in Sicily. The subsequent oils show geometric rocks and cave interiors in faceted browns. These are experimental, architectural forms in which we have views into receding passages, the eye being led through dim caverns with no colours other than those of rock and earth.

In Agrigento, Sicily, he drew villas and olive groves and in Amalfi sketched a number of fine images of the town buildings ascending the cliffs with fishing and pleasure boats moored in the bay below. Next, he travelled north via Perugia, Assisi and Ravenna to Florence where he spent some weeks in a campsite during the summer of 1964. He made many visits to the Uffizi, but complained of the tourists, the noise and the unbearable heat, and headed south again. He stopped at Siena, where he was struck by the warm red and golden colours of the buildings and climbed the 90-metre city hall spire to survey the Tuscan landscape. He also halted at the Etruscan town of Orvieto, with its big Romanesque-Gothic cathedral, and marvelled at the strange and macabre frescos after the works of Dante.

François stayed with Patricia and Dormel Gertenbach – old friends from Stellenbosch – in Vitinia, a suburb on the outskirts of Rome from where he made excursions into the countryside for a few days at a time. He liked Ostia, and at Spoleto he drew haystacks, medieval walls and spires. When he returned from a sketching expedition one evening, he actually allowed the Gertenbachs to see some of his drawings, a rare occurrence. He had to leave the room for a while and, on returning, he noticed that Patricia had turned one of the pages of his sketchbook. Such was the privacy of the man that he immediately closed the book and did not offer to show them any drawings again.

He remained with the Gertenbachs on and off for three months and Patricia, who did his washing, recalls how lightly he travelled, almost like a Bushman, with two shirts, two pairs of trousers, one pair of *velskoene* and a cardigan, two pairs of socks and two of underpants. The rest of his rucksack was filled with sketching equipment. When the couple were hastily recalled to South Africa for three weeks, Krige looked after their house and this gave him a good opportunity to get to know Rome again, 20 years on. He took time to visit his old haunts and go exploring in search of early Christian mosaics, a particular interest at the time. When his hosts returned, not an item in the refrigerator had been touched – François was determined not to be a burden to them.

Back in South Africa the artist was in for a surprise. For the duration of his period abroad he had sublet his Dorp Street apartment to Michael Schneider, a left-wing activist who, without Krige's knowledge, had used the flat as a base for making bombs to be employed in the anti-apartheid movement. The police had been tipped off and Schneider had fled the country. The flat was searched and François was questioned by detectives upon his return. The story has a strange twist, however. On his outward-bound voyage, Krige's ship had stopped at Tenerife in the Canary Islands where he visited friends. There was a serious gas explosion in the building he was staying in on the island, at exactly the time of the police raid on his flat in South Africa. There was much joking among his siblings, who teased him that they would turn over information concerning his various bomb-making escapades to the police.

FRANÇOIS KRIGE

80

THE OPEN WINDOW, CLIFTON 1960S
OIL ON CANVAS
91 x 66 CM
HUMPHREYS COLLECTION

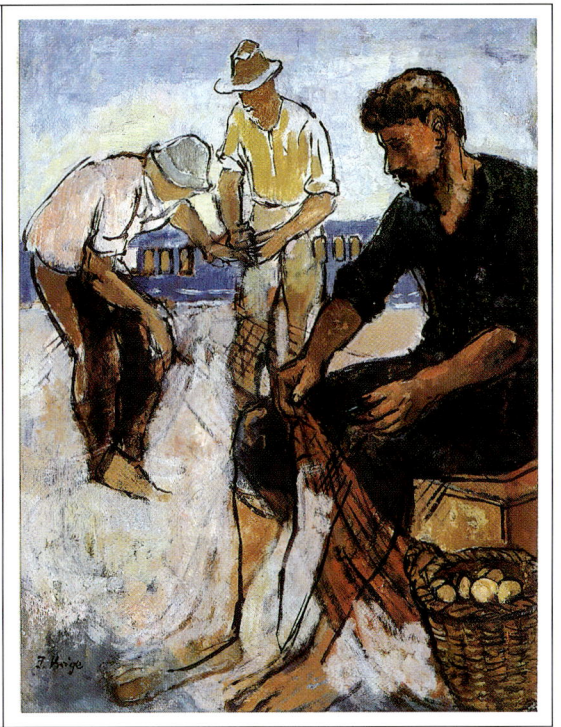

CAPE TOWN

1
PULLING OUT THE BOAT, C. 1950S
OIL ON BOARD
54 x 46 CM
WELZ COLLECTION

2
MENDING NETS, 1955
OIL ON BOARD
53,2 x 39,8 CM
PRIVATE COLLECTION

3
ONRUS, 1962–1965
OIL ON BOARD
53 x 70 CM
SANLAM COLLECTION

4
HOEDJIESBAAI, 1955
OIL ON CANVAS
50 x 65 CM
PRIVATE COLLECTION

FRANÇOIS KRIGE

82

1
REVIE, C. 1959
OIL ON BOARD
27 x 23 CM
PRIVATE COLLECTION

2
ANNA-MAGRIETA, 1940S
OIL ON CANVAS BOARD
38,5 x 32 CM
PRIVATE COLLECTION

CAPE TOWN

83

1
ONRUS LAGOON, C. 1960S
OIL ON BOARD
50 x 59,5 CM
PRIVATE COLLECTION

2
ORYX FOAL
CONTÉ

3
MAMRE MISSION STATION, C. 1960S
OIL ON BOARD
51 x 65 CM
PRIVATE COLLECTION

1
FETCHING WATER, PATERNOSTER, 1951
OIL ON BOARD
52 x 57 CM
PRIVATE COLLECTION

2
SUNFLOWER, 1955
OIL ON BOARD
45 x 34,5 CM
RUPERT COLLECTION

3
FROM THE ARTIST'S STUDIO, DORP STREET,
C. 1960S
OIL ON CANVAS BOARD
65 x 49,5 CM
WELZ COLLECTION

CAPE TOWN

85

POMEGRANATES, 1950s
OIL ON BOARD
34,5 x 49 CM
PRIVATE COLLECTION

FRANÇOIS KRIGE

86

LANDSCAPE, SOUTH WEST AFRICA,
C. 1950S
OIL ON CANVAS
58,5 x 75 CM
JAG COLLECTION

SMALL TOWN IN THE KAROO, 1950s
OIL ON BOARD
45,3 x 54,5 CM
PRIVATE COLLECTION

5. MONTAGU 1967-1994

The artist and the author, 1969.

It was six years before François asked Sylvia whether she thought they should get married. When she replied in the affirmative he said, 'Well, how about next week then?' Things were duly arranged and the couple arrived at the Wynberg registry office with two witnesses on 28 January 1966 – they wanted to keep it an intimate affair. Sylvia remembers it as the hottest day of the year and François, who had initially appeared in an ugly grey jacket and flannels, had been forced into his winter Harris Tweed. At the registry office a wilting François could not remember his year of birth so he had to call his mother to verify it. When she enquired why, he was forced to admit that he was getting married and in no time his mother had organised a drinks party at her home. Sannie, not finding anything unusual in her son's secret marriage, was, however, incredulous at his inappropriate attire.

Soon after the wedding the couple bought an 1866 thatched cottage on Long Street in the Little Karoo town of Montagu and Krige supervised the restoration to its nineteenth-century condition. It was a great relief for him to get away from the city and to simplify his life in a platteland village. Krige had sought a country retreat where living would be inexpensive and he could escape regularly into the mountains to be alone with nature. He had always loved rural settings and this town was to make the ideal home for the last decades of his life. He also enjoyed the privacy it afforded, far from family, friends and the art establishment. In the early years he refused to have even a telephone installed as he liked the idea of being incommunicado. However, guests kept coming – partly due to Sylvia's hospitable nature – and in exasperation François dubbed the house *Soete Inval* (Sweet Drop-in).

Montagu suited the artist perfectly, with its warm climate and porcelain-blue skies most of the year, even during the heart of the Cape winter, and wonderful varied topography and vegetation. For the nature lover it was a garden town with orchards and vineyards lining the main street. Krige also loved exploring the town's fine botanical garden filled with the region's indigenous plants.

The atmosphere and rhythms of the place must have reminded him of his youth in Stellenbosch and the Cape and Free State villages in which he grew up. Its slow pace and season-determined existence was exactly what Krige needed for his creativity and peace of mind. In spring he could paint the *vygies*, mountain blooms and the first roses in his garden. Summer brought the apricot harvest and days of scorching heat when he took refuge behind the thick walls of his home. Autumn was grape harvest time and the mountains became

vygies: mesems.

more defined, with russet colours suffusing vineyards and orchards. In winter snow appeared on the peaks, flowering aloes and proteas on the slopes, and bathing in the hot springs of the kloof was a frequent form of relaxation.

During the first year of their marriage, 1966 to 1967, François lived alone and Sylvia continued to run Gallery Shear in Cape Town, spending her weekends in Montagu. He took this opportunity to turn the entire house into a rambling studio and it was some time before Sylvia managed to carve out a living space free of easels and stacked canvases. This situation was eventually relieved when the cottage next door in Long Street was bought and François converted it into a large studio.

Soon after moving into the main house he, like Monet at Giverny, set to work creating a garden and tended his vegetable patch with pride, reaping lettuce, carrots, peas, sweetcorn, beans, radishes, and onions (which adorned the walls of the kitchen, Spanish style), while fruit and flowers provided a fresh flow of subject matter for still-lifes. His creative rhythm was seldom disrupted. He woke early to gather vegetables from the garden and sometimes there would be an early-morning swim in the thermal baths. After breakfast he would work out of doors or in his studio until lunch, followed by a siesta, after which he would again work undisturbed until dusk when he settled down for a whisky before dinner.

Sannie was one of the first house guests, visiting for a week to have her portrait painted. On her last day the old lady, a stern critic of her children's efforts, was permitted to see some of François's work, mostly still-lifes of flowers. She was most impressed:

Vir die eerste keer het ek verstom gestaan vir die groot talent wat François het. Miskien oor [hy] my kind is, het ek dit tot dusver aangeneem as iets gewoon, ek is nie die soort van vrou wat 'n lawaai maak oor haar kinders. Die Kriges is snaakse mense. As iemand hom vra, sê hy hy het niks klaar nie & die studio deur bly gesluit. Ek het lank gesit (die 35 jaar storie van my portret skilder) & parmantig uitgestap, nie links of regs gekyk nie. Gewonder of hy self sal aanbied om sy werk te wys.[1]

Krige had not done much etching since his training in Antwerp in the thirties. However, soon after arriving in Montagu he again became interested and Sylvia had an etching press made for him as a surprise gift. She wrote to Uys at the time:

F continues to paint well, his colours are very strong and bold. And this week he has ventured to try out the etching press. It's a messy business but with a little research and practice F should master it.[2]

A close family friend, Margaret Maskew, recalls that François was always out of sorts when printing his plates. She is an accomplished etcher herself and would help François with the 'messy business' of printing. To Sylvia's dismay Krige would do much of the work on the kitchen table between the kettle and the tea tray, his white overall and hands covered in ink. The etching press had a room of its own adjacent to the kitchen, the zinc and copper plates lining the walls on a narrow shelf round the room. He experimented with aquatint, lithography, monotype and mixed-media graphic work, but always returned to etching as his chosen medium, dry-point and hard-ground etching being his preferred forms.

Having a press in his home, François could again concentrate on this medium as he had been unable to do since Antwerp and he began to reinterpret images from his past, particularly his travels, and also to capture his new environment with the etching needle. He wrote to Uys about his press in 1968: '*Die ets pers wat my nou al 'n jaar in die gesig staar is nou in aksie en ek is besig om baie van die ou etse, sommige oor die dertig jaar en erg aangetas, verweer deur die verloop van jare, op te knap.*'[3]

Among the many fine Montagu etchings there are some delicate images of birds, Krige finding the etching needle particularly appropriate for rendering the soft effect of feathers. Perhaps the most powerful of these is an owl, the image exhibiting a commanding balance of hatching and cross-hatching in the feathers and a marvellous control of chiaroscuro across the body. *Cape Eagle Owl* derives from sketches done on the Montagu farm of a friend, Kenneth Knipe. The bird had a broken leg and Kenneth and François had managed to climb a tree and get hold of the creature (a stray talon opening Kenneth's scalp during the operation). Knipe and the local chemist managed to tie a splint to the leg and François produced images which capture both the dignity of the creature, but also its lethal nature implicit in talons and bill.

His etchings remain realistic, his methods traditional, and the guiding spirit of Rembrandt, his inspiration since the Antwerp days, is everywhere discernible. Like the master, he employs light, accurate touches, often with minimal expressive means. His use of the dry-point needle suggests mass and volume as well as tactile and physical qualities. The softer lines allowed him to show atmospheric and light effects, and he

---

Vir die eerste … : *For the first time I was astonished by François's great talent. Perhaps because he's my child I accepted it as commonplace, I'm not the kind of woman who makes a fuss of her children. The Kriges are funny people. If someone asks him, he says he's got nothing finished and the studio door remains locked. I sat for a long time (the 35 years of my portrait being painted) and walked out in a huff, not glancing left or right. Wondered whether he would offer to show me his work.*

'*Die ets pers …* ': '*The etching press which has stared me in the face for a year is in operation now, and I'm busy fixing up some of the old etchings, some of them from thirty years ago and spoiled and worn away.*'

---

[1] Sannie Uys in the Uys Krige Archive, undated (1968) letter to Uys and Taillefer (Uys's son).
[2] Sylvia Krige in the Uys Krige Archive, undated (1968?) letter to Uys.
[3] François Krige in the Uys Krige Archive, undated (1968) letter to Uys.

1
CAPE EAGLE OWL
ETCHING

2
BRINGING IN THE BOATS
ETCHING

3
AURORA DE JESUS MARQUES
PENCIL

'Dis 'n ervaring …': 'It's quite an experience to see such a ship negotiating the narrow gaps between islands, sometimes hardly more than thirty yards wide, calling for helmsmanship of the highest order.'

[4] François Krige, private family correspondence, letter to mother dated 2 September 1969.

always printed very few impressions, never allowing the fine web of lines to become blurred.

EUROPE

At Sylvia's birthday party in 1968 François, no doubt buoyed by the festive occasion and feeling guilty at not having bought his wife a present, rashly vowed to take her to Europe for a long vacation. The next time she was in Cape Town she decided to hold him to his promise and booked the tickets, presenting the voyage to him as a *fait accompli* upon her return. François capitulated and they decided that they would take their car with them on the ship in order to complete a long road journey through Europe.

The Kriges sailed to England in June 1969 where they spent over a month in London making the necessary pilgrimages to museums and galleries, and then toured the British Isles visiting the Cotswolds, Wales and Scotland. On the last day of their stay in Edinburgh, François heard about an important Rembrandt painting in Glasgow, so he insisted they take the train to see his favourite artist's work. Next they took ship for Bergen, Norway, and then sailed on to the North Cape (the northern tip of Norway), their cruise ship stopping in fjords along the way where Laplanders came on board selling pails of berries. François enjoyed the adventure: *'Dis 'n ervaring om te sien hoe so 'n skip deur die noue openings tussen eilande vaar soms seker nie veel meer as dertig tree wyd nie, wat stuurmanskap van die hoogste bekwaamheid vereis.'*[4]

They headed south via Denmark to Germany where François was again in search of Rembrandts. His guidebook directed him to Kassel where a feast of eighteen of the master's works awaited him. Being a man of the mountains, François also wanted to see the Swiss and then the French Alps and in Chamonix they took a cable car to view the glacier and marvelled at the spectacular views (his love of mountain climbing was, however, not indulged in on this occasion).

François felt at home in Haute-Provence and the Kriges stayed at medieval Sisteron in the first week of October, where he sketched extensively. There is a fine, economical drawing of a bridge below the town, the eye being led into the picture by a pedestrian, a car, a road and by selective use of shading. Visiting Aix-en-Provence – Cézanne's hometown – Krige was frustrated by avenues of traffic and disappointed that the town's galleries did not have a single painting by Cézanne. Out of sentiment and as homage to the master, he tried to find the road to Mont Sainte-Victoire, the mountain made famous in this Post-Impressionist's late works, but failed.

They headed west past Arles to Perpignan and Lourdes, but by this stage François was tired of strange hotel rooms and beds, constant packing and unpacking. He was sick of bad French drivers with their conduct on the road: *'audace, toujours le [sic] audace'*. He began to feel that his days of grand travel were over, and quoted Picasso in his own defence:

> *Toe Picasso skei van sy eerste vrou wou sy hom stroop van al sy skilderye – hy het daardeur sy vertroue in sy medemens verloor, erg teneergedruk geraak en 'n bekommerde vriend het voorgestel hul moet op reis gaan na Spanje. Picasso het die saak goed nagedink en toe die Talmud aangehaal, wat sê: 'drie dinge verswak die mens, die sonde, vrees en reis'.*[5]

The solution for the Kriges was to find a place where they could relax and remain for an extended time. In October he and Sylvia crossed the Pyrenees into Spain and traversed the Iberian Peninsula to the Algarve in southern Portugal, where they moved into the holiday house of a friend, Cynthia Bloch, in the village of Carvoeira. It was the perfect retreat. Their cook and housekeeper, Aurora de Jesus Marques, was a charismatic old woman whose portrait François took to sketching as she peeled potatoes or worked about the house. However, when Sylvia tried to get involved in the cooking, Aurora took François aside and told him quite firmly that 'four breasts in the kitchen simply do not work'.

The Kriges would buy a whole bucket of sardines from local fishermen and braai them over the coals along with some chestnuts, while sipping *vinho verde*. François was able to relive his pre-war Iberian experience and was in his element. Every day he went out sketching and captured scenes of peasants and farms. He did a series of a potter at work, kneading clay and working at the foot-driven wheel in a barn stacked with jars and vases. He sketched the Bloch home set among olive trees and vineyards, views across the open Algarve countryside and scattered farmhouses with tiled roofs and distinctive white chimneys.

From Carvoeira they made day trips to places like Faro, Lagos, Prince Henry the Navigator's Sagres and Cabo São Vicente, the southwestern tip of Europe. Krige became interested in the feats of the great Portuguese navigators and battled through Camoens's *The Lusiads* in Portuguese. Albufeira beach elicited a series of drawings of the fishing boats pulled up on the sand and cottages suspended on the cliff above; we can see Arniston and Paternoster in his vision of this simple fishing community. He made trips to nearby Silves and his ink and water-colour version of the town with its red roofs and ochre buildings is particularly good. He employs hue economically, defining and colouring only the areas of greatest interest and judiciously revealing the anatomy of the town by saying as little as possible.

After nearly two months they left Carvoeira and headed back north via Seville where Krige sketched the Tagus, with reflections of Seville's spires and palm trees hatched in the river water. The homeward route to Genoa where they were to board their ship was determined by artistic co-ordinates: the Moorish palace in Granada, the Quenca Museum, Toledo (for the El

SILVES
INK AND WATER-COLOUR ON PAPER

Toe Picasso skei ... : When Picasso divorced his first wife she wanted to appropriate all his paintings – the result was that he lost confidence in his fellow man and became very depressed. A friend suggested they take a trip to Spain. Picasso thought it over and then quoted the Talmud: 'Three things weaken man: sin, fear and travel'.

[5] François Krige in the Uys Krige Archive, letter to mother and Uys dated 17 October 1969.

Grecos), Madrid (for the Prado) and Barcelona (for the Picasso Museum).

The drawings from this period in Europe, particularly the architectural ones, are some of the finest of his career. Travelling light with no oils, he could concentrate on his draughtsmanship for a full six months. Whole villages, interlocking streets and roofs are suggested with a few deft lines, figures with even less. His mastery of the southern European townscape – the economy, fluidity, poetry of line drawing – is an aesthetic accomplishment.

THE MONTAGU PAINTINGS
HOUSE AND GARDEN

Since at least the Middle Ages the image of an enclosed garden has been a recurring motif in Western art, bringing with it the notion of refuge from the outside world and positing the idea of tamed nature as a harmonious realm. Krige engages with this tradition which probably found its greatest exponent in Monet. Indeed the similarities between the two painters and their endeavours deserve attention. Both artists retired to quiet farming villages in the countryside, within easy striking distance of the city (Montagu and Cape Town, Giverny and Paris). Both artists threw themselves into the cultivation of gardens and took to painting these and the produce that they harvested. Both employed a number of gardeners and set up studios in their gardens where they could work undisturbed. Monet took his creation to an extreme, creating a giant, controlled still-life, whereas Krige's remained a functional 'farm' garden, with fruit and vegetable harvests and a 'wild' mountainscape often discernible beyond the tamed space.

Particularly in the last decade of the artist's life, the Montagu garden became one of his chief inspirations and the paintings form an important, sustained thematic legacy. These should rightly be divided into two: those of his studio garden, which was an orchard of fruit trees where wild flowers were allowed to predominate, and those of the garden at his home, cultivated with vegetables, vines, roses and dozens of indigenous plants. In the latter he painted images of the enclosed space, with Sylvia occasionally seated somewhere in the foliage. These are often 'high' Impressionist in execution and sentiment.

Krige Home (1989) is a fine piece celebrating his garden in autumn. Blossoms riot across the canvas, from the blooming roses in the foreground to the red vine over the pergola behind. The foliage is handled in Impressionistic dabs and dashes of colour and light, often mixed with white, giving a shimmering effect. Shadows are described in purple which is echoed in the wisteria blossoms, while mauve is the unifying colour in the sky and is reflected on the walls. The composition is framed by vegetation while the mountains – which have little aerial perspective – press forward and 'close' the picture. In other versions of this scene the enclosed, 'fabricated' space (both garden and painting are realms fashioned by the artist) is further suggested by the unusual square (and hence 'defamiliarising') format of the canvas.

The studio garden was a tranquil place of refuge for the artist and I sometimes used to surprise him there. Once or twice he invited me into the studio, a quiet place filled with the smell of oil paints. All the rooms were lined with canvases facing the walls and François would carry one or two to the window so that they could be drenched by light. Never was I allowed to see more than a handful.

From this studio he painted the views in different directions: Long Street, his home seen through the trees, the museum, the neighbour's orchard and his own apricot trees. On the last occasion I was allowed into the studio it was a Monet-like impression of a tree from the studio garden that caught my attention. In this painting, *Blossoming Plum Tree* (1989), the iconic tree blossoms against a Montagu sky, filling the canvas in a joyous celebration of spring. The subject suits his 'high' Impressionist rendering. A cool receding sky is warmed by mauve effects and by the putty-coloured ground which is left bare in places. The solid branches of the tree, hewn predominantly in impastoed deep purples, blues and violets, dissolve into clouds of blossoms described in dabs of white and off-white delivered with a loaded brush (I found a number of François's grey hairs in these blossoms). The earth is painted in short horizontal brushstrokes which become increasingly blurred to create the illusion of recession. Flowers, purple shadows, leaves and clumps of earth speckle the ground, echoing the rendering of the tree. In the background stands another tree that has not yet broken out in blossom and as such creates a sense of temporal and seasonal continuity.

Montagu Museum (1990) offers another view from the studio garden. The sky is punctuated with violet clouds which are scumbled in dry paint over an even blue, giving the effect of

MONTAGU

93

MONTAGU MUSEUM, 1990
OIL ON CANVAS
71,5 x 87 CM
PRIVATE COLLECTION

light and movement. The church (now a museum) picks up the cloud colour and the pinks of the walls are laid on thickly with a palette knife, imitating the texture of the rough painted walls. The black roof is described in a host of dark pastel colours drawn in long straight brush marks while the shadows on the walls are a green-blue colour, reflecting the garden foliage. The cypresses and tree in front of the church are beautifully painted in stark contrasts of green and blue. Krige has introduced warm reds and oranges into the distant hill which has the effect of bringing it 'closer' to the viewer. The warm colours echo the soil in the immediate foreground and contribute to the unity of the image. The Long Street buildings are granted just the right amount of detail to give a sense of recession, also assisted by the corresponding diagonal path leading towards the church and echoing the road. These alleviate the strong horizontals of the foreground and middle distance as do the diagonals of the gables. Krige introduces a small figure, probably a gardener, into the left side of the picture, which gives us the scale and serves to evoke the small-town, Little Karoo atmosphere. The picture is dominated by an apricot tree rendered Impressionistically in dabs of brightly coloured leaves which reflect the sunlight. The paint has been thickly applied to the tree and soil of the heavily worked foreground. This gives a sense of relief and the warm colours certainly advance towards the viewer.

THE TOWN

Krige also painted in and around Montagu, particularly in Long and Church streets, with cottages, gardens, church and orchards featuring in many works. There is a series of oil paintings looking from the east and *Montagu Village* is a magnificent spring-time scene. The roughly worked foreground field is handled with broad brushmarks in a range of earth colours and greens, while a line of mauve-blossoming apricot trees carries the eye into the village. Indeed one is encouraged to read the painting from the bottom left corner as all the landscape's 'movement' originates here. Diverse brushstrokes, ranging from dragged horizontals to the vertical hatching of the mountain and the gestural calligraphy of the sky, make for a lively composition. The buildings occupy a narrow band on the picture plane and are a pattern of coloured cubes and triangles dominated by Kanonkop and the Langeberg which tower above them – the houses are rendered with a startling economy of means. The structure of the painting is carefully handled and judiciously placed verticals lend order and symmetry. For instance, three trees grouped in a line in the bottom right-hand corner are echoed by the church steeple and the two trees on either side of it. This is repeated in the three peaks of the distant mountain as well as the highest peaks of the three individual mountains featured. Furthermore, in each case this tripartite device suggests a triangle and the motif is carried through the composition with triangular-shaped mountains, roofs and steeple. The Langeberg are the dominating feature, their spring-green slopes and flesh-coloured rocks soaring to the summit of Bloupunt, whose shadows are described in blue. Both the shape of the mountain, the colour range employed and the parallel-hatched strokes, used directionally to define form, are reminiscent of Cézanne's famous *Mont Sainte-Victoire* series. The two ageing artists were both celebrating the countryside and the mountains they loved, the light and topography, the beauty of their Little Karoo or Provençal home.

LANDSCAPES

Krige would set out in the early morning to paint landscape scenes around Montagu. He explored the Koo Valley and the Barrydale Road and hiked into Kogmanskloof. He would try to reach the kloof early before the wind got up and Sylvia recalls how he was often back home by 9 am, furious at the southeaster which had blown his canvas over.

Krige was a member of the Worcester mountain club and would go walking in the mountains, especially the Langeberg. He loved hiking and swimming in the mountain streams and knew the flora and fauna of the Cape ranges intimately. His paintings of the mountains around Montagu show an acute understanding of nature, of how the rock was formed, twisted and contorted. His brushstrokes appear to take cognisance of the violent volcanic disturbances which once thrust the rock in different directions.

Krige loved to paint at Kalkoennes, the corner of a valley in Kogmanskloof where the cliffs cluster around a cottage. He and Sylvia first visited the spot in 1965 with the writer Jan Rabie and his artist wife Marjorie Wallace. They stayed in the cottage and were cut off by flood waters. Here Krige sketched the towering rocks, inquisitive dassies, and the Anglo-Boer War blockhouse built on a koppie commanding a bend in the river. In the early sketches of Montagu mountains we can

MONTAGU GIRL
CONTÉ

PAGE 95
MONTAGU VILLAGE, 1980S
OIL ON CANVAS
66 X 77,5 CM
PRIVATE COLLECTION

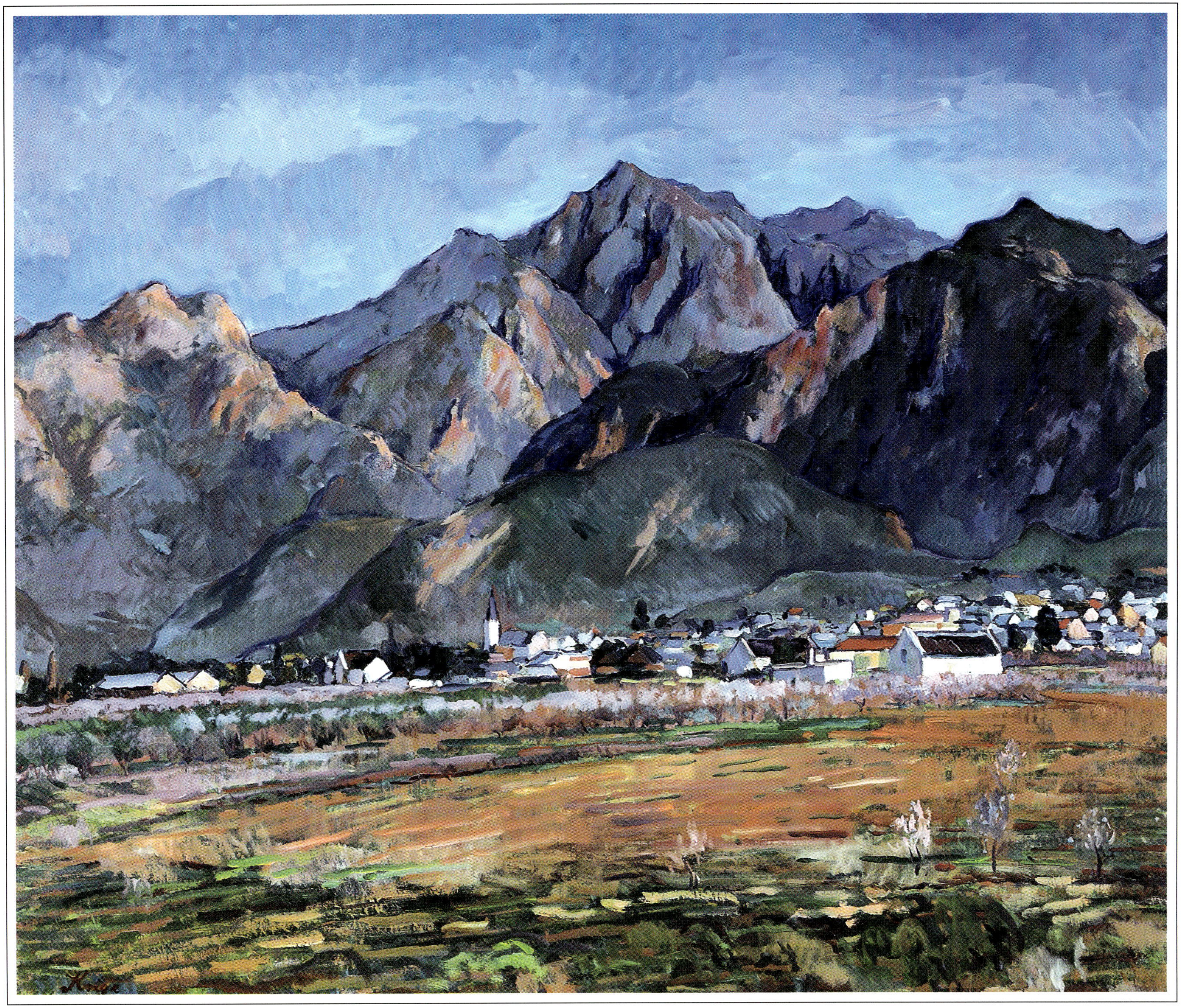

PORTRAIT OF A MAN, MONTAGU
CONTÉ

suikerbossies: protea, sugarbush.

skaamrosies: mountain rose, blushing bride.

bergkatjiepiering: wild gardenia.

already see François's sensitive portrayal of the rocks, capturing the crags and fissures with areas of parallel hatching to denote facets and shapes. These are preliminary sketches for a large series of canvases of the kloof, Aasvoëlkrans (Vulture Cliff) and the great rock portals at the entrance to Montagu painted over the next two decades.

The peak of Aasvoëlkrans rises up like a giant tooth, expressionistically depicted in dramatic colours. It became his *Mont Sainte-Victoire* and he painted it in every light condition. In one work, the rock is rendered in dramatic ochres and lime greens while in another softer sunlight brings out the creams and beiges of the rock. Sometimes he uses Impressionistic dabs of paint, while at others his technique is almost Fauvist with bright separated brushstrokes patterning the surface.

Aasvoëlkrans (1974) features a dramatic, even romantic sky hatched in broad diagonal brushstrokes in a whole range of blues, greens, mauves, purples and pinks. The cream underpainting along the top of the canvas is allowed to shine through, giving the sky – which in this painting is as important as the landscape – a dynamic and animated effect. Broken sunlight plays on the cliffs, sun on rock being portrayed in rich creams and pinks while the corresponding shadows are described in dashes of purple and violet. The direction of the brushstroke usually follows the form of the object described, but at times Krige introduces an 'unmotivated' dash of colour moving 'against the grain'. This gives a strong sense of animation and relief on the gnarled face of the rock. The two main pinnacles of rock are beautifully wrought in short, expressive brushstrokes while the rest of the mountain loses something in the Impressionistic handling of dark greens, and the swirling form in the bottom right corner of the painting is unconvincing. However, the immediate foreground is well handled with balancing areas of ochre ground, only partially mixed on the palette, in both left and right corners. The red earth in the left foreground is flattened due to the unmodulated hatching and consequently does not distract us from the vista with unnecessary detail close to the 'surface' of the picture. The craggy hill in the left middle distance is particularly beautiful with purple rocks, and rich fynbos punctuating the slope. Similarly, the mountains in the distance, described in a broader, thinner application and in cooler olive hues to enhance the aerial perspective, are successful. The composition is superb, the foreground creating a subtle U-shaped cradle in which the 'drama' of nature takes place. A series of diagonal lines created by the landscape rises from the bottom left corner of the picture up to the second highest peak but falls away rapidly on the right side. The focal point of most of these eidetic lines is the 'swirl' of landscape in the right corner.

Kogmanskloof, Montagu (1986) is an unusual, close-up subject and a daring execution, a painting with a powerful blue and purple keynote. It is a 'waterfall' of Montagu rock modelled in colour, a tumbling diagonal insistence of multihued directional strokes matched by diagonal, parallel-hatched brushstrokes in the sky. The celebration of Montagu skies became a feature of the later paintings, the sky rendered in soaring notes of blue, often worked roughly and confidently across large expanses of the support. The solid mountain is not seen as fixed, perhaps in reminiscence of its volcanic formation. Its rendering matches that of the clouds in a rich surface texture of webbed strokes, making the sky as permanent, or as transitory, as the cliff. The patchwork of colours and lack of any real aerial perspective create a tapestry effect close to the picture plane, which is enhanced by the square format – a feature of Krige's art during this period.

Friends of the Kriges, the Pienaars, had a farm deep in the Koo Valley and for many years the Kriges were asked to look after the house and dogs and cats for a period in the winter. Tolbos was a perfect place for Krige to work. The farm extended up the slopes of the Langeberg and the property was filled with proteas. The artist would swim in the mornings and then settle down to work, either painting still-lifes indoors if the weather was inclement, or roaming about the farm looking for subjects. The large number of landscapes from Tolbos feature wabooms, fynbos shrubs and the unique proteas of the area: *suikerbossies*, *skaamrosies* and the extremely rare *bergkatjiepiering* (found only near Montagu, a bloom which Krige painted repeatedly). Sugarbirds cling to the flowers against clear winter skies, while the blue, snow-capped Matroosberg and the patchwork green valleys of the Koo fill the background.

Sylvia recounts that she woke one morning at Tolbos to a snow-covered landscape. Outside the window stood a waboom laden with snow and she fetched a canvas and set up the easel at the window, commanding François to paint the scene. *Snow Tree* (1981) features delicate 'blossoms' of snow suspended like cotton balls on the branches, juxtaposed with strong viridian green touches. Quick, calligraphic brushstrokes feature

MONTAGU

97

Krige was a man of deep reflection, never more so than when he was alone in the mountains.

1
SNOW TREE, 1981
OIL ON CANVAS BOARD
44,5 x 59 CM
PRIVATE COLLECTION

2
KOGMANSKLOOF, MONTAGU, 1986
OIL ON CANVAS
74,5 x 74,5 CM
PRIVATE COLLECTION

3
AASVOËLKRANS, 1974
OIL ON CANVAS
64 x 90 CM
PRIVATE COLLECTION

throughout. The paint is thin and even smudged at times as the picture was produced *alla prima*, and therein lies its success. *Snow Tree* can be viewed as a companion piece to Caldecott's tree from the same valley, *Tree, Baths Kloof, Montagu* (1927). In both paintings the artists have singled out a lone tree against a mountainside, rendering what in effect becomes a *portrait* of a tree, such is the poetry of each image. The seasons are opposite, but in each the feeling for temperature, environment and atmosphere hits exactly the right note.

STILL-LIFES
During the Montagu years Krige concentrated on still-lifes for long periods, perfecting his technique and creating a large body of impressive works. Still-life presented none of the problems for Krige that a living model did, and days or even weeks could be spent working continually on a single subject. His still-lifes usually feature fruit or flowers from the district in combination with jugs, pottery, clippers and knives. His compositions employ some of the innovations of the French Impressionists and particularly Cézanne's great achievements in the genre. We see the same tipped-up platters and jugs and various distortions used for the sake of making a thrust into space more forcefully, or for isolating and 'holding' one plane in relation to other planes. Objects often appear to be sliding towards one, almost encouraging the viewer to reach out a hand to stop them. Traditional rules of perspective are occasionally suspended and elements are precariously balanced, swelling or shrinking according to their function within the composition. In effect we see the objects from different eye levels, resulting in a dynamic and often arresting rendering of space which holds the viewer's attention. The lines (often blue) that define the contours are firmly stated and used to emphasise a linear rhythm that flows through the picture. Krige's backgrounds are seldom mere backdrops, but are conceived as an integral part of the image so that the whole picture works as a harmonious unit. Table tops or walls are often broken into two planes creating an interesting spatial effect. Like the Post-Impressionists, he models using colour (hot colours 'approaching', cool colours 'receding') instead of traditional chiaroscuro and he likes to 'flatten' his backgrounds, thus creating a tension between two-dimensional and three-dimensional space, particularly when he uses African-print tablecloths. Colours are not restricted to recording the local hues of exact forms, but are repeated throughout the entire surface of the painting, often 'bleeding' into nearby objects.

Like Cézanne, Krige was less interested in light effects than in the arrangement of forms and colours and the balancing of masses. However, his intentions remained more realist than Cézanne's and he never pursued the French master all the way down the road of formalism and geometric method. Indeed, many images still lent themselves to a delicate, feathery Impressionist approach.

Krige's still-lifes are personal meditations and seem to invite introspection on the part of the viewer. He appreciated fruit and flowers as the products of nature, and also humble, unadorned, traditional objects like earthenware jugs and bowls, often made by his wife or potter friend, Hym Rabinowitz, which he felt represented an admirable sense of craftsmanship and of rural domesticity.

Before he acquired the Montagu studio, Krige would set up his still-life pieces in the kitchen, bedroom or living room, and for the days that these objects were being painted, they were not to be touched. One evening when Sylvia was visiting friends in Cape Town she received a distress phone call from Montagu: François couldn't find any potatoes to go with his dinner. Sylvia said they were on the table, to which her shocked husband replied: 'You didn't actually expect me to *destroy* my still-life, did you?!'

His vegetable and fruit still-lifes feature richly coloured spheres in which paint is laid down in a thick mesh of robust colour to create almost edible textures. We see his garden produce, from succulent peaches to mundane potatoes, sometimes voluptuous and sensuous, at other times austere and elemental.

Still-life with Fruit (1979) features glowing fruit in saturated, bleeding colours. There is a harmonious rhythm of hue and line with reds, yellows and greens echoing through the composition, while the blue tablecloth is painted over a red ground. The tipped-up bowl does not sit comfortably on the cloth which is calligraphically enlivened with marks denoting folds. The loose directional hatching 'pulls' at the blue sheet, adding dynamism. The horizontality of the bowl, sheet and composition is offset by the verticals of the stems and the darkened corner of the room, which divides the bowl in two. The diagonal arrangement of items lends depth to the composition as the eye is led from the closest lemon along the branch, leaves and peppers to the bowl. Colours respond to nearby primary colours, for instance, the pear picks up the red of the adjacent pepper in its own flesh. It is said that Krige considered this one of his most successful still-lifes.

The artist also made a vast number of still-lifes of flowers, ranging from relatively unsuccessful attempts at roses from his garden to a large body of magnificent proteas, the latter often painted in a 'super-realism' suited to the primordial-looking plants. We see *cynaroides*, *skaamrosies*, *bergkatjiepierings* and sulphurias, sometimes blossoming on the slopes of the Montagu mountains, but mostly in formal 'academic' pieces with mixed proteas in copper and earthenware bowls.

Bergkatjiepiering (1986) is executed on a very fine-grained canvas and the proteas are set starkly against a pale blue background. A wide and quite remarkable tonal range of greens, yellows and even purples is used in the leaves, which reach out like hands in every direction. (The leaves become brightly coloured during the flowering period, changing from yellow to orange to bright red or purple.) A bold outline encases the plants and this is appropriate to the strange flowers. The earthenware jug is well drawn, with its clay texture suggested in the sweeping, blended brushstrokes, but the muddy brown tabletop is less successful. The background is modelled in diagonal, parallel-hatched strokes, variously spaced to create a sense of 'breathing'.

Petunias (1978) is a particularly fine, small floral still-life with a daring use of colour. A diagonal pull is created by the pink petunias and Krige conveys the sensual, almost decadent feel of these flowers. The texture of the brass bowl is realised with dynamic strokes of sienna and cream to denote light. The bowl rests on an indeterminate surface with no dado line while the background has been reworked many times and the various hues are allowed to show through the scumbling in places, creating a marvellous texture and play of colour.

Still-life with Nemesias (1984) depicts these glowing pink flowers in a vase made by Sylvia, who had started a pottery school during their first years in Montagu. There is, for Krige, an unusually dark background over a lighter *ébauche* with an orange ground showing through and an interrupted dado line. Aspects of the image are reminiscent of Jean Welz's style of scumbling with a dark foreground surface and pink-and-yellow blossoms bright against a dark background. The shaft of mustard light on the back wall is an inspired device. The flowers are mixed wet-in-wet with a loaded brush on canvas.

Apart from fruit and flower studies, Krige experimented with a range of diverse still-life subjects: crayfish, animal skulls, dead birds and even O'Keefe-like shells. Perhaps the most successful of these is *Still-life with Fish* (1986), an oil of a silverfish and a hottentot, executed with great tenderness, a simple meal contained in the orb of an earthen bowl. Sylvia remembers that she bought them from a man selling fish on ice from the back of his *bakkie* in Montagu. François had to rush, because Sylvia insisted on grilling them for dinner that evening and the speed of execution results in the assurance and brilliance of this still-life.

The two fish lie head to tail in a blue dish and the composition is turned slightly on the diagonal. We look from above and the monochromatic, dark-burgundy background, painted over a light-blue ground which shines through, leaves nothing to distract the eye from the sphere, broken only by the heads and lifeless tails. The pink of one fish is repeated in the silver of the other, and the blue of the bowl (echoing the ocean from which they come) is reflected in both. The range of colours that Krige has put into each animal is astonishing: yellow, purple, green, brown and orange. These are hardly noticed at first glance, but the eye is captivated by this array and by the texture of the skin. The short parallel hatchings across their bodies is an excellent visual metaphor for their scales. Both heads are dislocated – evidence of violence here transformed into a thing of beauty.

NYALA
CRAYON

BLACK EAGLE
CHARCOAL

This humble image has biblical connotations and an archetypal feel.

PORTRAITS

In his portraits Krige has a penetrating intimacy and he depicts a calmness – even sanctity – in his sitters, who are almost always seated meditatively alone, never in a group. His studies of facial expressions give an implicit narrative and psychological dimension. Many people from the Montagu district sat for him: domestic workers and gardeners, the librarian's beautiful daughter, the butcher boy and Koos Kok, curator of Montagu's botanical garden, with whom he loved discussing the local fauna. Friends like Enslin du Plessis, Andrew Murray, Etienne Joubert and Fred Davis also feature.

In addition, there are a large number of family portraits from the Montagu period. Over the years he painted a whole series of his elderly mother and the fine *Sannie* is a reverential image of her. Weight is created on the right-hand side of the painting by the shadow of her hat and the light on her neck. The flowing lines of the floppy hat which frames her face are mirrored in her hand and fingers. The hand raised to her cheek is well drawn while the pose and foregrounding of the expressive gesture convey the idea that she is a thinker and writer. Her face is modelled with patches of colour ranging from pink to deep mauve.

Sylvia (1977) is a portrait of his wife in a colourful striped jacket, the browns of the gown matching the background. In her frowning look – Sylvia's normal expression when her usually animated face is at rest – he captures something of her strength, but also her generosity of spirit. Her face is well modelled in multi-toned facets of colour with a careful handling of shadow across them, and the rest of the painting is in broad, bold applications. The picture is divided into four unequal vertical bands – the outside ones dark, 'containing' the image – while her gown and undershirt continue the idea of stripes. This vertical insistence, a device which gives the composition a rigid structure, is broken by the horizontals of lips, eyes and brows, which, appropriately, form the focal points of the composition.

Krige painted many portraits of the farm labourers and workers of Montagu. In the nineteenth century the Realists and Impressionists had sought an 'honest' image of peasant life that was sincere, uncompromisingly frank and without sentimentality. Krige turned to the tillers of the platteland in a similar way to artistic forebears such as Millet and Courbet who always stressed the dignity of peasants. Living in Cape Town and travelling the coast of the Western Cape, Krige had recorded the lives of the Coloured fishermen on our shores; now that he lived in a land-locked Karoo town, it was to the rural and farming culture that he turned his attention. His figures seem almost iconic and he focuses nostalgically on a way of life that he perceived to be disappearing. The subjects are given a moral depth, a sensitivity and capacity for deep reflection, attributes that we also find in similar works by Rembrandt.

The nomadic Krisjan Swart, an old character from the district, features in a great many drawings, water-colours and oils, particularly in the late seventies. He usually appears with his billy-can, staff and sack of belongings, tramping the Karoo roads in *velskoene* and greatcoat. Krige gives him the look of an itinerant preacher or apostle, a lonely soul making his way across the arid landscape. The old man slept in the veld at night and was a loner, something which would have struck a chord with François. Breyten Breytenbach discusses the Krisjan series in his travel memoir, *Dog Heart*:

> *François Krige repeatedly paints Krisjan, Ai Byp's brother. The dark, gleaming canvases imbue the sitter with a melancholy glory. In this small village oasis Krisjan is painted as the emblem of a broken humanity. The folds in his face are pages blackened by history, marked in a foreign tongue. Krisjan is King Lear. His majesty and his massive presence fill the cloth. Krisjan is a deposed ruler seen through the eyes of Rembrandt. He comes from a long way away down the ages. Then François Krige paints Krisjan as Montagu knows him: a hang-about, bum, drifter, beggar, sleeping wherever the alcohol closes in upon him in rain or in sun, the sad nomad with filthy rags twisted around the head, an oversized and shapeless and torn overcoat, all his belongings in the one bag slung across his shoulder. In the past the old people trek through the mountains with across their shoulders all their belongings in bags made of soft skin.*[6]

The Rembrandt-inspired oil, *Krisjan* (1979), is one of Krige's finest portraits. There is an accomplished modelling of the face with economical, bold and assured brushstrokes. The tonal play of light on Krisjan's face is particularly well handled, illuminating his forehead and eyes. The scruffy, hand-me-down clothes and the greatcoat to ward off a Karoo winter speak of hardships endured. These elements are rendered in hatched

BOY WITH HAT, MONTAGU
CONTÉ

[6] Breyten Breytenbach, *Dog Heart (A Travel Memoir)*, Cape Town, 1998, p. 108.

strokes with only the slightest adjustment of tone and hue. The palette is unusually dark for Krige and he does not hesitate to use a lot of black. Shirt and collar are thickly scumbled and definition is retained through a few deftly over-painted lines. The white doek on his head adds character to the portrait and is an effective device to complement the dark greys, blacks, browns and Prussian blues. The mood and the emotion conveyed in this portrait are sombre, yet uplifting.

The seventies and eighties saw a great flowering of Krige portraits and in this period the figure of Joan Kroukamp, their domestic worker, is significant. There are also many studies of 'Joan with the sad eyes', of her sisters and other Coloured children of the town. In 1980 François produced an astonishing series of pencil sketches of Joan. There is extremely delicate line-work and fine cross-hatched shading over her face. She appears soulful, melancholic, with a face that glows, giving her expression a Madonna-like sanctity.

In *Hillary* – a portrait of ballet dancer Hillary Janks – the sitter stares back at the viewer with glazed eyes. Her vulnerability is further suggested in the drooping shoulders and white ruff around her neck. Line is minimised in the portrait and only her face is rendered in detail. There is an astonishing play of greens across the canvas with the dress and background echoing each other's rough brushmarks, while flesh pinks occur in the background and greens are repeated in her face. Krige regarded this as his most successful portrait of a woman.

Krige painted a large body of self-portraits during the Montagu period. The artist is usually featured with a blue-grey background and blue shirt, and always has the same watchful, oblique expression. There is perhaps vulnerability here, certainly deep introspection. In his self-portraits he grapples with his reflection, unsparing in his search for the essential man.

Self-portrait (1972) has a golden-yellow background which allows the keynote blue to show through the scumbling; his shirt has an accomplished play of blues and greens. The blues are perpetuated in his hair and beard and also in the curtain behind. The image is 'contained' by characteristic, darkened vertical shafts of blue on either side of the head. The artist looks

1
JUSTIN, 1970
OIL ON CANVAS BOARD
45 x 35 CM
PRIVATE COLLECTION

2
SANNIE, 1960S
OIL ON CANVAS BOARD
44,2 x 34,5 CM
PRIVATE COLLECTION

askance at us with a serious expression, perhaps even a diffident look in his eyes. Both his hair and the windowpanes are rendered in dry, chalky paint, while there is daring use of colour in his face, with dark flesh hues and even reds employed. The ear, however, is awkwardly drawn. The painting – particularly the golden background – was reworked later, as an older signature is discernible underneath the existing one.

In the late work, *Self-portrait with Buddhist Print*, the artist stares back at the viewer or himself with a melancholy expression. The canvas within the canvas is illuminated by a light source behind the artist and his face is largely in shadow. Perhaps there is the sense of approaching death in his look, in the shadow that creeps across his face and in the darkness filling the space behind his head. One of Krige's favourite images, a Buddhist print of ascending figures that he bought on his trip to the Far East in 1983, hangs on the wall behind. The figures appear to have religious significance and have 'halos', most appropriate for this 'death-theme' self-portrait. The almost luminous light in Krige's own hair alludes perhaps to the 'halos' of the buddhas behind. The objectivity of age allows the artist to look critically at the image staring back at him from the mirror and to analyse the ageing self.

ON THE ROAD

Each year the Kriges would journey to Cape Town and stay in Sylvia's Clifton apartment, but these were infrequent occurrences as François saw the trip to the city as a major expedition and turned the two-hour drive into a day's journey with plenty of stops, most importantly for his swim in the Du Toit's Kloof streams. Although he was always anxious to get back to his beloved Montagu, he did enjoy these periods in the city and produced a number of paintings in the flat. There are seascapes seen from the windows, although many of these are unfinished, some just *ébauches* with high viewpoints looking into luminous green and mauve water.

There were road trips much further afield than the Peninsula. Margaret Maskew recalls the time when Sylvia bought a kombi for her husband (he was initially furious at the extravagance), thinking it would be beneficial for his painting expeditions:

'I know my customer,' Sylvia said laconically, referring to François. 'He needs it for his work … I ask you! How can he pack all the equipment for a painting trip into the small car? Just think of the wet canvases alone, how much space they occupy, not to mention the camping equipment, the food, the cameras, the easel …'

François argued that they were living above their means, that the earth's natural resources must be conserved and that they did not need two vehicles. I detected however that he had already thawed towards the kombi but would not admit it.[7]

Sylvia's sister took charge of fitting out the vehicle with a bed, stove and refrigerator, and in time François could hardly hide his excitement. As soon as it was ready, he made plans for a trip to Namaqualand to see the flowers and this would become an annual pilgrimage. It was not long before he became quite possessive about the kombi, not allowing anyone else to drive it. Sylvia certainly knew her customer.

The Cederberg was a favourite hiking area and he was intimately acquainted with these mountains.[8] The muleteer-guides James and Frederick Joubert led Krige on many walks into the mountains. They would sleep under the stars or in trail huts, swim in mountain streams, climb in search of snow proteas and find pink nerinas on the mountain tracks. There are studies of plants and indigenous trees and sketches of the strange rock formations, contorted, pock-marked stones and mountainscapes. In one powerful oil a whitened cedar tree stands against rocks of a myriad ochres and browns, the gnarled bark imitating the shape of the rocks, while the sky echoes these dynamic forms. We see old James with his hat pulled low, sitting at a campfire, the night rendered in a symphony of deep, watercolour blues. There are drawings of Wuppertal, Dwarsrivier and Sanddrif, mountain hamlets with thatched houses, vine terraces, and washing hanging out to dry.

Each spring the couple would drive north in the kombi via Clanwilliam and stay in a hotel in Kamieskroon from where they could make day trips into the *vygie*-covered veld. Often the flower expedition would be extended into the far Northern Cape and Namibia. Augrabies, near Upington, was a regular destination, where Krige loved to paint the sublime rock formations, waterfall and gorge carved by the Orange River as well as the many species of aloe and succulent. He would set off each morning with his camera and sketching material while Sylvia stayed behind to read, collect stones from the river bed or fend off the baboons trying to steal their food. The paintings show a Pierneef-like rendering of geometric rocks in a reduced palette, klipspringers and dassies staring at the torrent of the Augrabies Falls.

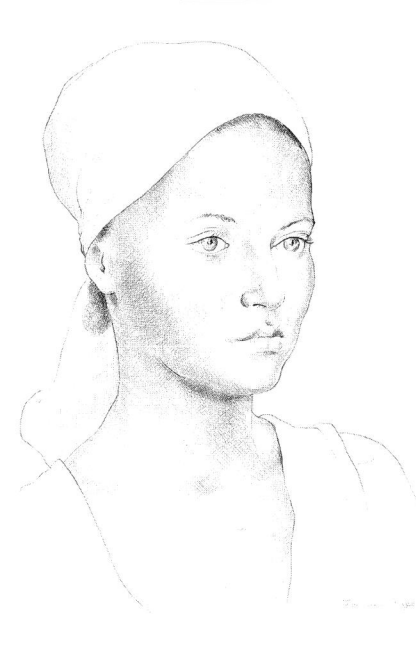

JOAN
PENCIL

---

[7] Margaret Maskew, *A Portrait of Uys Krige* (Wynberg, 1985), p. 37.
[8] Krige's knowledge of fauna, flora and mountain geography was exceptional. On one hike in the Groot Winterhoek with Montagu friends, the Biesenbachs, Jean and Gustav's eight-year-old son, Rymar, kept asking François unrelated questions: 'How high is that peak? What is this flower or that bird? What is the name of that stream?' and François was able to give him exact answers (which the others later checked and invariably found to be accurate).

On one trip, venturing as far east as Kimberley to attend the opening of an exhibition of his work at the William Humphreys Gallery, François was taken on a diamond mine tour and shown some of the big gem stones. So intrigued was he by the quality of light emanating from the diamonds that he painted a number of starkly geometric and stylised oils depicting the gems' facets of colour.

From the Northern Cape they would often continue into the Kalahari, and to the Gemsbok Park in particular. Here he would sit near waterholes and draw the wildebeest, gemsbok, hartebeest, springbok and other antelope coming to drink. On one occasion he spent hours sketching cheetahs at a kill from the open door of his kombi.

On longer expeditions, Krige always insisted on spending as much time in Namibia as possible, making more than half a dozen long trips during the Montagu period. He loved the breadth of the horizon and the country's emptiness, its silence and loneliness. This stark environment posed different challenges from the landscape of the Western Cape, softened as it was by vegetation and a more muted light. He had to come to terms with the vastness of the vistas which focused attention on individual forms in the desertscape. The glaring light and its effect on shapes and colours at different times of the day also had to be taken into account.

The Kriges camped in dry river beds and slept under the stars. From these camps François would venture into the desert to sketch the plants that managed to survive in this barren landscape: welwitschias, kokerbooms, euphorbias, tiny succulents and further north the upside-down tree, the baobab. He also enjoyed visiting the coastal towns of Namibia with their turn-of-the-century German atmosphere. Swakopmund and Lüderitz were the bases from where he and Sylvia sallied forth into the Namib Desert and it was here that they relaxed and enjoyed a few days of comfort. From Lüderitz they struck inland to the diamond-mining ghost town of Kolmanskop, the Fish River Canyon and north to Sossusvlei. In Swakopmund there are sketches of Sylvia drinking coffee at Café Anton, of the German architecture, fisherman's pier, palm-lined streets and the old railway station.

The couple made expeditions north along the Skeleton Coast past Terrace Bay as far as their kombi would take them before the dunes became impassable. In this wilderness they saw elephants burrowing in the sand for water and starving lions taking seals on the beach. The images show the solitary creatures of the desert, ostriches and gemsbok, lone verticals in an endless horizon. Water-colours reveal the pale shades of desert sand and sky. He sketched the dramatic mountains of Spitzkoppe and Brandberg, the oasis at Goanikontes, as well as the 'Pointillist' rock engravings (petroglyphs) at Twyfelfontein in the Kaokoveld: '*Daar in die verlatenheid by Twyfelfontein het ons op wonderlike rotsgravures afgekom – honderde van hul op reuse rotse uitgebeitel en seker een van die merkwaardigste tonele in Suid Wes.*'[9]

Namib Dunes (1975) presents a pattern of interweaving dune lines at Sossusvlei. The sand dunes in this part of the Namib Naukluft Park turn brilliant shades of red and orange at sunrise and sunset. The painting is both realistic and with an element of abstraction by nature of the subject matter, composition and 'flattening' effect of his style. Krige captures the almost organic lines of the dunes and the eye is led from the foreground along snaking dune ridges to the distant red slopes. He paints in thin, smooth washes, subordinating his characteristic brushstroke to the realistic effect he feels that the subject demands, and renders the sand in a range of warm creams, salmons and pinks while the sky is a monochromatic blue-green.

Krige was fascinated by the flora of the Namib and on one expedition he, Sylvia and Margaret Maskew camped for a few days beside an ancient welwitschia (the 'desert octopus', a prehistoric-looking plant which is thousands of years old). Sylvia remembers that it was her birthday, 14 October 1982, and a full moon rose over the desert. Krige made detailed sketches of the plant and later painted two imposing canvases of the subject. In *Welwitschia* (1982-87) our viewpoint is low to the ground as we look up at the spreading, tentacle-like leaves. The plain behind is dotted with these plants and the image suggests that we have been transported back into the earth's distant past. The horizontality of the composition – the expanse of desert sand and sky – and the use of aerial perspective in the middle distance gives us a sense of the open spaces of Namibia. From a rim of jagged, purple mountains the full moon climbs through leaves towards a pink sky. The effect is otherworldly, almost science fictional and the super-realist technique, unusual for Krige, is suitable for the subject matter. The experiment with super-realism is fairly successful in technical terms, but we can be thankful that he did not pursue this branch of his oeuvre and returned to a Post-Impressionist style, more suited to

KRISJAN
ETCHING

'*Daar in die …*': 'There, in Twyfelfontein's desolation, we came across wonderful rock engravings – hundreds of them, chiseled on giant rocks, and certainly one of the most remarkable scenes in South West.'

[9] François Krige in the Uys Krige Archive, undated (1968) letter to Uys.

his individual approach to line and colour, humble rather than monumental.

On some of the Namibian trips, the Kriges crossed the border into Botswana and on one occasion flew into Orapa airport in late June 1980, where they met up with their friends the Gregorys and then travelled by Land Rover north via Maun to Chobe, one of southern Africa's last great wilderness areas. They were often surrounded by elephants, François making some fine drawings of the beasts as they grazed alongside the vehicle, the quick assured strokes of his pencil capturing their bulk and grace.

At one of their camps in Savuti François woke one morning to screams coming from the ablution area. Dressed in his paisley pyjamas, toilet roll in hand, he ran to see what was the matter. A woman had encountered a lioness in the ablution block and first one lioness and then another brushed past François as they tried to get away from the hysterical tourist. The artist grabbed his sketchbook and jumped into the Land Rover, following the pride until they settled for the day. The flowing conté-crayon drawings of supine lions resulting from this encounter are very fine indeed.

Wildlife painting is considered a relatively specialised genre and surprisingly – given the wealth and variety of local fauna – is one that is infrequently embarked upon by the foremost South African artists. Krige is a notable exception and today can be considered one of the country's finest wildlife artists. His wonderfully economical images of wild animals are the product of years of careful observation. Because the creatures of the veld do not remain immobile for long, hundreds of preparatory sketches precede some of his images of southern Africa's fauna.

Many of his best wildlife drawings were done on safari in Botswana and Namibia, but there are also many portrayals of coastal animal life, such as seals and penguins, and even insects feature widely in his sketchbooks. But it is his depictions of birds that are perhaps the most accomplished. There are images of birds in flight, of eagles swooping to kill, talons menacingly outstretched, of swallows nesting at Kalkoennes, of dead birds, their feathers and skulls merging with the earth. Of all the birds of the veld, the elegant blue crane of the Karoo was the creature he most loved to draw, often in charcoal and wash, and there are dozens of studies. Many of his crane paintings are reminiscent of both Frans Marc and Maggie Laubser in their use of simplified animal forms on multicoloured, non-naturalistic backgrounds. The simplification of the subject matter and decorative compositions emphasise their beauty and the sinuous forms suggest graceful movement. The blue-grey birds with their snaking necks create intricate patterns and the stylisation accentuates the creatures' fine lines. The crane paintings are expressionist pieces and the scenes are set in idyllic fantasy landscapes.

TERUGBLIK: MEMORY PAINTING

The year 1976 was a terrible one for Krige. Political unrest (the Soweto uprising and the momentous political events in South Africa's history at the time influenced François in a peripheral but fundamental way), coupled with the arrest of his friend Breyten Breytenbach on treason charges against the apartheid state, was distressing enough. But Uys's near fatal car accident and his mother's death in the same year took a heavy toll on the artist. The extended Krige clan had gathered for Sannie's ninetieth birthday and the grand old matriarch was admitted to hospital soon afterwards. Her last conversation with François on the day of her death concerned his reluctance to exhibit:

'Wanneer gaan jy uitstal?' she asked, to which he answered, 'Ek het dit weer uitgestel.'

'Van uitstel kom afstel,' she said. 'Maar ek kan nie langer uitstel nie.'

He did eventually exhibit later that year, but did not sell many paintings and comforted himself with the pragmatic thought that if motorcar sales were dramatically down, how could he hope to be selling well? He had already begun relinquishing contact with the art establishment. There would be a few more exhibitions in a relatively short period and then he would begin painting for himself alone.

In the space of a few years Krige participated in a number of successful exhibitions: he took part in a travelling exhibition of South African graphic art to West Germany in 1978 to 1979; the South African National Museum of Military History organised a large exhibition of his war works in Johannesburg in 1980; he exhibited at the Association of Arts in Cape Town and then in Pretoria from where an artist friend, Leo Theron, wrote to Uys giving his impressions:

Die uitstalling is deurgaans van so 'n hoë gehalte soos wat ek selde in SA gesien het in die afgelope 20 jaar.

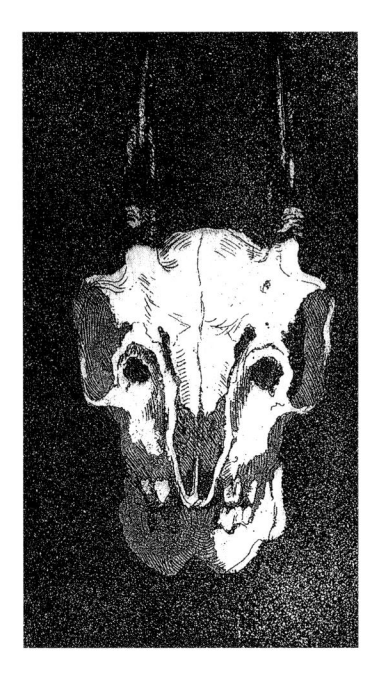

SKULL
LITHOGRAPH

'Wanneer gaan jy … ': 'When are you going to have an exhibition?' she asked, to which he answered, 'I have postponed it again.'
'Postponement leads to abandonment,' she said. 'But I can no longer postpone.'

Hy is ongetwyfeld 'n groot skilder, en daarby die mees beskeie wat ek ken. Sy kleurgevoeligheid is ongelooflik fyn ontwikkel en sy werk is 'achevé' tot 'n mate wat selde gesien word. Quel oeil! roep ek uit soos Degas [sic] meen ek, oor Monet gesê het.

Omdat hy so min uitstal is sy formaat des te groter.[10]

After these fairly successful exhibitions and his self-proclaimed last great trip abroad,[11] Krige finally turned his back on the public and the art community and pursued a personal, inward journey. He now had some financial security and Sylvia could be a buffer between him and the outside world. It was as though he began turning away from the present and rewriting his own history, paring it down, highlighting and romanticising certain aspects.

To some extent his reworking of past images and his practice of painting from memory might have been the response of an artist groping for subjects, going through his drawers and sketchbooks in search of ideas. Thus the revisiting of the past may not necessarily have been a totally unified strategy. However, the work of the mid-eighties reveals a sustained period of nostalgically reinhabiting moments from his youth, from the war years, from his period in Cape Town and most significantly from his early journeys to Namibia and Botswana.

It was a time for looking back over his life. He revisited the emotional space of the war and repainted scenes of bombed buildings in *Foggia* (1980) and the large troopship oil entitled *On Board Ship*. One version of *Four Body Bags* was reworked many times between 1981 and 1987. The haunting *Dead Tank Driver* (1987) is also a product of this mining of his past. It was painted in the year that Uys died and memories of his brother's proximity to death at Sidi Rezegh must have welled up in his mind at the time of Uys's passing. That charred figure could so easily have been Uys.

There was a nostalgic creative return to the years prior to the war, to the Karoo and the Malutis of his youth. Two important works result from his Lesotho period, evocations of his time spent in the mountains in the thirties. They were both painted in 1979 and inspired by sketches done as a young man. In the better of the two we see a naive genre scene of Basotho gathered in front of a cluster of rondavels which frame the composition. It is a contrived scene in which the figures, all wrapped in traditional blankets, have little relationship to or interaction with one another. Two men pour home-brewed beer, a woman grinds meal while another walks with a clay pot on her head across a pink-and-yellow ground. The painting is stylised with bright Basotho blankets adding a series of patterns to the composition, and there is a romantic, dreamy feel enhanced by the narrow range of hue and the colourful layered mountains. The image comes across as a painted memory: the figures even seem to float ethereally above the ground.

Funeral in the Karoo (1980) is a reworking of the watercolour-and-pen scene sketched in 1940. Here the memory of Courbet's egalitarian *Burial at Ornans*, reflecting the democratic social ideals of 1848, is even more apparent. Painting a group of Coloured labourers at a funeral in 1980 has equally powerful political connotations, but these are never directly stated. Where the Courbet work is a celebration of the people of Ornans, Krige's work lends dignity to the Coloured people of the Karoo.[12] The image can again be seen as a painted memory. The faces are not clearly characterised and the scene is archetypal and yet unmistakably local. Mourners gather around an open grave under a darkened sky; some weep, others are barefoot, a dog scratches for fleas. The *memento mori* skull-like head among the mourners of the 1940 version is omitted and we have a series of mother-and-child figures (there are in fact five – arguably six – with one mother breast-feeding) which convey the notion of life rejuvenating itself in this barren, funerary landscape. The preacher stands out above the others with the line of their heads forming a rhythm – echoed by the hills on the horizon – behind which the labourers' cottages are just discernible, linking the people closely to their landscape.

It was during this period that Krige also returned to his sketchbooks of the Bushmen for inspiration and transformed his drawings into a large body of significant paintings. There are the same intimate domestic scenes of women and children as he had sketched in the late fifties and early sixties. Naked boys hunt and venture out across desert sands like adolescents on a Greek frieze. Hunters track antelope over a dry, open plain (Krige's romantic vision even places a young hunter in the context of a welwitschia plant, which does not grow anywhere near the Bushman regions). These are nostalgic works informed, perhaps, by personal experience of change, loss and ageing, and his return to these Bushman images suggests an attempt to arrest time or deny the loss.

In *!Kung Girl* (1984) the monumental figure sits on her haunches with a calabash before her. The reduced palette

---

Die uitstalling is … : The exhibition is of such high quality throughout as I have seldom seen in South Africa in the past 20 years.

He is without doubt a great painter, and more than that, the most modest. His colour sensitivity is unbelievably finely developed, and his work is 'achevé' to an extent seldom seen. Quel oeil! I exclaim as Degas [sic], I think, said of Monet.

Because he exhibits so seldom his stature is so much greater.

---

[10] Leo Theron in the Uys Krige Archive, letter to Uys dated 27 September 1979.
[11] Soon after his seventieth birthday in 1983 Krige decided to make one last trip on his own overseas, this time to Asia to fulfil one of his mountaineering dreams: to walk in the Himalayas. He flew to India and then on to Pokara in Nepal where he hired a Sherpa guide to hike in the foothills of the Himalayas. They trekked through stone villages and along the banks of streams lined with shrines. He lived on stale yak butter, lentils and rice and lost over seven kilograms during a few weeks (only the biltong and dried fruit Sylvia had packed for him saw him through).

Before returning to South Africa he travelled further east, via Bangkok to Taiwan (to see Chiang Kai-shek's famous art treasures) and Japan. In Taipei it was the art of the Sung period that particularly intrigued him, but he could not cope with modern international travel and longed to get back to his garden in Montagu:

Daar was tye wat ek gevoel het ek spat uitmekaar. Die aankoms en uitvaart uit stede en lughawes 'n nagmerrie wat ek nie graag weer sou herhaal nie. (At times I felt close to bursting. The arrivals and departures from cities and airports were nightmares I do not wish to repeat soon.)
(François Krige in the Uys Krige Archive, postcard to Uys dated 21 November 1983.)
[12] In Courbet's paintings the peasants and lower classes who had been politically sidelined after the failures of 1848 began reappearing in Realist art, which was unpatronising and lent them dignity.

presents a symphony of ochres and browns while the indefinite background is partially a result of deficient recall but is also appropriate to the monochromatic desert landscape. This content-less, neutral and yet dynamic space (created by vigorous brushwork) seems to locate the !Kung girl outside time and almost situates her visually in the artist's memory. Indeed the strange lack of context in this and other Bushman works of this period suggests an attempt to hold on to what has passed – for him and for the people he had lived with in the Kalahari – by letting them literally float outside a concrete time/space dimension.

Unlike a conventional portrait, this girl is turned away, adding mystery and drawing attention to her characteristic pose. Outline is emphasised, the figure not being allowed to 'breathe', which enhances its solidity, and there is a Japanese-like stress on silhouette. There are interesting negative spaces around her arm, but her hand is awkwardly rendered, probably as a result of Krige's drawing without a model.

The artist paints many of the family scenes he had so enjoyed drawing, exhibiting balanced compositions, 'rhythms' of figures and accomplished colour harmonies. Negative spaces offer interesting shapes while interlocking figures sit closely packed, pressed into the canvas space, thereby suggesting the close-knit nature of their clan. But it is the 'princess' who occupies much of his attention in the studio work. He places her in the context of a domestic group or standing alone on the desert sand. She is adorned with ostrich-eggshell decorations, often holding a calabash, with a tortoise-shell cosmetic box for buchu powder round her neck. Krige 'creates' a woman who stares self-assuredly back at us, an exotic and remote Other from the old man's African travels into the past.

Krige's mnemonic eye is remarkably assured: 25 years later he remembers colours, shapes and details accurately. That so much remained in his mind's eye and could be recalled with the aid of his economical drawings is impressive, but the art is flawed. Drawing realistic figures from memory poses a whole range of difficulties and the 'portraits' certainly suffer from lack of models. Without sitters, the facial features generally remain indistinct and this leads to a kind of stereotyping of the exotic of which Irma Stern can also be accused. The archetypal exotic stands in a timeless space with his/her primitive accoutrements: ostrich eggshells, bow and arrows, kaross and calabash. The drawings done *in situ* do not suffer from this problem of recall and are the more successful Bushman works.

It is probable that during as many as three of Krige's expeditions to Botswana (1960, 1962 and 1972) he stayed with the Barakwena people.[13] These sojourns resulted in a number of drawings of this clan which were used in his grand Gauguinesque paintings executed in the Montagu studio many years later. The Barakwena, or River Bushmen, are a group that cannot be easily identified as either Bantu or Bushmen, and many of them live in the region of Rakops to the southeast of the Okavango delta in Northern Botswana. Like their Bantu neighbours they grow crops, fish and keep livestock, but are also hunters and gatherers.

The paintings were done in the mid-eighties from Krige's earlier sketches and these memories are romanticised. A series of large-format paintings of figures on a river bank (possibly the Boteti or Okavango) deserves attention. They are paradisiacal evocations from his past. The banks of the rivers are verdant, goats graze in the shade of large trees while a flautist provides musical entertainment for reclining female figures. An idyllic village of round mud huts is discernible on the banks of the river. There is little or no work being done and in this Arcadia there is none of the threat of the wild and of the harsh climate. We are in a 'timeless' sphere of the artist's recollection, an old man in the last decade of his life turning away from the present and journeying back nostalgically into the past.

Barakwena Woman with Calabash is a monumental figure on a large support. A dark-skinned Barakwena woman sits on her haunches gazing out of the frame at the river where a *mokoro* glides by and at the village tucked among the trees on the far bank. Behind her another woman pounds millet, an archetypal scene suggesting domestic village life. She is in partial silhouette and her body has a greenish-bronze cast like a statue, the green also reflecting the leafy canopy above her. There is even the suggestion of a carved wooden statue here – indeed her body colours are repeated in the hue of the tree behind. The painting is a dream-like recollection and the 'ghostly' calabash (left unfinished) on the ground beside her appears as though it has faded faster into memory than the statuesque woman, whose body is nonetheless already drifting free of the ground. The figures and main elements also seem to float on the yellow surface, cut-outs suspended in time and in the artist's memory.

The Barakwena paintings are so reminiscent of Gauguin that it is appropriate to look briefly at the differences and similari-

---

[13] No letters, accounts or photographs of these trips to the Barakwena remain and clues can be gleaned only from the paintings and sketches themselves. Krige referred to them as the Barakwena people of northern Botswana, but he also made sketches of the Okavango people round Rundu during his expedition with Bjerre in 1957 and these may also have been used as inspiration for the paintings of the eighties.

In *Kalahari* Bjerre noted that at Rundu on the Okavango River they came upon kraals hidden behind palisades made of pointed poles. He noted that the 'Okavangos' were friendly people living in an earthly paradise and his description has much in common with Krige's later paintings:

> They grow a little maize, tend a few cattle, and fish in the river with spears or large baskets and traps. Many of the Okawangoes [sic] have a traditional arrangement with the Bushmen who live further inland by which the Bushmen bring them wild fruits, roots, berries, nuts, and in exchange they take a share of the maize harvest. (p. 79)

ties in approach of the two artists. Firstly their styles are alike. Krige's adaptation of Impressionism was similar to Gauguin's: the flattening of Impressionist space, the continuous outline, the colourful parallel hatching, the increased smoothness of surface and broadness of hue. Their ideological positions are also not entirely dissimilar. Krige's initial trips to Botswana were not a romantic voyage to seek the 'child-savage' like those of Gauguin, but his artistic revisiting of the past *was* an idealistic, sentimental journey, if a more personal and inward one. Gauguin's travels to Tahiti were a quest for the primitive, Krige's were anthropological, albeit with a nostalgic complexion. Gauguin's was an ideal vision imposed on Tahiti and he gave free reign to his tendencies towards decorative symbolism. He presented a colourful, idyllic South Sea Island existence, a life in harmony with benevolent nature, in which the human figure was at one with the landscape. Krige's was initially a different intellectual approach, but in those grand Barakwena paintings some of Gauguin's stylisation is there and Krige's attempts to bring characters from his past to life on canvas fail in a similar way to Gauguin's (exhibiting romanticisation and stereotyping of the exotic).

LAST YEARS

In 1990 Krige was encouraged to make a last trip to Europe: the draw-card was the Van Gogh retrospective in Amsterdam. The journey started in the Dutch city and Krige made five trips to see the Van Goghs. Next it was London to view the galleries, particularly the various Egyptian collections, and then to Paris for an Impressionist feast. But he became tired of international travel and had soon had enough, asking Sylvia to cancel the German, Austrian and Spanish legs of the trip. Possibly his approaching cancer was already weakening him, but one thing was certain, he wanted the peace of Montagu. He returned and entered a feverish period of work. Perhaps the artist already knew that he had only a few years to live and there was so much more that he needed to paint.

Although François felt most comfortable at home in Montagu, he continued to make sporadic sketching expeditions to his favourite locations. The Kriges spent three long vacations in the beach house of their friends, the Repkos, in the coastal hamlet of Eersterivier in the Eastern Cape. The last Eersterivier holiday took place in 1991 and I joined them there for my Easter break. Here François sketched and painted a number of seascapes and impressions of rock formations, some being reworked on each successive visit. Perhaps he was recalling Monet's fine painting of the rock arch at Étretat, *The Manneport*, when he painted the great archway at Eersterivier, waves crashing against the rocky base.

The most successful of the seascapes is *Eersterivier Beach* in which fingers of rock reach out across the canvas towards oncoming surf. Painted *en plein air*, dirt has got mixed in with the sky, which is handled with thin, turpentine-diluted oil. Pinks and violets, and even some greens, warm the sky which threatens a southeast gale with clouds smudging the horizon. The description of the rocks relies heavily on line and brushstrokes generally follow form. The sparse foreground with just the barest suggestion of scrub and stones is particularly well handled. The use of a hard line for the rocks and the total lack of this in the ocean sets up a contrast in style that matches the different elements. Much of the sea and rock is painted wet-in-wet, the colours only partially mixed on the palette.

The painting is a good example of Krige's mature style: multi-hued sea and sky, calligraphic, line-based drawing, and economical rendering of unimportant detail derived from his drawing technique. The sea is painted with a bold brush that imitates the crashing and rolling surf. The horizon line divides the canvas in half and the colours and brushstrokes used in the sea are appropriately echoed in muted form in the sky, as the clouds emphasise the effect of the rolling surf. There is a deliberate lack of a focal point, the eye being encouraged to range across the wide seascape scene, to experience the sea air and light.

While at Eersterivier, Krige also experimented with a kind of Pointillism as he had done on one or two other occasions in his career. The results are disappointing and the images lack life or plasticity. This disciplined and meticulous style did not suit Krige and he had neither the carefully balanced composition nor the consistency of method of a Seurat (the dots appear on a pale wash sky, rather than as colour fields built up with dots). The approach is too derivative, without any of the Krige flair he brings to his usual, eclectically Impressionist approach.

I arrived at the beach house in early April 1991, my car loaded with oil painting equipment. I was going to watch my uncle very carefully and try to learn some of his skills – at least that was my intention. The house was set on a slope overlooking a wild section of coast where waves thundered against the rocks. Spray plumed high through a blowhole; nearby I would

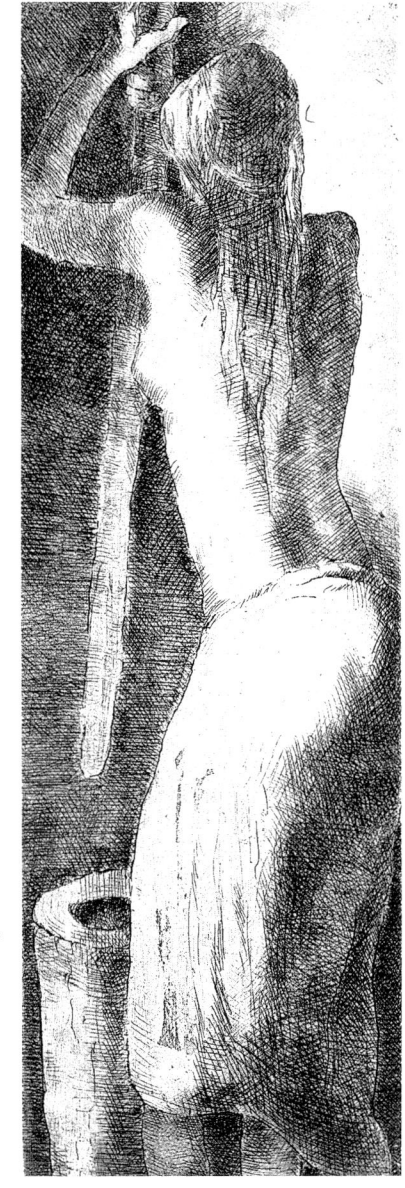

BARAKWENA WOMAN POUNDING MILLET
ETCHING

find François with a sketchpad on his lap, drawing the wave-carved rocks in conté.

In the evenings we would sit and watch the sunset as the sea breeze ushered in a light mist. I was delegated to fire duty and braaied every night. Later we would settle down to a game of Scrabble, although François generally sat to one side, absent-mindedly twirling a strand of hair and sipping his whisky or drawing on his pipe. I fired questions at him about his technique, about the Impressionist palette, about the spelling of a word in our game. He would pause endlessly and then give measured and concise replies, twisting that loose strand of white hair all the while. Out in the darkness we could see the lights of fishing boats riding on the swell and hear the artillery of the surf.

I was not able to learn enough from François. By the time I woke in the morning he was long gone, sketching up or down the coast among the boulders and dunes. While out surfing in the bay, I would see him clambering over rocks, sketchbook in hand, naked save for his black bathing briefs and a big straw hat – almost like a Bushman artist on the move. One mid-morning I found him on the veranda of a beach shack, sheltering from the southeaster and working on the Pointillist piece he had brought with him from Montagu to be reworked on this vacation. I sat watching him apply the dabs of paint, long contemplative pauses between each touch. He was clearly distracted by my presence, so I left him in peace.

One morning when the weather was too foul to venture out, François set up his easel in the bedroom to paint the scene below us, a rock formation named Table Mountain. I quickly set up my own equipment in the lounge and resolved to copy the scene, paying careful attention to my uncle's technique. I borrowed his oils, lightened my palette, raised and blurred the horizon, copied his broad brushstrokes for the beach sand, added red and green accents to my sea and sky as he did. We completed our small oils in a couple of hours. Mine was a complete failure, but somehow François found things to praise in my piece and offered some words of encouragement. His *Eersterivier Étude* was a masterful, consummate seascape oil sketch.

After two weeks, city commitments and the autumn chill drew us back to Cape Town. I was due to leave for Europe and when I visited him again in Montagu the following year, he was already terminally ill. The period at Eersterivier was a brief glimpse of my uncle as I had never seen him before, and I cherish that Easter as one of my happiest memories.

In 1992 and 1993 Krige continued to work but the pain became extremely debilitating. In the paintings we start to see shaky brushwork and a more sketchy application of colour. He states only the essentials in these final works which are, appropriately, mostly still-lifes, nature being brought into the home to be near him to the last.

Still-life with Roses (1993) was his final painting and he dedicated it to his wife. He was already bed-ridden and Sylvia picked a bunch of pink and white roses from the garden, propped him up on pillows and set up the canvas next to his bed. There is rough and confident use of the brush, a lifetime of experience in the casual strokes of dry paint over a muted ground, the odd loose stroke left to stand. Here at the end of his life there is nothing superfluous – he is supremely in charge of his materials. Throughout his career he had struggled to capture roses; how to get the light, delicate feel of petals without being too 'fussy'. In this, his last painting, he hits exactly the note. It is a rapid work with deft application of white in the 'dreamy' roses and, as with so many of his single-sitting études, the result is beautiful.

Breytenbach recalls his last visit to the dying man:

The painter has always had the appearance of a Renaissance youth. The cheeks are red, the neatly trimmed beard and hair swept back from the broad forehead are still of a golden colour despite his years. It is only when he shifts the body to find a more comfortable position that you see in how much pain he must be. Then he unconsciously starts twisting a lock of hair in his fingers, as if he were again a fearful and uncertain child …

His hand has made so many movements, has travelled the extra mile over unexplored spaces. The hand may be knobbly now, uncertain in striking the match, but the whole being is as invisible and right *as a Bushman's arrow, and the blue, intelligent eyes mirror something which the others have not yet seen.*[14]

In the last year of his life a flurry of attention was paid to the artist. A rose was named after him,[15] a television programme was made about him, a book of his drawings was published and he was made an honorary freeman of Montagu. He bore all the attention with equanimity, but it did not sit comfortably with him.

During the final months the pain prevented him from working and he would lie on the veranda under the vine pergola

---

Sylvia Krige at the opening of an exhibition of her late husband's paintings (1999). Sylvia established the Krige studio in Montagu, a living memorial to both François's work and the delightful home and garden they made together.

[14] Breyten Breytenbach, *Dog Heart (A Travel Memoir)*, pp. 114-15.
[15] This Old English rose, red in colour, was cultivated by Ludwig Taschner in Pretoria. It was thought that the classical shape (seen in old rose still-lifes) would be particularly suitable to be named in honour of Krige.

appreciating his garden and watching the birds that came to feed. Here at the end, after a lifetime of resisting, he was drawn back into the heart of the family, surrounded by the hub of activity, the wine-tasting and chutney-making that is Sylvia's world; and having let go of the privacy of his studio, I think he secretly enjoyed it. His wife and his sister, Suzanne, nursed him and say that his intellect remained sharp until the end. On his deathbed he made Sylvia promise to destroy all the paintings he had marked with an X, after he died (this task has regrettably been carried out).

Breytenbach tells of the news of Krige's death:

> *When he is dead the colours fade and for a while the birds do not return to the garden. Not even the owl which sometimes hooted on the roof. It is as if they know. During the previous weeks ordinary folk – brown ladies with headcloths and their hands clasped under their aprons, brown gentlemen in blue overalls turning their hats awkwardly with rough fingers – come regularly to ask after the health of meneer François. Sylvia looks at them with her green eyes, she greets them solemnly, she informs them exactly of the position.*[16]

François died of cancer on 19 February 1994 in great pain and during the last days even large doses of morphine could not afford him relief. In his will he left his studio to the National Botanical Institute, the Cancer Research Trust and the South African Nature Foundation. His family decided to buy back the building and convert it into a gallery in which his work could be exhibited. His architect brother-in-law, Revel Fox, restored the building which is today the François Krige Studio, housing a permanent collection of his work.

Krige's nephew, Bernard Joffe, summed up François's reclusiveness in a humorous note read at the opening of the studio in 1995:

> *François would have loved all this attention. I can picture Oom François, dressed in a white Elvis Presley outfit of silver sequins, shiny leather boots and a pair of wrap-around sunshades, shadowed by an entourage of groupies and paparazzi. Smiling at the flashing cameras, enjoying the fuss and attention! Tap-dancing through the studio, in and out rooms, enjoying the great new spaces.*

STILL-LIFE WITH ROSES, 1993
OIL ON CANVAS
44,5 x 34,5 CM
PRIVATE COLLECTION

[16] Breyten Breytenbach, *Dog Heart (A Travel Memoir)*, p. 116.

FRANÇOIS KRIGE

110

1
KRIGE HOME, 1989
OIL ON CANVAS
55 x 62,5 CM
PRIVATE COLLECTION

2
WILDEBEEST
CONTÉ

3
EERSTERIVIER BEACH, 1990s
OIL ON BOARD
60 x 90,5 CM
PRIVATE COLLECTION

4
PEACH BLOSSOMS IN VINEYARD, 1980s
OIL ON CANVAS
61 x 75,5 CM
PRIVATE COLLECTON

TOLBOS FARM, 1987
OIL ON CANVAS
59,5 x 90 CM
PRIVATE COLLECTION

FRANÇOIS KRIGE

112

STILL-LIFE WITH FISH, 1986
OIL ON CANVAS
44,5 x 60 CM
PRIVATE COLLECTION

STILL-LIFE WITH QUINCES, 1979
OIL ON CANVAS
40 x 64,5 CM
PRIVATE COLLECTION

FRANÇOIS KRIGE

114

1
STILL-LIFE WITH PAWPAWS, 1980S
OIL ON CANVAS BOARD
44 x 59 CM
PRIVATE COLLECTION

2
STILL-LIFE WITH POTATOES AND ONIONS, 1988
OIL ON CANVAS
48,5 x 59,5 CM
PRIVATE COLLECTION

3
STILL-LIFE WITH PEACHES, 1988
OIL ON CANVAS
38,5 x 47 CM
PRIVATE COLLECTION

4
PETUNIAS, 1980S
OIL ON CANVAS BOARD
35 x 35 CM
PRIVATE COLLECTION

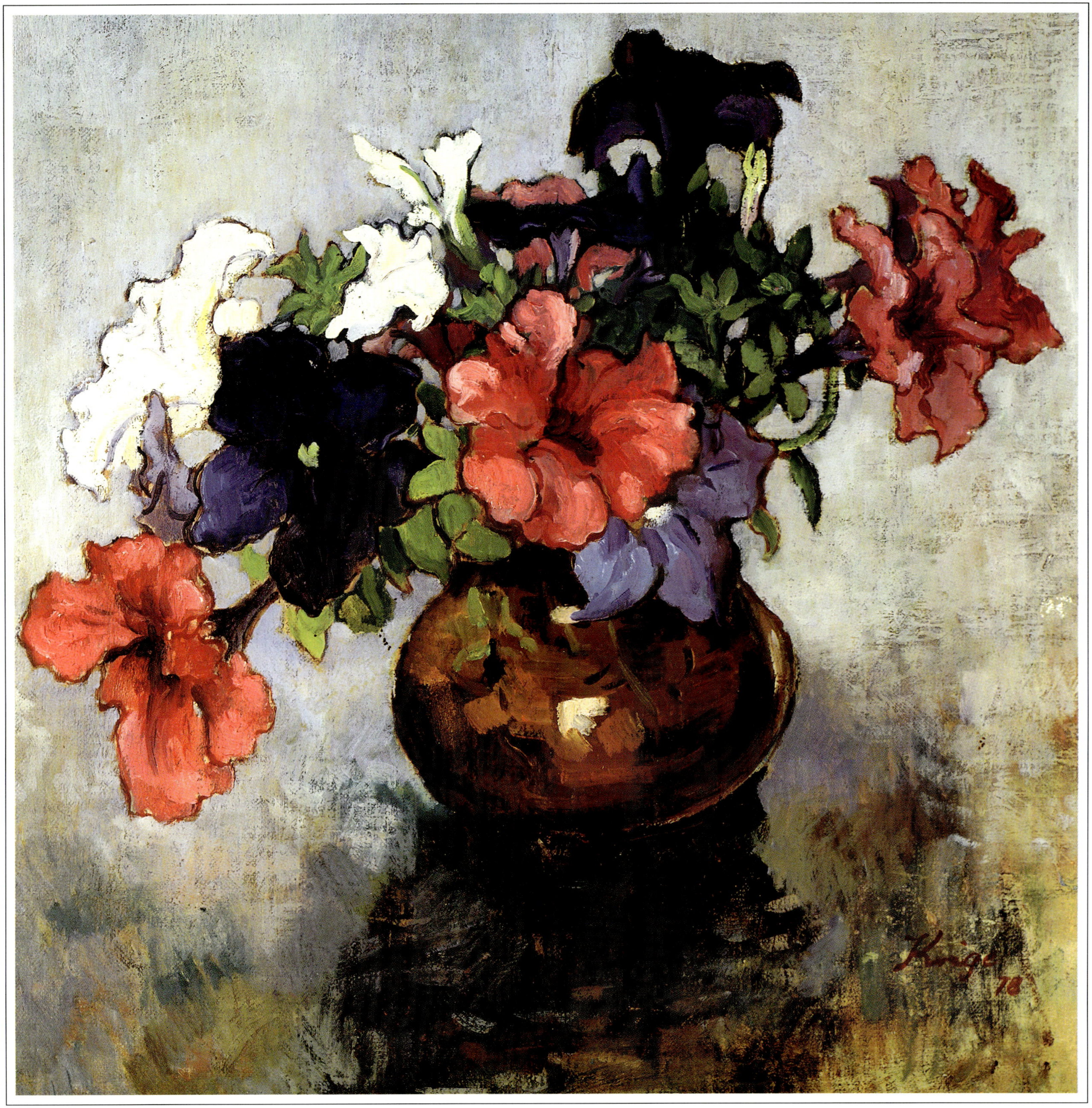

4

FRANÇOIS KRIGE

1
STILL-LIFE WITH NEMESIAS, 1984
OIL ON CANVAS
44,6 X 37,2 CM
PRIVATE COLLECTION

2
STILL-LIFE WITH PROTEAS, C. 1970S
OIL ON CANVAS
60,3 X 65,3 CM
FNB COLLECTION

BERGKATJIEPIERING, 1980s
OIL ON CANVAS
65,5 x 60,5 CM
PRIVATE COLLECTION

FRANÇOIS KRIGE

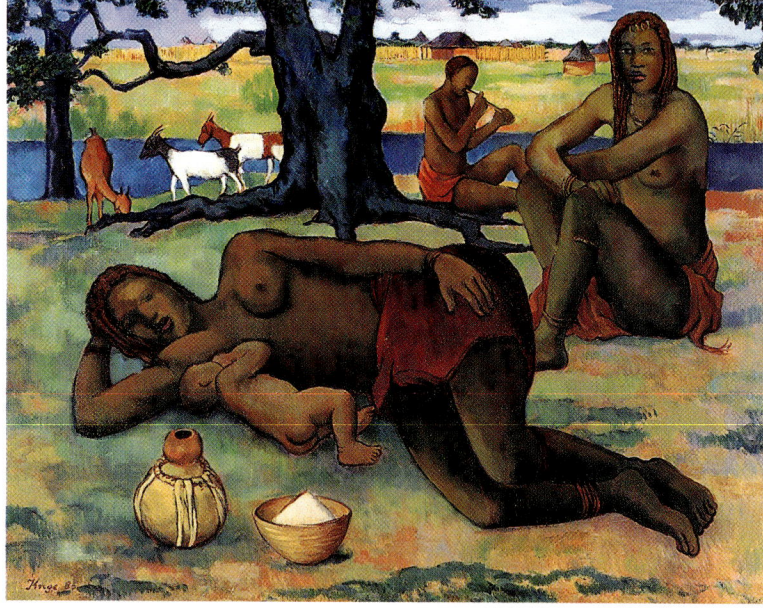

1
!KUNG GIRL, 1984
OIL ON BOARD
59,5 x 49,2 CM
PRIVATE COLLECTION

2
BARAKWENA WOMEN, 1985
OIL ON CANVAS
71,5 x 90 CM
PRIVATE COLLECTION

3
WELWITSCHIA, 1982–1987
OIL ON CANVAS BOARD
59,5 x 90,5 CM
PRIVATE COLLECTION

4
BUSHMAN GROUP, 1984
OIL ON CANVAS
65 x 55,5 CM
PRIVATE COLLECTION

FRANÇOIS KRIGE

120

BASOTHO VILLAGE SCENE, 1979
OIL ON CANVAS
70 x 95,6 CM
PRIVATE COLLECTION

FUNERAL IN THE KAROO, 1980
OIL ON CANVAS
70 x 95 CM
MONTAGU COLLECTION

FRANÇOIS KRIGE

122

ABSALOM, 1988
OIL ON CANVAS
61,5 × 51 CM
PRIVATE COLLECTION

1
KLAAS, C.1970S
OIL ON CANVAS
44,5 x 37,5 CM
RUPERT COLLECTION

2
KRISJAN ASLEEP
CHARCOAL

FRANÇOIS KRIGE

1
THE DRIFTER
MIXED MEDIA

2
HILLARY, C. 1970S
OIL ON CANVAS
64,5 x 54,5 CM
PRIVATE COLLECTION

3
FANIE, 1980S
OIL ON CANVAS
60 x 50 CM
PRIVATE COLLECTION

SELF-PORTRAIT, 1972
OIL ON CANVAS BOARD
50,5 x 39,5 CM
PRIVATE COLLECTION

FRANÇOIS KRIGE

1
SPANISH GIRL, 1977
OIL ON BOARD
59,5 x 49 CM
PRIVATE COLLECTION

2
SYLVIA, 1977
OIL ON BOARD
60 x 44 CM
PRIVATE COLLECTION

3
BUTCHER BOY, 1980s
OIL ON CANVAS
75 x 62 CM
PRIVATE COLLECTION

3

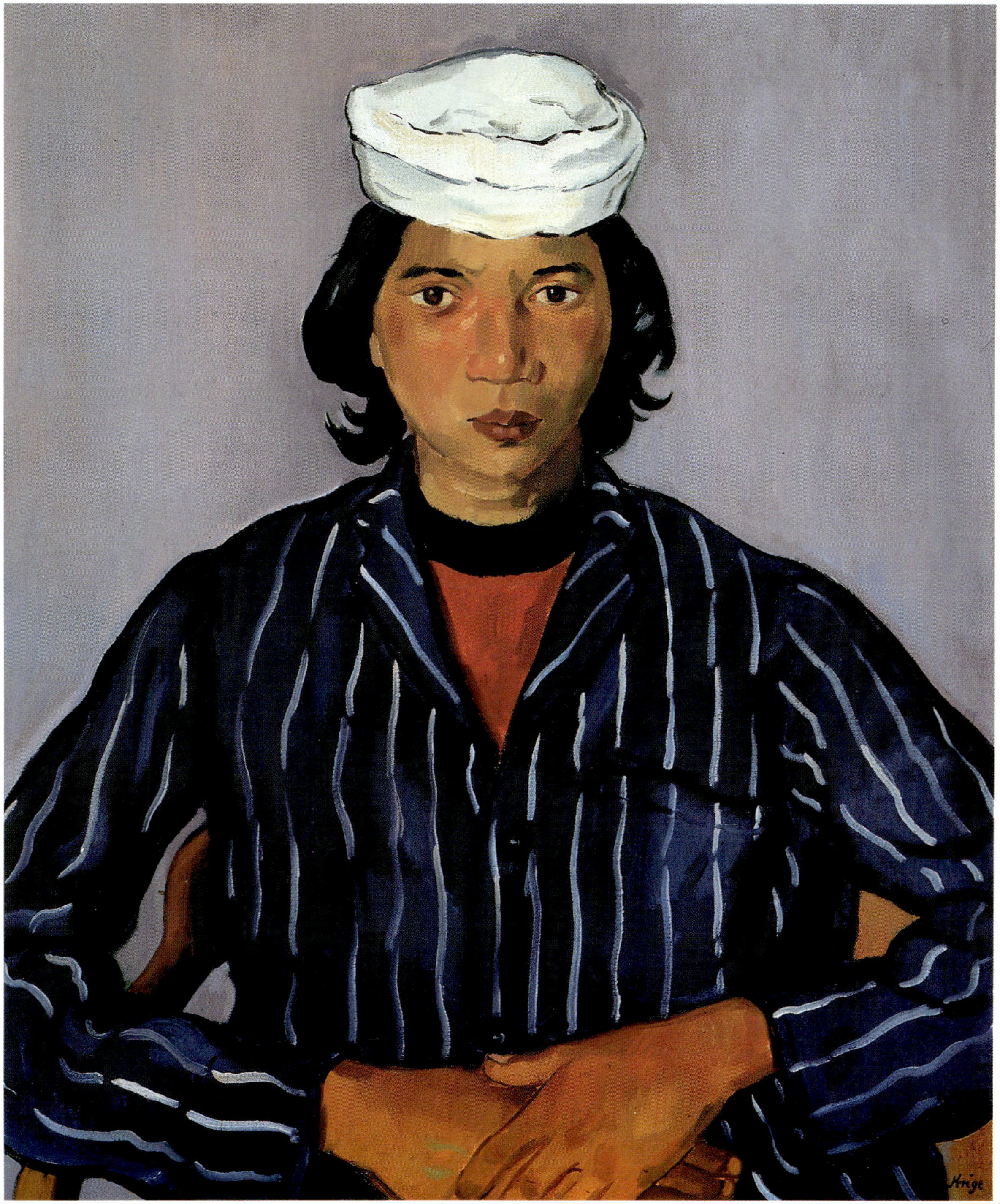

2

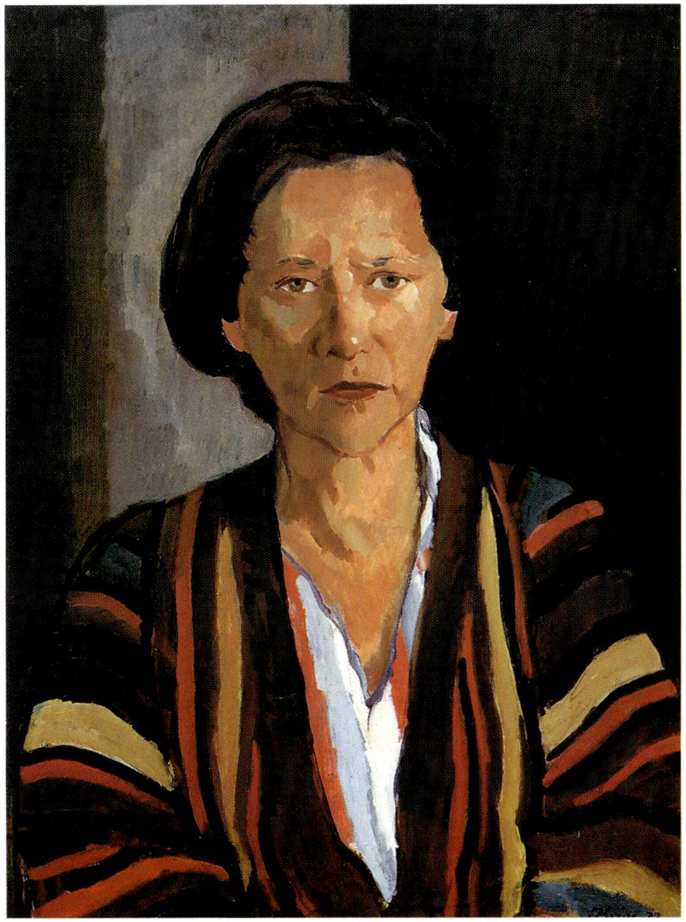

FRANÇOIS KRIGE

128

KALBASSIE, 1968
OIL ON CANVAS
66,6 x 54 CM
PRIVATE COLLECTION

CONCLUDING REMARKS

Krige's was an increasingly reclusive life, dominated by his work and less and less subject to the 'distractions' that separated him from it. His dedication to his art did cut him off from other people, yet his need for privacy never communicated itself as a lack of warmth or a rejection of others. The fact that he was the youngest son in a line of strong brothers with successful parents should also be noted. His relationship with his famous and flamboyant brother Uys was complex. It was as though the younger brother consciously shied away from the limelight Uys courted. These familial relationships add dimensions to the conditions of François's reclusiveness in ways I have intimated in this book. His self-effacement was certainly not unrelated to his need to find an identity through his work and to distinguish himself positively from his successful siblings.

His relationship with the art establishment was also one of frequent reticence and withdrawal. Again his effacement is perhaps to be both admired and respected, as well as regretted. Despite the fickleness of an establishment which he was perhaps right to treat with caution, many would have valued more contact with an artist of such talent and integrity.

Other sources of his reclusiveness may have related to the lack of a sense of 'belonging' in social, cultural and political terms. He felt that he did not belong in a greater Afrikaner community which subscribed to increasingly exclusivist notions of culture and identity during his lifetime. Nor, given his background, did he feel entirely comfortable in English-speaking South Africa.

We have seen that Krige maintained more or less the same style of painting throughout his life and experimented only in a circumspect way, returning always to his personal technical and indeed emotional approach. There was François's unique use of line, his economy, handling of colour, and his attempt to capture the light, colours and textures of the South African subject. His emotional approach exhibits an integrity which is conveyed not only in technical terms (his austerity and economy), but also in his choice of subjects. This approach was humble in a way that translated itself into a form of morality.

CITADEL, PORTUGAL
PEN

It is Krige's serene communion with his subject, his reverence for it, that touches us, as well as his humanism, which emanates from the work. Neither his style nor subject matter nor technique are original, but it is the unpretentiousness, the intimate knowledge of his subject and the truth of his vision that affect the viewer.

Neville Dubow writes of his painting:

> *There can be few artists who apply their paints as carefully or as knowledgeably. The patient layers of underpainting invariably found in his work finally emerge as something rather more than technical achievements.*
>
> *One feels that these layers of paint are going to endure - for as long a time, perhaps, as the values of the artist who put them there will continue to command respect.*[1]

Krige was, it appears, concerned about what would 'endure'. And it is probably for this reason that he made his wife promise to destroy many of the inferior works. Throughout his career he sought to create a sustained world of beauty in his art. It is as though he takes his viewers and gently leads them into a way of seeing that is aesthetic, harmonious and true and perhaps even inherently moral. This 'vision' that he wished to leave behind once he was gone - his oeuvre - was a very definite one, and he wanted nothing to detract from its sustained beauty. If he had had the chance, I think he would have destroyed many more canvases in order to keep this vision 'pure'. We can be thankful that he did not, but his motives are understandable.

François's pictures were an intimate part of him and he found it difficult to part with them. When prospective buyers visited he would often tell them to come back the following year as he had nothing to show, despite a studio packed with finished canvases. Such was his attachment to his work that if he saw one of his paintings in a gallery he would buy it back. His friend Dirk Marais tells another story of the artist's close relationship with his art. Marais was asked by François to return a painting he had bought to the studio so that he could varnish it. François was delighted to see his picture again and when the time came for the painting to be returned, the artist shyly asked if he could keep it a little longer.

'But why, François?' asked Marais.

'I just don't think the background is quite right,' replied Krige.

'But François, I like the background as it is!'

To which the artist replied, 'If you don't like the changes, I'll scrape them off.' François could not be parted again from the painting - his progeny - for months.

François Krige is certainly one of this country's finest draughtsmen. Some of his oil paintings seem heavy with the density of the material, with their bold, sculptural outlines and fields of scumbled colour, whereas his drawings are free, light and effervescent and arrest one with their economical brilliance. And it is his sketch-like, unfinished or under-worked paintings - those that employ the deftness and economy of his drawings - that are often the most striking. But many of Krige's major oils are formidable and deserve a significant place in the country's painting legacy. Some, it is true, appeal through their linear composition and graphic quality, but there are also those which sing with the brilliance of a gifted colourist. His greatest achievements in this medium are in still-life and portraiture: studio-based, meditative images that present us with an austere self-expression. *Still-life with Fruit*, *Petunias*, *Still-life with Fish*, *Krisjan* and *Hillary* surely rank as some of the finest South African paintings of the second half of the twentieth century.

NANNY
CRAYON

[1] Neville Dubow, 'François Krige's Paintings Reflect His Permanent Values' in *The Cape Argus*, 13 November 1959.

CONCLUDING REMARKS

1
KRISJAN, 1979
OIL ON BOARD
69,5 x 50,5 CM
PRIVATE COLLECTION

2
BUSHMAN WOMAN WITH CHILD
CRAYON

THE ETCHER (SELF-PORTRAIT)
ETCHING

The Art of François Krige: An Appraisal
by Stefan Hundt

Accepted criteria for acknowledgement and recognition in contemporary art have changed dramatically in recent decades. By the time South Africa rejoined the international art world in the late nineties, François Krige had passed away. Krige still painted in the nineties and would have been aware of some of these dramatic changes in the international art world. During his travels abroad he would have been confronted with contemporary art that was at times objectless and conceptual, but he found such art incomprehensible and confrontational in its flagrant disregard for traditional practices. The present vogue for experimentation in the contemporary art world, combined with a revival of avant-garde bravura, dominates the current South African art scene and overshadows the past.

Looking at South Africa today, two traditions of art-making coexist: the first is characterised by terms such as *cutting edge, installation, text-based* and *conceptual,* and its *modus operandi* is most often confrontational and 'anti-aesthetic'. The other is rooted in a tradition of craftsmanship, image-making and aesthetic experience in and for itself – a context in which Krige's work should still be valued and appreciated. While South African artists presently vie for recognition with their European and American contemporaries at international exhibitions and biennials, the market for traditional South African painting, as reflected in the auction market, is booming. Perhaps this is an indication that the work of Krige and his contemporaries is finding a new relevance albeit not a current aesthetic one.

In the present context Krige's work would be considered a vestige of the past. Like many of his contemporaries Krige rapidly developed a recognisable style and approach to painting that he retained until the end of his life. His deliberate isolation from the art establishment and his reticence to exhibit later in life, make Krige's work somewhat of an unknown entity today. Despite later attempts by well-meaning individuals to provide Krige with public recognition, few works have to date entered public collections.

Esmé Berman, in her book *Art and Artists of South Africa,* sums up Krige's contribution:

François Krige was regarded in his youth as a Golden Boy of SA painting. He was one of several promising members of the New Group who experienced similar premature acclaim: each of these painters stepped into the limelight and one by one they receded from the ranks of the avant-garde.

Written almost twenty years ago, Berman's commentary is not inaccurate and reflects the critical reception of Krige's work at the time. No doubt his consolidated style of painting which persisted into the eighties, was seen as retrogressive by the art establishment. In 1949, at the age of 36, Krige had already received the Gold Medal from the *Suid-Afrikaanse Akademie vir Wetenskap en Kuns* (South African Academy for Science and Art), an accolade most painters only hope to receive much later in life.

The concept of the avant-garde has gone through considerable reformulation – being different now than in the previous decade. To consider Krige's work in relation to the 'avant-garde' of today would be futile. His approach and reason for painting provides little or no consideration of such a notion. However, much of Krige's inspiration derives from the nineteenth century European avant-garde – Impressionism and Post-Impressionism.

Krige's choice of subject matter, style of painting and relocation into the country town of Montagu, mirrors the relocations of Van Gogh, Gauguin, Pissaro and Cézanne to Provence in the south of France. Many similarities exist between the landscape and light of the Klein Karoo and that of Haute

AN APPRAISAL

KAROO SCENE, 1940
OIL ON CANVAS
50,5 x 46,5 CM
RUPERT COLLECTION

Provence lending themselves naturally to the adoption of techniques elaborated by these painters in France. Although Krige's intentions may have been very different, the recurring similarities in paint application and use of colour between his work and that of Van Gogh, Cézanne and Gauguin are obvious.

With the exception of the paintings done as a war artist and a series of paintings featuring Bushmen, Krige's choice of subject matter remained confined to traditional categories – primarily still-life, landscape and portraiture. In his earlier works his approach to his subject matter remains realistic and predominantly anecdotal.

Landscapes are often places that Krige frequented or had purposely visited. Whilst in Europe, his itinerary through Spain reveals a predilection for the countryside and villages which still maintained a traditional lifestyle. No doubt these experiences of rural peaceful Europe were to influence his choice of and relationship to his subject matter in South Africa. Many of his excursions in South Africa before and after the war were to remote parts of the eastern Free State and Lesotho and later in life he sought out places where the rapid industrialisation and modernisation of the sixties and seventies had not encroached too visibly. And where it was noticeable, he preferred to renounce this in his private thoughts and not in paint.

In *Small Town in the Karoo* the tiny village is painted in enhanced red warm hues of desert sand under a partly cloudy sky. Viewed from a perspective that floats above the hilltops overlooking a herdsman with a herd of goats, the image takes on a magical character reminiscent of the style of the American Gothic painter Thomas Hart Benton. Similarly, in *Karoo Scene* of 1940, the imminent dawn or sunset creates an atmosphere of anticipation – much like one experiences at the beginning of a new story. The herdsman, his back to the spectator, provides the first character in a narrative to follow. Where the figures in these paintings provide the image with narrative possibilities, Krige's later landscapes provide almost none. In *Hoedjiesbaai* the results of a successful day's fishing are presented in the foreground whilst the picturesque fishermen's huts, devoid of people, make up the background. His paintings of Montagu and the surrounding countryside exclude figures entirely. Although the farmland is visibly worked and cared for, there is no evidence of those who toiled in the lands. Where the fruits of such labour are visible or presented, the hands that picked or caught them are seldom present. Not that Krige felt these subjects unworthy, as evidenced by the paintings of working fishermen and the numerous portraits of farm-hands and workers.

Krige had a self-conscious relationship with the landscape he painted. It was a vehicle for a contained personal vision that clung nostalgically to a pre-industrialised past. No motor vehicles, street poles or telephone wires interrupt the clarity of the scene. In this vision there is no place for any evidence of the encroachment of modernisation, only for Krige himself and his subject. Where painters of the previous century had struggled to come to terms with the peculiarities of light and topography in the South African landscape, Krige transformed them with a painterly language that fixed his vision within the internal mechanisms of the paintings themselves. The completed canvas was only the last piece of evidence resulting from a prolonged and complicated process of integration that he struggled with in every painting. Unlike the Impressionists whose landscapes symbolised the possibilities for leisure of a rising middle class, inviting the spectator to participate, Krige's landscapes remain the property of his eye and mind. The viewer always remains a spectator leaving little room for participation.

Krige's trips into Namibia and Botswana, undertaken specifically to visit the Bushmen, provided him with an array of imagery which he sensitively recorded in drawings he made during his stay. His experience of a supposed care- and stress-free lifestyle remained a source of inspiration for paintings he produced much later.

Krige's series of paintings of the Barakwena reveal a different aspect of Krige's temperament. In *Barakwena Women* (1985), one is transported into an idyllic rural scene. In the foreground a women lies suckling her baby, while another looks at the viewer (obliquely outside the picture). A characteristic calabash and bowl filled with mealie-meal animate the foreground. In the background a herdsman sits on a riverbank playing a pennywhistle. Distant huts and trees punctuate the horizon. The landscape is represented in colours and tones one would associate with a subtropical climate. Painted some twenty years after his visit to the area, this 'African arcadia' presents a romanticised image of a rural life no longer possible.

Similarly in *Basotho Village Scene* Krige presents an idealised vision of a Basotho hamlet in a valley surrounded by mountains where various figures in the painting are busy with characteristic domestic activity. The use of heightened colour and the abstractness of the surrounding landscape obscures the location of the village, while the vague undefined shadows add a timeless aspect to the image. This is a Basotho village remembered and rendered timeless, the people and animals fixed into place, static and immobile. Unlike Alexis Preller's appropriation of Mapoch and Sotho imagery as a vehicle for creating his own unique African symbolism, Krige's paintings only intimate possibilities for symbolic interpretation. In the context of the rest of his work, the presence of an intricate symbolic content seems unlikely. The simplification of forms, the static composition and enhanced colour are conventions employed by Krige to fix an idealised vision feeding off a personal nostalgia of past experience.

In *Funeral in the Karoo* (1980) Krige captures a particularly poignant moment. The congregants bury a loved one in a landscape that echoes their sorrow and their state of wealth. A simple hole in the ground a short distance away from their homes, surrounded by a desolate and textureless landscape, sets the scene for the inevitable. This painting speaks eloquently of his empathy and feeling for the particular circumstances of these people. However neither the composition nor the figures invite any participation by the spectator. This burial is an intimate private affair for those who knew the deceased.

Krige rarely evokes strong emotions with paint. His approach is more meditative than expressive. Looking at Krige's late self-portraits one sees a man not at ease with himself; the eyes are often filled with doubt, perhaps even anxiety. A self-portrait done in Antwerp in 1937 shows Krige as a young man with a hat and pipe in front of a window. The paint is applied in a self-assured manner and the youthful face is open and accepting. Later portraits present a much older, reserved and perhaps even a cynical Krige looking at himself with some doubt and scepticism. The tension between artist and image is made more tangible with the almost plain background in the *Self-portrait* (1972) which foregrounds the face. In the later *Self-portrait with Buddhist Print* the print in the background softens this serious facial confrontation.

In a broad range of portrait studies, Krige shows himself to be a demanding artist. Few of the sitters seem entirely comfortable, and silence seems to surround them as if they were not supposed to speak. In *Hillary* and *Spanish Girl* this silence enhances the serenity of their facial features providing a more relaxed accommodating space around the sitters, whereas *Krisjan* looks decidedly uncomfortable on his perch. *Absalom*, for that matter, seems to have just finished commenting on something betraying an understanding between him and the painter that Krige does not seem to have achieved with many of his sitters. Even in the portrait of Sylvia, Krige seems more intent on achieving a particular formal balance than evoking the character of the sitter. In contrast, his drawings are executed with a lightness of touch and confidence that reveal an artist skilled in the medium and at ease with his subject matter. In his numerous portrait drawings such as *Basotho from Mokhotlong* (1946), Krige conveys a comfortable and relaxed rapport with his sitter, as if at that point in time the conversation had been broken off to provide an opportunity for the conversants to catch their breath. In essence Krige's drawings are snapshots, which contain both that brief moment in time as well as the familiarity which only comes with repeated encounters.

The portraits of children, however, betray a more sensitive and intuitive Krige. In *Justin* and *Revie*, Krige captures the simultaneous combination of fascination and anxiety in both children's faces as they watch the artist applying paint to canvas. In *Revie* the short brush strokes quickly applied (probably out of necessity), provide a particularly charming rendering of the child's face at that moment. No contrived over-painting or reworking of the surface lends the painting a cheerfulness not present in other portraits by Krige.

Although Krige's still-life paintings often employ Impressionist compositional conventions, with their predilection for fleeting light and colour effects, they deviate considerably from these. Rather, his still-lifes are concerted attempts at fixing, permanently, the particular shape and tone of each individual peach, quince or fold of a tablecloth. The paintings look worked, as layer after layer and tone on tone are remodeled and re-modulated to accommodate the colourful interaction of a white tablecloth with a yellow pear as in *Still Life with Quinces and Pears* (1988). In *Still Life with Potatoes and Onions*, the wooden table surface is modulated with a range of colours providing suitable localised complementary colour interactions that lift the vegetables towards the picture-plane. Not all of Krige's still-lifes are successful though. His use of paint remained within a narrow textural range. Paint is rarely applied in a thick impasto or abstract manner where form and material battle for recognition. In this respect, Krige's flower paintings, although botanically accurate and colourwise enchantingly attractive, remain texturally flat and do not show the painterly

BLUE CRANES, C. 1980S
OIL ON CANVAS
65,5 x 54,5 CM
PRIVATE COLLECTION

effervescence of his late Montagu mountain landscapes.

Krige's *oeuvre* stretches over a period where change became the dominant driving mechanism of the arts. Having escaped the parochial art world of South Africa to study and travel in Europe, Krige returned with a broad repertoire of painting and drawing skills that he employed conscientiously throughout his life. His membership of the New Group emphasised his colleagues' admiration of his painting technique and for many years he stood as an equal amongst painters such as Gregoire Boonzaier, Irma Stern and Maggie Laubser. However the Post-Impressionist palette and conventions he had adopted, so similar to Gauguin and Van Gogh, changed only slightly over the many years he worked in Cape Town and Montagu. His early work found considerable acclaim and resonance in the art world of his time. Despite rapid and radical changes in this environment, Krige's later work remained the same – almost becoming a nostalgic longing for the past. Krige remained a member of that generation of artists who saw their primary task as engaging with their environment in modernist terms. What mattered most was the act of painting and the personal and unique expression that the artist could impart to a motif in a particular medium. No further justification was required – a notion that the politicised South African art establishment turned increasingly hostile towards. Breyten Breytenbach, in the foreword to this book, makes an apt observation about South African painting being

> *too loaded with meaning, often too clever by half, reflecting the ingrown toenails of living in the colonies, mortally afraid of being irrelevant or euro-centrist (as if we don't all learn from the same tradition!), worried about not being sufficiently committed or ironical or funny.*

Krige's painting stands out in stark contrast to the prevailing attitude that Breytenbach decries and remains a cogent reminder of the balance between history and the contemporary. Fortunately, Krige's contribution is at last being recognised outside the critical light of contemporary practice and will remain an important part of the evolution of South African art history.

AN APPRAISAL

BLOSSOMING PLUM TREE, 1989
OIL ON CANVAS
82,5 x 65 CM
PRIVATE COLLECTION

LIST OF COLOUR ILLUSTRATIONS

PRELIMINARY PAGES
Self-portrait with Buddhist Print (1980s) p. 7

INTRODUCTION
Barakwena Woman with Calabash (1980s) p. 13

2 Self-portrait with Hat, Antwerp (1937) p. 43
Merry-go-round (1940) p. 44
Portrait of a Man (1930s) p. 45
Basotho Store (c.1930s) p. 45
Basotho Women Dancing (1950s) p. 46
Still-life with Spring Flowers in a Terracotta Vase (c. 1930s) p. 46
Suzanne (1939) p. 46

3 Dead Tank Driver (1987) p. 53
El Alamein A/A Gun and Crew (c. 1942) p. 60
On Board Ship (1980s) p. 61
Italian Girl (1944) p. 62
At Home, SAAF (c. 1942) p. 62
Foggia, Winter (1944) p. 62
Nature Morte (c. 1943) p. 63
Grave-diggers, Sidi Rezegh (1943) p. 63
In Convoy (South African Sailors in Action) (1940s) p. 63
Sturrock Graving Dock (1945) p. 63

4 The Open Window, Clifton (1960s) p. 80
Pulling out the Boat (c. 1950s) p. 81
Mending Nets (1955) p.81
Onrus (1962-1965) p. 81
Hoedjiesbaai (1955) p. 81
Revie (c. 1959) p. 82
Anna-Magrieta (1940s) p. 82
Onrus Lagoon (c. 1960s) p. 83
Mamre Mission Station (c. 1960s) p. 83
Fetching Water, Paternoster (1951) p. 84
Sunflower (1955) p. 84
From the Artist's Studio, Dorp Street (c. 1960s) p. 84
Pomegranates (1950s) p. 85
Landscape, South West Africa (c. 1950s) p. 86
Small Town in the Karoo (1950s) p. 87

5 Montagu Museum (1990) p. 93
Montagu Village (1980s) p. 95
Snow Tree (1981) p. 97
Kogmanskloof, Montagu (1986) p. 97
Aasvoëlkrans (1974) p. 97
Justin (1970) p. 101
Sannie (1960s) p. 101
Still-life with Roses (1993) p. 109
Krige Home (1989) p. 110
Eersterivier Beach (1990s) p. 110

Peach Blossoms in Vineyard (1980s) p. 110
Tolbos Farm (1987) p. 111
Still-life with Fish (1986) p. 112
Still-life with Quinces (1979) p. 113
Still-life with Pawpaws (1980s) p. 114
Still-life with Potatoes and Onions (1988) p. 114
Still-life with Peaches (1988) p. 114
Petunias (1980s) p. 115
Still-life with Nemesias (1984) p. 116
Still-life with Proteas (c. 1970s) p. 116
Bergkatjiepiering (1980s) p. 117
!Kung Girl (1984) p. 118
Barakwena Women (1985) p. 118
Welwitschia (1982-1987) p. 118
Bushman Group (1984) p. 119
Basotho Village Scene (1979) p. 120
Funeral in the Karoo (1980) p. 121
Absalom (1988) p. 122
Klaas (c. 1970s) p. 123
Hillary (c. 1970s) p. 124
Fanie (1980s) p. 124
Self-portrait (1972) p. 125
Spanish Girl (1977) p. 126
Sylvia (1977) p. 127
Butcher Boy (1980s) p. 127
Kalbassie (1968) p. 128

CONCLUDING REMARKS
Krisjan (1979) p. 131

APPRAISAL
Karoo Scene (1940) p. 133
Blue Cranes (c. 1980s) p. 136
Blossoming Plum Tree (1989) p. 137

INDEX

Page numbers in *italic* indicate images

A

Aasvoëlkrans 96, *97*
Absalom 122, 135
Allied Soldier 57
Almeira 29-31, 33
Anna-Margrieta 71, *82*
Antwerp 32-3
Armstrong, Brigadier 50
Asia 105n.11
At Home, SAAF 49, *62*
Aurora de Jesus Marques 90, *91*

B

Barakwena Musician 72
Barakwena Woman pounding Millet 107
Barakwena Woman with Calabash 13, 106
Barakwena Women 118, 134
Basotho 37, 105
Basotho Elder 40
Basotho Store 45
Basotho Village Scene 105, *120*, 134-5
Basotho Women Dancing 37, *46*
Batiss, Walter 36, 37-8, 39-40, 73, 76
Baumann, Mizzi *see* Krige, Maria Magdalena (Mizzi)
Bawcombe, Philip 50, 51-2, 59
Belgium 31-2
Benton, Thomas Hart 134
Bergkatjiepiering 99, *117*
Bethlehem 36-7, 38
Biesenbach family 102n.8
birds 89, 104
Bjerre, Jens 73-5, 106n.13
Black Eagle 99
black soldiers 50, 54
Bleeker, Jacob 67
Bloch, Cynthia 91
Blossoming Plum Tree 92, *137*
Blue Cranes 104, *136*
Bo-Kaap 69
Bontebokskloof 19
book illustrations 9, 26, 65, 72-3
Boonzaier, Gregoire 36, 69, 78, 136
Botswana 73-6, 104, 106-7
Bouman, A C 26
Boy with Hat, Montagu 100
Braque, Georges 14
Breugel, Pieter 32

Breytenbach, Breyten 9-12, 100, 104, 108, 109, 136
Bringing in the Boats 90
Bushman art 39-40, 73-4
Bushman Boy with Bow and Arrow 76
Bushman Boy with Playing Stick 73
Bushman Girl grinding Wheat 75
Bushman Group 119
Bushman Woman with Child 131
Bushmen 13, 39, 65, 73-7, 105-7, 134; *see also* Barakwena
Butcher Boy 127

C

Cairo 56-7
Caldecott, Stratford 24, 36, 69, 98
Campbell, Mary 29
Campbell, Roy 26, 29
Cape Coloured culture 65-7, 105
Cape Eagle Owl 89, *90*
Cathcart 22, 23-4
Cederberg 102
Cézanne, Paul 11, 14, 24, 25, 38, 90, 94, 132, 134
  and still-life 69, 70, 98
Chagall, Marc 14, 42, 72
Citadel, Portugal 129
Cobra group 12
Cope, Jack 77
Courbet, Gustave 42, 100, 105

D

Davis, Fred 100
De Klerk, W A 72
De Kooning, Willem 12
De Villiers, Johanna 17
De Wet family 20, 21
Dead Tank Driver 50, 53-4, *53*, 105
death 21
Diaz, Daniel Vázquez 31
Donkergat 12
donkeys *1*, *28*, 30-1, 65
Dorp Street Studio 68-9, *84*
The Drifter 124
Dryfsand Bo-op Halfaya Pass 48
Du Plessis, Enslin 100
Du Toit, M L 26
Dubow, Neville 14, 130
Dufy, Raoul 67, 70

E

École de Paris 12
Eersterivier Beach 107, *110*
Eersterivier Étude 108
Eitemal 65
El Alamein 50-1
El Alamein A/A Gun and Crew 49, *60*
Empire Exhibition, 1936 34
Epstein, Jacob 78
Erhlich, George 78
The Etcher 132
etching 32, 33, 34, 43, 89-90
Europe 27-36, 79, 90-2, 107
Expressionism 24, 25, 42, 68

F

Fanie 124
Fetching Water, Paternoster 67, *84*
figure studies 14, 24, 32-3, 37, 42, 70-1
First View of Mersa Matruh 52
fishermen 65-7
Fishermen 67
Fishermen (Almeira) 35
Fishing Boat 11
Foggia 58
Foggia (1980) 105
Foggia, Winter, 1944 62
Four Body Bags 54, 105; *see also Nature Morte*
Fox, Justin *88*, *101*, 107-8, 135
Fox, Revel 18, 68, 109
Fox, Revel Junior 71, *82*, 135
France 31, 90
From the Artist's Studio, Dorp Street 84
Funeral in the Karoo 11, 42, 105, *121*, 135

G

Gallery Shear *64*, 78, 89
Gaugin, Paul 11, 14, 25, 68, 106-7, 132-3, 136
Germany 34
Gertenbach, Dormel 79
Gertenbach, Patricia 79
Goya, F J de 31
Grave-diggers, Sidi Rezegh 54, *63*
Green, Lawrence 65
Gregorie family 104

H

Hillary 101, *124*, 130, 135
Hoedjiesbaai 67, *81*, 134

I

Impressionists 24, 70-1, 92, 94
In Convoy (SA Sailors in Action) 48, *63*
Italian Girl 58, *62*
Italy 34, 58-60, 79

J

James Joubert, Cederberg 5
Janks, Hillary 101, *124*, 130, 135
Japanese art 14-15, 25, 68
Joan 101, *102*
Joffe, Bernard 109
Johannesburg 25-6, 41-2
Joubert, Etienne 100
Joubert, Frederick 102
Joubert, James *5*, 39, 102
Justin 101, 135

K

Kalahari 15, 40, 65, 103
Kalbassie 128
Kark, Victor 27, 34
Karoo Scene 133, 134
Klaas 123
Knipe, Kenneth 89
Kogmanskloof, Montagu 96, *97*
Kok, Koos 100
Krige, Arnold *16*, 18, 22, 47, 50, 68
Krige, François *2, 9, 16, 17, 19, 24, 27, 47, 55, 58, 70, 78*
   artistic works *see under* title of work or specific topics: book illustrations; etching; figure studies; landscapes; memory painting; portraits; self-portraits; still-life; technique; war art
   character 9, 14, 17-18, 129
   exhibitions 34, 36, 47-8, 60, 64-5, 78, 79, 103, 104-5
   marriage 64-5, 88
   relationship with Uys 22, 24, 25-30, 37-41, 68-9, 72, 129
Krige, Jacob Daniel (Japie) *16*, 17-18, 23, 71, 79
Krige, Jacobus (Bokkie) *16*, 18, 22, 23, 26, 27, 47

Krige, Lance 28-30
Krige, Lydia 47
Krige, Maria Magdalena (Mizzi) *16*, 18, 27, *27*, 38, 40, 47, 68, 79
Krige, Susanna (Sannie) 18, 19-20, *23*, 27, 31, 68, *68*, 88, 89, 100, *101*, 104
Krige, Suzanne 18, 22, 23, *46*, 68, 109
Krige, Sylvia *64*, 77-9, *78*, 88-91, 100, 102-4, 108-9, *108*, *127*, 135
Krige, Uys 11, 15, *16*, 18, 23, *27*, 34, 77, 104
   as POW 49, 51, 52, 59, 105
   Ballade van die Groot Begeer 66
   'Die Diefstal' 20-1
   The Dream and the Desert 19, 20
   Na die Maluti's 37-41
   Sol y Sombra 9, 65
   'Two Daumiers' 50, 52-3
Krige, Willem Adolph 17
Krige family *16*, 17-24, 68
Krige Home 92, *110*
Krisjan 11, 39, *124*
Krisjan (1979) 100-1, 130, *131*, 135
Krisjan Asleep 123
Krisjan (etching) *103*
Kroukamp, Joan 101, *102*
!Kung Girl 105-6, *118*

L

Ladybrand 26, 36
landscapes 14, 24, 31, 52, 64, 71-3, 94, 96, 134
Landscape, South West Africa 86
Laubser, Maggie 25, 36, 136
Leipoldt, C Louis 47
Lesotho 36-41, 42, 64, 105
Levson 26
Lewis, Neville 47
Lindsay, Major R N 56, 60
Lipshitz, Lippy 36
Lock, Frieda 36
Long, Geoffrey 47, 49, 51, 56
Louw, W E G 34
Luxor 57

M

Malherbe, Colonel E G 56-7, 59-60
Mamre Mission Station 83
Manet, Edouard 11
Mantegna, Andrea 34
Marais, Dirk 130
Marc, Frans 14, 104
Maskew, Margaret 89, 102, 103

Matisse, Henri 10, 14, 37, 70
McCaw, Terence *27*, 36, 37-8, 40, 41
McKillop, Minnie 21
memory painting 104-7
Mending Nets 67, *81*
Merry-go-round 42, *44*
Mersa Matruh 51-2
Meyerowitz, H V 22
Michaelis School of Fine Art 22-3, 36
Michelangelo 11
Millet, J F 100
Miners 45
Molofo, Setha *27, 31*, 39, 40, 41
Monet, Claude 68, 89, 92, 107
Montagu 13, 15, 72, 88-9, 92-102, 132, 134
Montagu Girl 94
Montagu Museum 92, *93*, 94
Montagu Village 94, *95*
Moodie, Major Derrick 49
Mostertsdrif 19-21
Mougi, Philoman 50, *50*
Murray, Andrew 100
Muybridge, Eadweard 77

N

Namib Dunes 103
Namibia 73-5, 102, 103-4
Nanny 130
Nature Morte 54, *63*
Naudé, Hugo 24, 32, 36
New Group 14, 36, 48, 132, 136
Nile River 57
Nude 46
Nude (1962) 69
Nyala 99

O

Obidos, Portugal 8
Oerder, Frans 32
O'Keefe, Georgia 99
Old Woman Reading 45
On Board Ship 61, 105
Onrus 21-2, 42, 68
Onrus 81
Onrus Lagoon 68, *83*
The Open Window, Clifton 80
Oryx foal 83

P

Paternoster 66-7
Peach Blossoms in Vineyard 110

Pedrella, Vincenzo 59
Petunias 99, *115*, 130
Philoman Mougi 50
Picasso, Pablo 11, 14, 91
Pienaar family 96
Pierneef 76, 78, 102
Pinker, Stanley 78
Pissaro, Camille 132
Plantinga, Poppie 64, 65
Pohl, Victor 65
Pointillism 107
Pollock, Jackson 12
Pomegranates 70, *85*
Portrait of a Man (1930s) *45*
Portrait of a Man, Montagu 96
portraits 11, 14, 22, 24, 32, 49-50, 70-1, 100-2, 134, 135;
    see also self-portraits
Portugal *8*, 91, *129*
Post-Impressionists 14, 24-5, 71, 98, 103-4, 136
Preller, Alexis 36, 135
Prowse, Ruth 22, 36, 69
Pulling out the Boat 81
Pyper, Sannie 41, 64

R

Rabie, Jan 94
Rabinowitz, Hym 98
Rembrandt 11, 14, 32, 33, 71, 89, 90, 100
Repkos family 107
Retief, Piet 17
Revie 71, *82*, 135
rock art 39-40, 73-4
Rogan, Captain Doug 49-50
Rome 59-60
Rouault, George 42
Roworth, Edward 36
Rubens, Peter Paul 32

S

Sannie 100, *101*
Sannie Uys (etching) *68*
Schneider, Michael 79
sculpture 23
Sekoto, Gerard 36n.20
Self-portrait (1972) *3*, 101-2, *125*, 135
Self-portrait (conté) *15*
Self-portrait with Buddhist Print 7, 102, 135
Self-portrait with Hat, Antwerp (1937) *3*, 33, *43*, 65, 135
self-portraits *3*, 132

Setha 31, 39
Seurat, Georges 107
Shear, Sylvia *see* Krige, Sylvia
Shepherd, Rupert 69
Sidi Rezegh 52-4
Silves 91, 91
The Sisters 78n.15
Skull 104
Small Town in the Karoo 72, *87*, 134
Snow Tree 96, *97*, 98
South African Academy for Science and Arts 64, 132
South African Exhibition 1933 26
South African National Gallery 22, 36
South African National Museum of Military History 47, 104
South African Railways and Harbours 60
South African Society of Artists 36
Spain 28-31, 33-4, 92-3
Spanish Girl 126, 135
Stern, Irma 24, 25, 36, 42, 106, 136
still-life 69-70, 98-9, 134, 135-6
Still-life with Fish 99, *112*, 130
Still-life with Fruit 98, 130
Still-life with Nemesias 99, *116*
Still-life with Pawpaws 114
Still-life with Peaches 114
Still-life with Potatoes and Onions 114, 135
Still-life with Proteas 116
Still-life with Quinces (1979) *113*
Still-life with Quinces and Pears (1988) 135
Still-life with Roses 108, *109*
Still-life with Spring Flowers in a Terracotta Vase 46
Still-life with Veld Flowers 70
Sturrock Graving Dock 63
Sunflower 70, *84*
Suzanne 22, *46*
Swart, Krisjan 11, 39, 100; *see also Krisjan*
Sylvia 100, *127*, 135
Symbolists 25

T

Taschner, Ludwig 108n.15
technique 14-15, 31, 49, 129-30
    oils 24-5, 68, 97, 103
    see also under figure studies; still-life
Theron, Leo 104-5
Thomas, Elizabeth Marshall 73
Tolbos Farm 96, *111*

U

University of Cape Town 22-3
Uys, Dirkie 17
Uys, Jacobus 17
Uys, Nols 20
Uys, Piet 17
Uys, Susanne *see* Krige, Susanne (Sannie)
Uys family 17, 19

V

Van der Post, Jan J 65
Van der Post, Laurens 73
Van Dyk, Sir Anthony 32
Van Gogh, Vincent 14, 23, 24, 25, 64, 70, 107, 132, 134, 136
Van Melle, Jan 47
Verwoerd, Hendrik 47
Vesuvius 59

W

Wallace, Marjorie 94
war art 15, 47-63, 105, 134
Welwitschia 103, *118*
Welz, Jean 99
Wenning, Pieter 32, 36, 69, 70
Wildebeest 110
wildlife 65, *83*, 99, 104, *110*
William Humphreys Gallery, Kimberley 103
Woman on a Donkey 28
woodcarving 22-3
World War II 14, 41, 47-60

Y

Young, Francis Brett 65

Z

Zandhoogte 18
Zerffi, Florence 69

List of subscribers

SPONSORS' EDITION

Steve Bales	Robin Moser
Judge E. Bertelsmann	Steve Phelps
Graham Britz of The Post House	The Ramsay Family
Jim Gerard Paul Broekhuysen	Mark Read
Fernwood Press (Pty) Limited	Sybil Sieff
Stephen Handler	Judy Smuts
Philip & Rilla Jacobson	Jean Turck
Advocate A.P. Joubert SC	Dr H. J. van Wyk
Brett Kebble	A. Wapnick
Jack Koen	Christo Wiese
Dave McCay	Jeremy Woods

COLLECTORS' EDITION

Dr & Mrs S.E. Baumann	Rita Meininghaus
Hester E. Borgelt	Dr Danie, Daniel & Christiaan Olivier
The Brews Family	Dr L. Reissig
Graham Britz of The Post House	Dion Pierre Rossmeisl
Chris Calitz	Teja Jean Rossmeisl
Elsie Calitz	S.A. Library
P. Coetsee	Sybil Sieff
Helena Cohen	Marius Stanz, Fairland
C. de Wit	Pieter & Pam Struik
Jalal & Kulsum Dhansay	Peter & Caroline Trengove Jones
Fritz G. Eckl	J.A. Janse van Rensburg
A.G. Farndell	N.P. Janse van Rensburg
Lydia Gorvy	Anton Gusinde von Wietersheim
Basil E. Hersov	D.J. Wakefield
Graham Leslie	Thys & Jennie Wessels
Aubrey Luck	J.A. (Jerry) Windell

STANDARD EDITION

A
Lorinda Alberts
J.L. Allen
Keith Allen
Monica & Michael Amm
Hennie Aucamp

B
Basler Afrika Bibliographien
Dr Nicolas Exner Baumann
Peter & Ann Baumann
Yvonne Becker
Vaughan & Linda Beckerling
John R. Beecroft
Alan & Sonja Begg
Jeanette Benater
John & Susan Benjamin
Penny & Neil Berens
M.C. Bergh
Bernardi Auctioneers
Wendy Bertie
Giulio Bertrand
Frieda Beukes
Christine Beyers
Clive Biden
Gustav & Jeanne Biesenbach
BKS Group Engineering & Management
C. Yudelman Bloch
L. Blumberg
Mrs Susan Bolton (née Krige)
Gregoire Boonzaier
Frikkie en Hettie Booysen
Klaus en Hester Borgelt
M.F. Bosazza
Marcia H. Boshoff
Leonard Bosman
Alice Botha
Amanda Botha
Theunis Jacobus Petrus Botha
Charles Bower
E.N. Brink
Mary Bristow
H. Brits
Dr Hubrecht Brody

Amelia Brown
Diana Brown
Dr B. Buitendag
Carl Schlettwein

C
Reverend F. Claerhout
B.J.D. Clapham
Dr & Mrs D. Clark
Andrew Collins
Trudie Conradie
Syd Coosner
C. Cornew
Viv & Rob Jedeikin Cunliffe

D
Johan & Riana de Beer
Marlene de Jongh
Fred de Kock
Mev. A.B. de Villiers
Mnr. A.J. de Villiers
I.E. de Villiers
Dr L.H. de Villiers
Professor Pieter de Villiers
Lydia M. de Waal
Caroline de Wet
Dr Nic de Wet, Somerset West
Nicole de Wet
D.J.S. de Wit
Mr & Mrs H.C. Devine
Lisa, Vincent & Marcus Di Bella
In memory of Martin Di Bella
Coba Diederiks
Karen V. Dixon
Iris Madeleine du Plessis
Jacobus & Karen du Plessis
J.C.M.D. du Plessis
Deirdre du Preez
J.P. du Toit

E
Mr & Mrs R. Ehrlich
Carolyn Einhorn
Marion Ellis
Tonnie Erasmus

Jeanie & Jonathan Erickson
Einhard & Dagmar Erken

F
Ian & Carrol Farlam
C. Faure
John Faure
Martin Fleishman
FNB (A Division of FirstRand Bank Limited)
I.S. Fourie
Mev. S E Fourie
Y.C. Freedman
Richard & Else Friemelt
Lorraine A. Frost

G
Erich & Nicole Gaertner
Advocate J.J. Gauntlett
Alice Gilbert
David & Nicky Glasser
M.M. Glyn
Martha Going
Cecil Golding
Dr G.J.M.R. Gorter
Maureen Götte
David Graaff
Patricia Graham-Collier
Helen Grell
Anton Grobbelaar
Francois Grobbelaar
Dr J.P. Grobbelaar
Kobus en Thelma Grobbelaar
Meyer en Dillie Grobbelaar

H
Lisa Hager
Lorna & Poul-Ejnar Hansen
Wolf-George Harms
J.O.C. Hart
Jacqueline Heaton & Johann Scholtz
Mr & Mrs G.F. Hellström
Sheila Henderson
S.L. Hertzikowitz
Lucia & Renier Holtzhausen

Birgitta Hope
N.S.H. Hughes
Erika Huntly
David en Martie Hyman

I
Franz Irlich

J
Stephen L. Jaffe
Josandra Janisch
Jaco Jansen
J. Jawno
Johan Carinus Art Centre, Grahamstown
Johannesburg Art Gallery
Ralf Johannsen
Dr Carel P. Jooste
T.J. Joubert

K
Glenda Kacev
J.C. Kannemeyer
Dave King
Laetitia Knox-Davies
Dr Harold König
Colleen & Walter Köppe
Yousef & Daryl Koutnik & Rana Tayyar
Philip & Michele Krawitz
G.P. Kriegler
Hennie & Sandra Krige
Johan Dawid Krige
John & Rinske Krige
M.I. Krige
Naomi Krige
Taillefer Krige
Herman Kruger
Denis & Joan Krupp & Family

L
Glenn & Mallory Lambert
Dr A. Landman
Mrs S. Le Roux
Sjaan le Roux

P. & U. Lee
Dawina Lemmer
John Lennard
M.I. Leveson
Mike & Jill Levett
S.S.E. Lewis
Freda Stevenson Lloyd
Jan en Hester Lombard
Tenk Loubser
Mrs Shëlagh M. Lubbock

M

B.H.L. Macdonald
Dirk Marais
Hennie en Anna Marais
Rob & Cheryl Marconi
Mev. Maria Mars
Martins Prokureurs, Bloemfontein
Osvaldo Marucchi
Ignatius Marx
J.S.P. Maynard
Ian McCall
Jill McIlleron
H.S. McKenzie
David & Karen McLennan
C. McNeill
S. McNeill
C.W. Meaker
E. Meaker
E. Melamet
L.S. & P.L. Melunsky
Charlé en Suzanne Meyer
Professor en Mev. Daan Meyer
E. Meyersohn
Werner Migliarina
D.E. & S.A. Milton
Dave Minnaar
Marlana Möller
Sarah Morris
Egon & Evonne Möslein
F.P. & S.W. Mountford
Dr J.E.C. Mullen
J.G. Müller
Mike & Ann Munnik
Lyndall Murray

N

A. Naude
C. Naudé
Gerda S. Nel
Douglas Newton
Sarah Newton
Mrs G.A. Nikschtat
P.A. Nisbet
Ronald & Valda Norwitz
R.S. Nussbaum

O

Oliewenhuis Art Museum, Bloemfontein
Magda Olivier
P.T. Olivier
Renier Oostehuizen
Robert Ornduff
A.D.P. Ovenstone

P

Paul Roos-Gimnasium
Roydon C. Peden
Ben J.P. Pienaar, Stellenbosch
David Porter
Allan Powell
Mev. A.B. Pretorius
Tarisa Pretorius
Mrs Susan Prins
Uwe Putlitz

R

Annatjie Rainsford
Miles Rasmussen
Mr & Mrs Len Raymond
T.H. Rebok Fine Art Restoration
Jan Repko & Margaret Rutherford
Herculine J. Retief
Susan Reyneke
R.B. Ritchie
Simon Roberts
Robertson Museum, Robertson
Coetzee Roux
Christine Roux
L.M. Rowe

Mev. M. Rüde
Ina Rupert
Jan Rupert
J.A. Rupert
Peter Rush
Dr Brendan Ryan

S

Gordon Schachat
Robbie Schilz
Genard Russel William Sizer
Stuart Andrew Sizer
Carol & Brian Slavin
Agna Smirnoff-Krige
J.H. Smuts
M.J. Snyman
Ines & Basil Stathoulis
George F. Stegmann
Johan Steyn
Catherine Stock
Mr & Mrs Gerrit Streefland, Breukelen, Holland
S.J. Streicher
The Strydom Gallery

T

J.E. Telian
Deleine Terblanche
Annette Theron
Corder Tilney
Mel Todd

U

M.R. Unite
W.E. Uÿs

V

Mev. M.J. van Alphen
Corinne van den Berg
Carine van den Heever
Leo van den Heever
Johannes van der Horst
Dr Robert H. van der Linden
Desmond van der Merwe
S.W. van der Merwe

Van der Post House, Philippolis
Professor H.H. van der Spuy
H.K. van der Spuy
Hendrik J. van Eck
Danie van Niekerk
E.J. van Niekerk
Joan van Reenen
Nicki van Reenen
Willie van Staden
Anna-Maré van Wyk
Retha van Wyk de Vries
Professor G. van Wyk Kruger
J.R. van Zyl
R. van Zyl-Smit
Vernon Veale
Dori Verhoog
F.P. Verster
Professor W.J. Verwoerd
Marlene Visser
Tanya Vosloo

W

Dr Gavin Watkins
Professor Ian B. Watt
E.S. Weinberg
Dr A.G. Wesley
Liezl Helena Wessels
Thys & Jennie Wessels
Westerford High School
Val & Dave Whittaker
Colin Whittle
Stewart Whyte
D.H. Wilson
www.vgallery.co.za

Y

Neil Yeats

Z

David Zetler